D0759945

NONVERBAL
COMMUNICATION
OF AGGRESSION

ADVANCES IN THE STUDY OF
COMMUNICATION AND AFFECT

A Continuation Order Plan is available for this series. A continuation order will bring delivery of each new volume immediately upon publication. Volumes are billed only upon actual shipment. For further information please contact the publisher.

ADVANCES IN THE STUDY OF
COMMUNICATION AND AFFECT

Volume 2

NONVERBAL COMMUNICATION OF AGGRESSION.

Edited by

Patricia Pliner, Lester Krames, and Thomas Alloway
Erindale College
University of Toronto
Mississauga, Ontario

Symposium on Communication and Affect,
4th, Erindale College, 1974.

PLENUM PRESS • NEW YORK AND LONDON

Library of Congress Cataloging in Publication Data

Symposium on Communication and Affect, 4th Erindale College, 1974.
  Nonverbal communication of aggression.

  (Advances in the study of communication and affect; v. 2)
  Includes bibliographies and index.
  1. Nonverbal communication—Congresses. 2. Aggressiveness (Psychology)—Congresses. I. Pliner, Patricia. II. Krames, Lester. III. Alloway, Thomas. IV. Title. [DNLM:
1. Nonverbal communication—Congresses. 2. Aggression—Congresses. W3 SY508K
1974n/BF575.A3 S989 1974n]   V. Series
BF637.C4S9 1974   156'.2'52   75-28122
ISBN 0-306-35902-2

Proceedings of the Fourth Annual Symposium on Communication and Affect
held at Erindale College, University of Toronto, March 28-30, 1974

© 1975 Plenum Press, New York
A Division of Plenum Publishing Corporation
227 West 17th Street, New York, N.Y. 10011

United Kingdom edition published by Plenum Press, London
A Division of Plenum Publishing Company, Ltd.
Davis House (4th Floor), 8 Scrubs Lane, Harlesden, London, NW10 6SE, England

Printed in the United States of America

Contributors

PHOEBE C. ELLSWORTH
Yale University, New Haven, Connecticut

STEVE L. ELLYSON
University of Delaware, Newark, Delaware

RALPH V. EXLINE
University of Delaware, Newark, Delaware

BENSON E. GINSBURG
*Professor of Biobehavioral Sciences, University of Connecticut
Storrs, Connecticut*

CARROLL E. IZARD
Vanderbilt University, Nashville, Tennessee

BARBARA LONG
Goucher College, Towson, Maryland

E. W. MENZEL, JR.
State University of New York, Stony Brook, New York

ROBERT E. MILLER
*Department of Psychiatry, School of Medicine, University of Pittsburgh
Pittsburgh, Pennsylvania*

STANLEY C. RATNER
Michigan State University, East Lansing, Michigan

HARVEY SARLES
*Department of Anthropology, University of Minnesota, Minneapolis
Minnesota*

Contents

CHAPTER 4

Patterns of Emotions and Emotion Communication in "Hostility"
and Aggression 77
CARROLL E. IZARD

CHAPTER 5

Communication and Aggression in a Group of Young Chimpanzees 103
E. W. MENZEL, JR.

CHAPTER 1

Language and Communication—II: The View from '74

Harvey Sarles

Department of Anthropology
University of Minnesota
Minneapolis, Minnesota

The study of aggression is a most important facet of modern behavioral interests. Its understanding and control is necessary to ensure our very continuity. It is a part of our existence which has nonetheless eluded deep understanding in spite of its having attracted concern and attention in the political, psychological, and philosophical traditions to which we are heir.

In the context of the ethological and comparative studies which have surfaced in the recent past, it has gained a wider, perhaps newer, sense because it appears to be an attribute of social animals in addition to man. We hope that we can extrapolate from knowledge about other animals to some sort of deeper, perhaps "biological," insights into man's nature and behavior.

While I share these hopes, I remain concerned about a number of issues or ideas which an overzealous biologism can carry on its ideological wings. We are in a paradoxical period where hard tissue and bodily form seem to be more plastic than was suspected (Enlow, 1968), while behavior is claimed to be less susceptible to change and learning than we had thought. As a person who has come to these issues primarily as a behavioral field-oriented (human) linguist, I am aware that we are heirs to curious traditions of human nature which have made us appear extranatural: "language," "mind," and "rationality" being some terms which encapsulate the essence of the human uniqueness arguments. Lorenz, for example, defines natural human behavior as preceding reason, language, and culture in his book, *On Aggression* (1966).

My approach to thinking about issues of human nature and behavior in a comparative framework has been through the metaphor of language. Some of the current ideas I have fought; others I've attempted to bypass. Some seem to be conceptual; i.e., earlier ideas of language have seemed so overwhelmingly "self-evident" that the only way to transcend them is to rethink them in some critical, historical context.

I believe that the so-called affective components of our nature are bound up in the same or similar conceptual traditions and are fraught with the same conceptual difficulties. To attempt to shed some light on the positions and ideas that I find myself occupying, fighting, abandoning, rethinking—let me review a paper I had published in *Current Anthropology* several years ago (Sarles, 1969).

In this article, I responded to a *Science* paper written by G. G. Simpson (1966) in which his ultimate definition of human nature was directly linked to language.

I claimed, among other things, that not only was Simpson's position unnecessarily dualist, but that any definition of language was more suspect than he or linguists of that era were willing to admit. Language is not in my view either peculiarly human or peculiarly individual—but we are social interactional creatures just as were our forebears.

Since that time, linguists' definition of language has indeed become open to debate; the implicit issue of man's sole ownership of language has become explicit, pushed especially by the work of the Gardners on chimpanzees (1969) and by the increasing abandonment of linguists by psychologists (Salzinger, 1970).

My original paper was presented in two parts—the first being a critical description of how human linguists and animal communication experts (callists) have some similar and some surprisingly different ideas and methodologies, with but little awareness of their assumptions and with a rather blind application of these ideas to subjects that they may not fit at all. The second part was a modernized program of research based on Darwin's original outline for the study of expression and emotions.

During the past several years I have thought and written about the variety of subjects a good deal—some of my views have changed (especially on the nature of faces and of the so-called insane). In the area of emotional expression, the literature has developed considerably, pointing in two virtually contradictory directions. The field of human ethology has gained a literature, if not exactly a substance. In fact, there may be two fields splitting and emerging—one which is essentially psychological–individual, the other more anthropological–social—as they tend to approach the same apparent subject matter from two quite different perspectives.

In this chapter I wish to mirror the earlier paper and to consider the language issues first; then I will point to some research directions especially from the anthropological–social perspective in which language is some subset of communicational behaviors not easily separated into discretely reified entities.

On Language

The principal dilemma in raising the issue of the nature of language is that virtually everyone believes he knows what language is, that each of us is an instantiation of a normal human speaker and thus "knows" in some deep sense what language is. In my personal experience, however, there seems to be little actual agreement about the very nature of language.

It is difficult to gain a critical sense for the underlying issues since most linguists and callists use the term as if there is universal, self-evident, and exhaustive insight and agreement into its very nature. People do tend to agree that language is in some sense unique to man—but in which senses remains unclear.

In my view, this belief about human language is strictly an insider's picture. Our so-called knowledge about the "talk" of other species is derived principally from an exclusionary article of faith concerning the uniqueness of man: other species get the leftovers. These views about man's uniqueness are based less on fact and evidence and more on a western theological assertion that man alone has a mind or soul. Since this position is based on some idealized conception of man, it also has a tendency to push us to distinguish normal man from non-normal man in ways similar to how we distinguish man from animals. That is, this arena of thought and research intrinsically carries the very seeds of social Darwinism.

What, then, is language? Where is its locus? What is its purpose? The term language remains little more than a metaphor which prejudges the observation and analysis of verbal behavior and arranges the data to fit whatever the prevailing view is. That is, we still don't know in any deep sense beyond what we can perform—and that we are unlikely to gain any insight into our performances unless we relook at language and linguistic ideology and sweep away some underlying brush.

It's not that we do not have theories about language. The history of western philosophy was and principally is predominated by inquiry into the nature of language.

There have been two main sorts of theories—one an "*object*" or "*word*" theory, the other an "*idea*" or "*sentence*" theory. But both have been linked intimately to theories of human nature and to human development. That is, our theories of language have always been exclusive theories of human nature. These theories have been based primarily on ideologies which related man, not to nature, but to western conceptions of the deity.

Consider how language has been conceptualized as human nature: Man has a soul, psyche, or mind—this makes him unique. Attributes of mind include intentionality, will, consciousness, rationality, creativity—the lexicon varies in the hands of different writers. The body is a residual phenomenon—what the mind is not!—and the emotions are thrown in on one side or the other, and occasionally even disappear. They tend to be sort of intermediate, occasionally intermediary, between mind and body.

One important thing to note in mind theories is that bodies curiously do tend to disappear. As our soul (the real me) ''leaves'' the body after death (Aristotle's metaphor), it has some sort of existence of its own—the mind, per se. As we are able to conceptualize minds without bodies, we are able to construct verbal behavior as an attribute of mind. This, in turn, seems to legitimatize the notion of language, per se—also disembodied in peculiar ways. (Later, we will note how these thought constructions also have enabled us to create studies of facial expression which, in my mind, are also essentially disembodied!)

The dualist thought construction, which sanctions us to disembody the mind, also contributes to the disembodiment of language and has helped legitimate certain other notions as well. For example, it is usual in the context of language to mention the term communication. Language, it is said, functions to enable us to communicate. Not having a very clear idea of what language is—except that it exists per se, and it's what other animals cannot do—we heighten this house of cards by speaking of a *function* of language.

To extend the bodiless metaphor a bit further, consider our prevailing notions of communication—as the passage of new information called messages. It is a configuration of symbolic interaction, the meeting of minds. In fact, the literature, which is admittedly science fiction, carries the ability of humans to interact with other sorts of bodies (like your favorite Martian) and is willing to admit that mutual intelligibility doesn't require human bodies or even human existence. Intelligent life—another metaphorical extension of our concepts of language—exists out there in the same sense as our primordial ancestors finally discovered or were given intelligence, as if logic, etc., were sitting around waiting for man to develop into it. May I suggest that some missing links are not merely in Olduvai Gorge, but also in our pictorial theories of the development of man?

Since there seems to be little actual doubt that we have bodies—or that we are bodies—we might reasonably ask what these bodies are doing while we speak, if indeed they are doing anything. Is it possible that they contribute something to language? Or are they purely epiphenomenal, a place in which our minds accidentally reside (and a dirty place, for some of us!)?

Well, bodies may have disappeared from theories of mind and language, but they haven't been entirely neglected. On any library shelf full of books on the mind, there are one or two about the body. And it is important to note what has happened to it, because its historical treatment has figured heavily in our conceptualization of language, especially as justifying support for the particular views of language to which we are heir.

The body is the place where the mind resides. In Western thought it seems inconsequential that our bodies are shaped or formed as they are. Rather, the essential person is one whose development is toward understanding, rationality. He gets language first *in order to* communicate later. I think it is worth pointing out that our stories about human development are parallel to or the same for the development of man and for each individual man. Our theories of learning also run parallel and tend to exclude the body from view and from analysis as part of language or intelligent behavior.

This theoretical stance pushes us toward a theory of communication which is very troublesome because it appears to require communication to be a meeting of the *minds*. Messages or information flow from one metaphorical telegraph system to another, using the body or facial expression as the transmission device. But, as in telegraphy, this sort of thinking suggests that the face and body are as passive as the telegraph line in the transmission of messages. Facial expressions have no "being," but are some sort of surface reflex of deeper structures. Language theories are the same, inasmuch as the behavior or sound is the vehicle for message transfer, not the message itself. In other words, the observable behavior of language in current linguistic theories has very little to do with the meaning of the messages.

This leaves the empiricist in the very uncomfortable position of either having to find some other nonempirical way into his data (the meaning) or virtually having to deny that interactors can really communicate or understand one another.

This is one of the disjunctions of theory and method which separate linguists from callists. Callists have only sound behavior to observe and have inferred, or imbued their subjects with, a semantic—albeit a simple one. Human linguists have been unwilling to do this, and semantics continues to be problematic; callists have been overly willing (in my opinion) to impute meaning to verbal noise and have been extremely naive in making judgments about the similarity and differences of animal sounds as they strike the human ear or are run through a sonograph. Events of the sort which callists are willing to call "the same" can literally make human languages unintelligible.

But even here, the human uniqueness theorem has apparently substantiated the callists' moves, since other animals can be chauvinistically assumed to be much simpler than we are. For example, the notion that other animals are locked in to a stimulus-bound present here-and-now has permitted callists to act as if the observed behavior has no history or context. If two animals' speech were directed toward or about a third conspecific out of sight of the observer, no one would ever know with present methods, and we could continue to analyze our observed data without fear of gaining any deeper insight into other species' cognitive ways. Given the variety of species on earth, we could continue to taxonomize and compare our apparent data far into any foreseeable future. And in the prevailing mood of biologism, I can even imagine that such non-data can be extrapolated to man, as part or parcel of his so-called innate/genetic linguistic endowment. I suspect that this is more truly science fiction than any of our stories about "intelligent" life on other planets.

In many ways, the era which promulgated these ideas is rapidly passing. But without any apparent theoretical underpinnings I fear that we are likely to carry these notions with us—under our breaths, as it were—while observing such obviously communicative events as facial expressions seem to be. Perhaps it is worth pursuing the underlying model further.

The major difficulty, as I see it, is encapsulated in ideas about the nature of communication and of the presumed nature and role of the individual organism. In the traditional notions of mind, it is the individual who gets or learns language and is *then* enabled to communicate with others. In the beginning is the squalling, dumb organism. Only gradually does he begin to be able to "speak his mind." Maturity, in Piagetian ideology (Piaget, 1963), has principally to do with increasing rationality or problem-solving ability. It continues the linguistic philosophers' view that logic or rationality has some sort of overarching existence—we grow into it, as it were.

This picture of man carries with it an "origin story" of man, which focuses on how man is different from his predecessors. Instead of looking at all of the uniquenesses of man, including our very special eyes, mouths, and faces, these stories make it appear that we are special in extranatural ways which exclude our bodies. Language, mind, consciousness, will, rationality, soul—all are terms which encapsulate these human differences.

Without making any strong claims that other species have language precisely in the human sense, let me point out that the data base for these claims is nonexistent. The methods used by callists are derived from prior ideas of human uniqueness, that is, that we have *human* minds and other species do not. No one has, for example, seriously suggested that we observe humans speaking in the same ways as we observe other animals—by calls related to their behavior—because we have already assumed that we know what the differences are about. (I have, incidentally, suggested that no other species could possibly discover that humans have language, if they used the methods which we use to examine the speech of other species! [Sarles, 1971])

Not only have these theories of human uniqueness affected our observation, analysis, and interpretation of the communication of other species, but they have also strongly affected the very formulation of theories of human language. Indeed, the current theories of linguistics are based on a dualism which parallels the mind/body, human/animal distinctions that come to us from long theological traditions.

Our very ideas about human thought derive from progressive evolutionary assumptions about the mind of man being created or formed in order to understand the deity. It is just those aspects of our thought and speech which tend to be called language. They are said to be "free," "creative," "non-stimulus-bound," "the message," "langue." Hardly any linguist (except possibly myself) has been willing so far to observe human verbal behavior in the same sense as callists must observe nonhuman verbal behavior. Linguists preselect from the stream of speech what they believe and agree to be language—no one seems to know if this represents about 90% of the total amplitude of ongoing speech, or, say, as little as 10%. In order to get intelligible speech over a background noise, speech needs to exceed noise by only several percent. So it may well be that linguists attend to only a small portion of the speech signal—while callists are struck with observing 100% and believe that they must relate the total animal speech stream with its co-occurring behavior. If any other species did, in fact, have language in any sense, the possibilities of our discovering it appear to be nil with present methods. We are fully into an era of descriptive taxonomy based on a very partial, if not totally inaccurate, theory about nonhuman language.

Where does this leave human language theory? In my view, it must be unsound. And the ideas derived from it are equally suspect, as are those which parallel it. That is, I am suspicious of any ideas about human behavior which are like our mind/body dualistic theories, in which the individual is the repository of mechanisms which stimulate others to respond. Theories of individuality smack of the same sort of theology which says that the individual is where the soul is, and that each of us is unique because we have unique minds. By focusing on the presumed uniquenesses of man and individual man, we risk not seeing that each individual exists in and is dependent for his survival on a variety of interactional networks. He must always, in my view, know how to communicate—before and after birth. Language, as I conceive of it, comes much later. It appears, in other words, that communication is prior to language, not the reverse as our human uniqueness stories would make it appear. And the recent ethology bolsters this communication view in the sense of showing that man *derives* from social species—he did not become social and communicative after he "stumbled" upon language.

Each of us must in some sense already *know* about himself vis-a-vis others; he is likely to derive his own view of himself as he interacts with others. While not wishing to deny the mind as the "hard" behaviorists do, I suggest that the individual is not merely a thing which grows, develops, and becomes more and more rational by essentially preformed stages. He is a dynamic, processual thing who is observed and molded within the cognitive structures of those around him. In this sense, rationality and logic are statements about the ways adults think. They don't exist in any sense independently of human thought and being—as tempted as we may be to believe that they do, and in spite of the attempts of modern logicians and linguists to market their view exclusively.

Consider that part of our existence which seems to be the most sturdy and continuous and nonplastic: our bony structure. Let me contrast two ways of thinking about, for example, "how we get to look the way we do." I believe that these are parallel to a developmental-stage versus a dynamic view of interaction and communication.

The first story is, of course, the one we all believe: that we look like our parents in some sort of genetic mix. Whether we favor our mother or father more is explained away, rather than explained, except that we do! We get bigger and look more and more like ourselves. The great changes in our faces are attributed to age and gravity, as if these imply natural processes that are independent of other aspects of our being.

The other story—which is gaining substance in the developing field of functional anatomy—is quite different (Enlow, 1968). We come to look the way we do in complex interactional fashions. Our very bony structure is in constant flux and is determined to a very large degree by constant soft tissue interactions. The soft tissue—mainly muscle tissue—I see as amenable to the same "habits" as our tongues in forming dialects. Dialects, we know, are an individual's muscular adjustments, which are very much like those around him. We speak the way our families do, and we are highly susceptible to change, particularly when we are young. As orthodontists have pointed out, the thrusting of the tongue is a great mouth-shaping force, and most of us native speakers of English sit and think with our tongues on upper teeth or alveolar ridge, pressing with some degree of force. The very form of our face, our bony tissue, is molded in the interactional dynamic in which children respond to how their parents believe they look.

In communicational-linguistic terms, this implies that expression is very much part of an interactional nexus. What shows up on an individual face is susceptible to interpretation by those around him, and those facets of expression which are interpreted consistently are the ones the individual tends to use consistently. Whatever preformed expressive abilities are manifested by the infant, for example, it is those which are meaningful and sensible to its mother which are acted upon and reinforced. The individual becomes, in my view, the expressive instantiation of that person to whom his family responds. It is tricky to separate that person who is "one's family's son" from that "son-as-a-person," one way of stating the existential dilemma that all of us find ourselves in. (It is tempting to suggest that the traditional dualism between mind and body be recast as the dualism in one's self between the interactional self as defined by others and the essential self.)

This sort of interactional notion also implies a quite different view of normality and abnormality than a stage-developmental one. The recent history of psychometrics pushes us toward the notion that any factor of form or behavior has a population distribution and that popularity and normality are kinsmen, if not twins, conceptually. This type of notion cannot help but seem persuasive particularly when it is bolstered by biopolitical notions such as "success."

In a reply to the article on which this chapter is based, G. G. Simpson (1970) chided me for criticizing those animal communication specialists whose work had only confirmed their beliefs about nonhumans and language. His critical tone confirmed for me the fact that animal behaviorists and some other biologists have a view of nature which makes man appear to be not merely unique (as are all species), but to be just a wee bit extranatural, outside of nature. His notion of language is the metaphorical vehicle by which he justifies this claim. But note also that he elected to appeal to a particular normative sense to convey his ideas, and that this appeal carries a greater intellectual load than it appears at first glance.

In Simpson's words:

> For myself, I am aware of the obvious fact that animals communicate. It seems equally obvious to me that they do not use language, as I and most others have defined that word. Over some span of time in some group of primates some form of communication did evolve into language. That does not make the surviving nonlinguistic forms of communication of other primates and other animals either primitive or defective forms of language, especially as man retains such forms of communication *in addition to* language. [italics mine]

Clearly man has what other animals have, plus he has more, namely, language. Whatever Simpson has in mind by his definition, I believe there is very little agreement on what language means. Even for linguists, the definition is in flux. The important point, in my view, is that Simpson's view is a mind/body dualism in which mind and human become coterminous through the appeal to a reified something called language. I find this totally circular.

Simpson went on to quote himself and to explain himself:

> What I actually wrote was, "Language is also the most diagnostic single trait of man: all normal men have language; no other now-living organisms do."
> Until someone finds a normal man who cannot acquire language or another now-living organism that can, I take this to be an acceptable provisional truth.

In casting about for some reasonable way to characterize human uniqueness, Simpson uses a method that modern linguistics has called "the clear-case" (Chomsky, 1965, p. 19). That is, while one's total definition is really quite fuzzy, one can make it appear reasonable, correct, and even popular by appealing only to those aspects of it about which everyone seems to agree. (In my actual experience, it turns out that if you disagree, you get called either incompetent or crazy!)

Underlying the method, and justifying its provisional nature, is some sort of promise that it will eventually elucidate some essential aspects of its subject matter—in this case, human nature.

But what about the notion of normality—of some sense of the "ideal" man who lurks beneath the observable behavior—that Simpson claims we all agree to be language. I suggest that normal and ideal are terms which carry along a great deal more than the mere concepts of "provisional definition" or "working hypothesis" appear to imply.

My reply to Simpson's remarks (Sarles, 1970a) pointed out that there are indeed a number of now-existing human beings who are adjudged to be *abnormal* in form and behavior. I suggest that our ideologies, which seem to imply an extranatural status for ordinary-normal men, also shield a potential implication for those whom *we* claim to be abnormal: namely, we tend to think of them in ways similar to those in which we think of animals. What else could a "lack" of language or defective or deficient language imply in a world view where the very definition of man depends on his having language?

What is really wrong with those people who speak peculiarly? Abnormally? Again, as in other aspects of theories of development, there seem to be two very different views. In the unfolding notion of normal development, there is something intrinsically "wrong" with those who are abnormal. Within the context of a dynamic, interactional view, the problem is seen to be much more complex.

Keep in mind the fact that the recent recipients of the label of "abnormal and deficient language" have been, increasingly, persons from minority backgrounds, and that the locus of their "problem" has increasingly been claimed to be in their central nervous systems or brains (Baratz & Baratz, 1972). "Minimal brain damage" is a label by which we can trick ourselves into justifying these essentially political–social judgments of abnormality-with-respect-to-the-majority, by claiming that such people had the sort of genetic endowment which limits the possibilities of their speaking (and thinking) normally.

In the *Realpolitik* of speech pathology, it turns out that the story is more involved. If the person "looks right," then the pathology is generally considered to be small. So, as far as I can tell, one's face *and* language both affect how he will be judged.

Consider the population which seems to provide our very facial stereotype of stupidity: namely, Down's Syndrome/mongoloid children. Their mouths tend to remain open and their tongues to hang out. We interpret this look to mean that not too much of interest is going on in their heads. As a population they are considered to be "retarded" in thought and language.

Are they really retarded? What is their problem?

As I have suggested elsewhere, the question of Down's children may very well be a social–perceptual problem of adult–child relationship. In my personal observations of very young (2 to 4-month-old) Down's infants, the clearest fact about them is that their external facial movements are extremely limited: very "sharp" eyes moving against a relatively blank background, little hint of a smile or other affective expression. I surmise that their external facial muscles are not working properly, possibly due to an intrinsically muscular or nervous innervation problem.

Now, without our making any strong assumptions about the nature and quality of their minds, which might indeed be "peculiar" in some sense, it seems reasonable that the very *definition* of them as retarded will suffice to produce the typically retarded person. That is, if parental perception of them is that they are very limited intellectually, that's how they will turn out.

There is obviously much more to this story, part of it being that the mothers of such children get less affective response/feedback from their children than they seem to know how to deal with and tend to alter by very slight steps the quality and type of interaction. These children are, in other words, not terribly "interesting." But this may have only to do with how we adults conceptualize faces—it may not have very much to do with intellectual capacity in any deep sense, except that a child who is treated peculiarly is likely to respond to such a treatment in kind.

Consider how any child "gets into" others' faces as part of the general problem of how anybody knows about others' bodies. Consider further that the Down's children appear to operate in this venture starting with a muscular endowment which is undoubtedly different from that of the ordinary infant. Not only is this a problem in adult perception, but let us assume that the child himself will attempt to "model" others' faces—however infants do this. That his face turns out to "look stupid" is probably just as surprising to him as the "intelligent" child's face, which turns out to look "smart," is to him.

What I'm suggesting is that the questions of thought, language, intelligence, and all that these terms imply, should be considered in their conceptual and behavioral-interactional dynamic. Our theories of normality may lead us to believe that such attributes of individuals as I.Q. are really "fixed" in some nonplastic sense, but I believe it is fascinating to attempt to reconceptualize these problems in other terms.

Some of the ramifications of these moves point to a new understanding of what it may mean to look or be stupid, but just a wee bit stupid. Teachers seem to get a great deal of their feedback about what's going on in their students' heads from watching their faces. Teachers must make rapid judgments about whether a point is understood, and by whom. Their data are primarily facial expressions. So a student who either looks stupid in some static overarching sense, or whose look is interpreted as confused or stupid, will have some effect on the conduct of any class. Depending on the teacher, his or her mood, patience, etc., that stupid-looking student may get a lot of teaching energy—or more likely, apparently, he will begin to be treated differently from the bright-looking students.

All of this, I believe, does go on rapidly and subtly in classrooms. One must be quite careful in college teaching, for example, to choose "good" students for feedback. If one is trapped into using a student who is mainly attracted to the teacher for other than purely intellectual reasons, it may create long-term havoc in that class, that course, and the personal lives of teacher and student.

All of us seem to have pretty well-formed pictures of what we mean by intelligent looks, and we operate in terms of our own pictures. Surely they tend to become our prevailing operating truths, in some cases, irrespective of what may really be going on in the minds of our students.

I believe further that many of us are highly susceptible to "reading" faces of various people in particular manners, similar to how we react to different forms of speaking. It is very easy to believe—along class lines—that people who use forms like "ain't" and "he don't" are not merely lower class, but also uneducated and probably stupid. To the extent that educators can "spot" poor people, we must remember that we are reacting to bodies, and particularly to faces. I believe—with only a bit of tongue in cheek—that the junior college movement is a mechanism whereby many students who do not look like proper university students somehow learn to look proper enough so that we university teachers will not merely dismiss them out of hand.

Aspects of Language

To return to our earlier discussion, this excursion was prompted by G. G. Simpson's claim that only "normal humans" have language. My claim, to the contrary, is that concepts like normal and language are much more complicated than a comparative framework would make them appear, and that these notions, in particular, are based on a tautological definition of humans being human *because* they have mind and language. Simpson, Chomsky, and essentially all dualists simply deny the possibility of comparing so-called animal speech and human language.

In the context of a model of human normality or ideal behavior, these concepts also carry the possibility of labeling any person who is considered to have abnormal or less-than-normal language as animallike. In Simpson's formulation, normal humans have what animals have—plus we have language. Therefore, animals have *less* than humans. It is tempting to apply such a deficit model to those humans who, like animals, have peculiarities or abnormalities of language. It is apparently more tempting and easier to believe our own judgments of this sort when the retarded also "look different."

How can the human uniqueness formulation be bypassed or somehow transcended in the search for variables which may lend new insight into the natural condition of man and other social animals? Using language variables as an exemplary area of relationship, I suggest that it will be more immediately useful to reexamine the nature and definition of (human) language, rather than merely extrapolating from the verbal output of other animals to man. Not only are they presently noncomparable, but many of our very notions of other animals' behavior is derived from these definitions of human uniqueness.

In the remainder of this chapter, several ideas will be explored that will point toward some redefinitional aspects of language which are more likely shared by other species. Included in these are alternative perspectives of viewing human language: e.g., how could other species discover that we have language; how do developing humans discover that fact? Second, we should carefully study the history of linguistic thought, to discover the underlying issues and assumptions which govern our very conceptualization of human language—and which may then lead to postulating alternative lines of thought. Another line is to observe language, not as a *Ding an sich*, but as behavior: movement, vibrations, and tensions which characterize the stream of speech. The nature of intelligibility in real time remains obscure. What is the nature of *context*? Language study has always moved from structure to context; yet contextual studies remain a promise in the putative future. Lastly, what are tone-of-voice phenomena, often called paralanguage? Affect, emotion, etc. are considered to be epiphenomenal to human language. In order to be potentially comparable to animal languaging, can we reconceptualize paralanguage and show that it has some part in the actual semantics of the interaction?

Considering language as behavior, it becomes less clear that human language is as unique as our assumptions would lead us to believe. Languaging is a set of muscular phenomena involving the usual parts of the vocal apparatus. But, from an interactional dynamic perspective, there is much more to it.

For example, language behavior is not only hearable—musical tones impinging on auditory nerves as Helmholtz (1954) characterized it—but it is excitingly visual. Young children's poetry is a visual "trip." "Baa, baa, black sheep" may sound good, but it also involves major visual lip changes in each syllable, and in speaking baby talk, parents virtually explode their lips apart, dealing in tension and distances far outside the ordinary interactional parameters of facial movement. Every time the low vowel (aah) is sounded, the mouth is wide open and the visual mask as it might appear to the infant is increasingly intricate as the teeth and rapidly moving tongue are exposed. Considering that humans are "into" faces more than any other interactional surface and that parental faces likely loom very, very large to infants, the visual aspects of speech and language production should not be underestimated. Yet the linguistic literature virtually omits the fact that external faces are involved in language production.

Parenthetically it may be noted that saliva is also a major factor, in human speech at least. We must have and manage proper sorts and amounts of saliva to be able to speak at all. I suspect it is also involved in hearing and intelligibility since it is at present forming on the upper tips of tensioned tongues of most listeners and readers.

Thinking about language from a behavioral point of view also forces one to consider the fact that speaking and listening take place largely in interactional settings. Modern linguistics acts as if this fact is inconsequential to linguistic theory. That is, our theories of grammar imply that language is in each person's individual mind, that the presence and active participation of other people in speaking and hearing has essentially nothing to do with language (Chomsky, 1968).

The assumption that human language is only or even principally a grammar consisting of all sentences is to me merely an assumption. I believe that language is not even "learned" in any direct, straightforward manner, but that verbal and other behaviors occur in dialogues in which linguistic correctness is quite secondary to linguistic, cognitive, and behavioral *sensibility*. Children, in my view, do not produce or generate phrases and sentences and then somehow learn semantics; rather, the mother–child relationship is a dialogue of questions and responses through which the parental picture of the world is constantly "laid upon" the developing child. This approach, I believe, not only has interesting implications for studying normal language development, but it suggests that abnormal language is a relational, not just an individual, phenomenon (Sarles, 1970 b).

From this perspective, the fact that speakers have and use their faces and bodies becomes an obvious and interesting fact. The proverbial outsider—the Martian observing humans or us observing nonhumans—is more likely to note that speech does not occur in the sorts of vacuums that the rationalist linguist creates in his monochromatic ideations.

In considering the question of whether any nonhuman could possibly discover that we have language (if, indeed, we do), it is clear that most of us have in mind the nonterrestrial creature who is somehow "intelligent." Considering the sorts of science fiction about, we might note that the bodily form of the creatures is inconsequential to the "fact" of their intelligence. Mathematics and logic transcend nature in those intergalactic fantasies which will ultimately have only computers left trying to manipulate one another.

I sincerely doubt that even the most well-meaning nonhuman could discover that we have language unless he already believed that we did—before he began his study. If we wipe out the civilizations that have cropped up in the past 30,000 years or so, we would have appeared as Desmond Morris's vision of *The Naked Ape* (1967). Using the methods—and assumptions—that we apply to the so-called speech of other terrestrial creatures, there is no way in which the observer could separate the stream of speech into "message" or "grammar" and all the tone-of-voice stuff which is in speech pretty constantly. If the outsider was an honest, hard-nosed naturalist empiricist, he could not even tell when a loud message was directed to the contiguous body or to the errant child behind yonder tree. How could any outsider distinguish, say, loudness from anger? Even if a fight ensued, no one could say why, with any degree of certitude. A well-directed whispered insult, on top of a history of bad relations, can be more provocative than the loudest verbal assault!

I believe that present conceptualizations of (human) language, drawing on the origin myths of human uniqueness, do not permit any way out of our dilemmas. That is, much more of the same sorts of linguistic or paralinguistic studies will not possibly lend any new insight into the nature of language—human or any other. Are there any ways around or out of our conceptual hang-ups?

In the history of dualist thought, which is essentially the history of our linguistic and human nature ideology, the mind has reigned supreme; the human body has disappeared. It is the happenstance locus for the mind and soul (Vesey, 1965). In science fiction, and in much of the current fiction called science, the dualist is subtly at work in indirect and insidious ways.

Linguistic theory has throughout this century posited two sorts of speech. In different eras they are called "deep versus surface" (Chomsky, 1965), "langue versus parole" (Saussure, 1959), or "competence versus perfor-mance." Behavior and body are either passive vehicles for the transmission of the real or deep language, or they virtually disappear. Our language theories are disembodied. The body is little more than the telegraph line which transmits the message. The body is not the message; paralanguage is not the message.

On the contrary, I suggest that the human form has a lot to do with human language, cognition, logic, and rationality. Not only do children's auditory nerves get titillated by speech, but they seem to like their speech "face on." Speech pressure hits the entire face and body. It may well be that the stuff of language, which effectively gets to the auditory nerves and interpretation cen-ters, is censored and shaped by those unique and special shapes which we all recognize as humanoid. It may well be that the listener who is passive in some of our communication theory mythologies is "holding" his facies in the sort of tensioned fashions that deliver his "favorite" sorts of sounds. The more active appearing speaker "reads" the tension and variation in the listener and relates the message to what he thinks he sees—and feels, as well, in my estimation. It is worth recalling that the sound spectrographic techniques that are widely used in animal speech studies seem to presume that auditory nerves are essentially panspecific. It seems, to me, a curious presumption!

More optimistically, I believe there are ways around these dilemmas. But they require some commitments to rethinking and reconceptualization. Why not, for example, study contextual variables directly in human language?

I had noted years ago, in a study among Tzotzil-speaking Mayan Indians in southern Mexico, that I could usually tell what sort of person was speaking to another, well before I comprehended the language in the ordinary sense, e.g., man and older women, adult with child. This was also observable while working at a psychiatric institute—I could usually tell from the hall what sort of person my medical colleagues were speaking to without hearing what was being said—wife, colleague, patient. And in my own household I can tell from upstairs whom my wife is talking to—often the specific person—just by the vague tones that drift up through floors, around hallways, and up the stairs. What sorts of things in those voices did I respond to; what do they represent; how might they affect the comparative study of language?

One of my students just finished a dissertation examining what she calls the "nonlinguistic" content of speech in English and Japanese (Benjamin, 1974). She took short (½-second or so) excerpts from ordinary speech in different contexts. The fact is that other people do know, with a fairly high degree of agreement and certitude from the voice of the speaker alone, a good deal about the situation, the speaker, the hearer, their relationship. The stream of speech carries our age as a constant message, for example, although we Westerners seem to be more in tune with this than the Japanese. We can tell if a person is speaking to one person or to lots of people, even in another language.

While this muddies the waters of cross-species linguistics, it is one suggestive example of how thinking ethologically has forced a few of us to reexamine our presuppositions about human language. Benjamin and another former student have done a parallel video-tape study of the human face in different contexts, which showed that an audience was also sensitive to the contextual changes as they are revealed on an individual face (Benjamin and Creider, 1973).

I suggest that a method which proceeds by these sorts of methods of "peeling off" the contextual and relational elements in speech first will ultimately yield more insight into the nature of human (or other) language than one that proceeds by assuming that we know a priori what the nature of the deep or message aspects of language are.

The difficulties in any such study—intra- or interspecies—is that the behavior is likely to be much more complex than we have thought. By reducing, or attempting to reduce, the actual complexity, we are likely, in my opinion, to obscure as much as we can elucidate. Again consider human language. Unless we are only tonal or phoneme-formant analyzers as all of our acoustic theory suggests, it remains unclear how we understand each other, especially in real time. It turns out, for example, that entire words can be cut out, literally excised from actual conversation, with little or no loss of intelligibility (Pollack & Pickett, 1964). This means, to me, that that information which *we* think of as a given word is more than that. If words can be cut out with no loss in intelligibility, information about that word must be present at other points in a given sentence (Sarles, 1967). This presents a real dilemma for the naturalist-descriptivist since, no matter how careful and accurate he is, the data which occur at a given instant may convey information about other instants, and not merely about themselves. Animal communication scholars have tried to get around this problem by claiming that nonhumans are stimulus-bound and tied into the present here-and-now (Busnel, 1963, p. 69). In other words, our view of history and context for other animals is extremely simplex.

We should remain dubious that simplex observations, even carefully done, can yield insight into more complicated worlds. All the scientist need do is discount some of his observations, or make his simplex pigeonholes wide enough to accommodate apparent aberrancies, to keep his science "pure."

Consider this example—eliminated from linguistic purview on the ground that it is extralinguistic. There is an old Stan Freberg record called *John and Marcia*. The record, the acoustic behavior, consists phonemically of just two words, repeated several times: She says, "John", he says "Marcia"—nothing else. But they simultaneously "tell" a long story: meeting, greeting, loving, lovemaking, departing. Where is all this information—on the record, only in our minds? The fact that there is continuity in speech, that there is a story, a mutual history, is not part of linguistic theory. And its possibility has apparently been eliminated from the study of other animals' speech, as well.

In other studies, always attempting to keep in mind a cross-species perspective, I have found that we are very context-bound, or context-congruent observers. By cutting a film in pieces to compare similar gestures, I noted several years ago that the accompanying speech sounded much different than I had noted it when listening in the ongoingness of the original film. It may well be that an immediate task of understanding other species and ourselves is to get some more insight into the sorts of observers we are. One method for doing this is to "break context," and match what we observed "in context" with the differences that show up out of context.

To conclude, studies of verbal behavior in different species have not been very directly comparable. While very few of us, if any, believe that others share all of the features of human languages, there seem to be whole landscapes which have not yet been explored.

Reasons for this include the exclusive, theological preorientation of the human linguist in his proclamation that human language is coterminous with human being. If one believes that things are intrinsically noncomparable, he has every right to suspect his own motives in trying to compare them.

Animal callists—professed comparativists—have not been sufficiently demanding of themselves or of human linguists, either to proceed in similar fashion, or to force themselves and linguists to gain each other's perspectives. In my experience, many biologists have overly accepted the extranatural definition of man contained in current linguistic formulations and have not yet demanded the same rigor of themselves in looking at humans that they apply in observing other species. If we desire more real knowledge about man, the comparative approach is crucial. But if we all begin with fictions about man, I am afraid that we'll end up with the kind of novel, biologized myths that have sold so well in the past few years.

I have tried to suggest a potentially rich direction for doing comparative work in verbal behavior. This is to reexamine and rethink the ideas which had led to the current theories about human language, to show that a very narrow, restrictive set of variables has been thought to characterize all of human language. I am convinced that human speech is a much more intricate process than it has been thought to be, and one which is potentially studiable. I think the comparison of human language and animal communication suffers from misconception, not from discontinuity!

I am leery of current extrapolations from nonhumans to humans, not because it is difficult, but because we have often defined nonhumans more as deficient humans than as rich interactors in their own social–cognitive terms. In trying to find some primary essence of humans or other, which would seemingly allow us to cut through or bypass the complexities of life, we may have impoverished our theories about the human condition. If, as I suspect, the study of aggression runs in any way parallel to the history and traditions of linguistic thought, we should continue to be as critical and careful of how we *think* about the problems of comparison as we are about the observations we make.

Acknowledgment

My thanks to Janis H. Sarles for a careful and critical reading of this work, and to Mischa Penn for his continuing intellectual advice and support.

References

Baratz, S., & Baratz, J. Black culture on black terms: a rejection of the social pathology model. In T. Kochman (Ed.), *Rappin' and stylin' out: communication in urban black America*. Urbana: University of Illinois Press, 1972.
Benjamin, G. R. The non-linguistic context of speech in Japanese. Unpublished Ph.D. dissertation, University of Minnesota, 1974.

Benjamin, G. R., & Creider, C. A. Social distinctions in non-verbal behavior. To be published in *Semiotica*.

Busnel, R. F. On certain aspects of animal acoustic signals. In *Acoustic Behavior of Animals*. Amsterdam: Elsevier, 1963.

Chomsky, N. *Aspects of the theory of syntax*. Cambridge: MIT Press, 1965.

Chomsky, N. *Language and mind*. New York: Harcourt, Brace and World, 1968.

Enlow, D. *The human face*. New York: Harper and Row, 1968.

Gardner, B. T., & Gardner, R. A. Teaching sign language to a chimpanzee. *Science*, 1969, *165*, 664–672.

Helmholtz, H. *On the sensations of tone*. New York: Dover, 1954.

Lorenz, K. *On aggression*. New York: Harcourt, Brace and World, 1966, Chap. 13.

Morris, D. *The naked ape*. New York: McGraw-Hill, 1967.

Piaget, J. *The origins of intelligence in children*. New York: W. W. Norton, 1963.

Pollack, I., & Pickett, S. M. Intelligibility of excerpts from fluent speech: Auditory vs. structure context. *Journal of Verbal Learning and Verbal Behavior*, 1964, *3*, 79–84.

Salzinger, K. Pleasing linguists: a parable. *Journal of Verbal Learning and Verbal Behavior*, 1970, *9*, 725–727.

Sarles, H. B. The study of intelligibility. *Linguistics*, 1967, *34*, 55–64.

Sarles, H. B. The study of language and communication across species. *Current Anthropology*, *10*, (2–3), April-June 1969, 211–221.

Sarles, H. B. Reply to Simpson. *Current Anthropology*, 1970, *11*, 1, February 1970:72. (a)

Sarles, H. B. An examination of the Question-Response system in language. *Semiotica II*, 1970, *1*, 79–101. (b)

Sarles, H. B. Could a non-H (possibly discover that humans have language)? In Hewes, Stokoe, Westcott (Eds.), *Language origins*, Linstock Press, Silver Spring, Maryland, 1975, in press.

Sarles, H. B. *The search for comparative variables in human speech. A symposium paper: animal communication vs. human speech—a discontinuity in approach or in evolution?* Paper read at the annual meeting of the Animal Behavior Society, Reno. 1972. (a)

Sarles, H. B. *The dynamics of facial expression*. Paper read at the annual meeting of the International Association for Dental Research, Las Vegas. 1972. (b)

Sarles, H. B. Facial expression and body movement. In T. Sebeok (Ed.), *Current Trends in Linguistics* (Vol. 12). The Hague: Mouton, 1975, in press.

Saussure, F. de. A course in general linguistics, W. Baskin (Tr.) New York: Philosophical Library, 1959.

Simpson, G. G. The biological nature of man. *Science*, 1966, *152*, 472–78.

Simpson, G. G. On Sarles' views on language and communication. *Current Anthropology*, 1970, *11*, 1, February 1970:71.

Vesey, G. N. A. *The embodied mind*. London: George Allen and Unwin, 1965.

CHAPTER 2

Visual Behavior as an Aspect of Power Role Relationships[1]

Ralph V. Exline and Steve L. Ellyson[2]

University of Delaware
Newark, Delaware

and

Barbara Long

Goucher College
Towson, Maryland

Introduction

There is an intriguing paradox inherent in the shared glance. On the one hand, there is the suggestion that willingness to engage in mutual glances is a means of establishing union with another (Simmel, 1969)—a suggestion which is supported by empirical evidence that affiliative motives (Exline, 1963) and loving relationships (Rubin, 1970) are characterized by relatively greater amounts of mutual looks than are their opposites. On the other hand, there is the suggestion, also backed with empirical evidence, that a mutual glance elicits threat displays between subhuman primates (Hinde and Rowell, 1962; Hall and Devore, 1965; Jay, 1965), that the fixed glance of one human is associated with another's accelerated movement away (Ellsworth, Carlsmith, & Henson, 1972), and that, in specified circumstances, the one who first breaks off a mutual glance is socially subordinate (Edelman, Omark, & Freedman, 1971), while one who

[1] Research reported in this paper was supported by funds from Contract No. 2285 and PHS Grant 1 TO1 MH11473.
[2] Now at Beaver College, Glenside, Pennsylvania.

looks steadily at another in silence is perceived to be more dominant than one who looks briefly (Thayer, 1969).

The senior author's first systematic study of visual interaction illustrates the paradox, for those who valued affiliation more than achievement significantly reduced their mutual glances in competitive as compared to noncompetitive situations, whereas those who valued achievement more than affiliation showed the reverse trend (Exline, 1963).

This book is concerned with the nonverbal communication of aggression, and our discussion will focus on the darker side of eye engagements, though we will deal more with power and control than with aggression per se. Power, control, aggression—the concepts are closely linked, for how often is one who gives little indication of interest in influencing or controlling the actions of others likely to be described as infringing or encroaching on another's rights or territory?

In the light of the theme of this symposium it is of interest that the first empirical study of eye engagements which we found reported in the psychological literature was one in which eye control was used as a measure of aggressiveness. In 1921, H. T. Moore and A. R. Gilliland of Dartmouth College published a paper entitled "The Measurement of Aggressiveness." They reported that the ability to maintain eye contact with another while performing a series of mental additions was more characteristic of aggressive than of nonaggressive persons. "Aggressiveness" was determined by asking students and faculty at Dartmouth College to rate 89 advanced undergraduates on the trait of aggressiveness. The values of the American Establishment are suggested as we read that the aggressive man is likely to be "vigorous, positive and masterful . . . less likely to shrink from notice, to avoid argument, [and] to display a lack of nerve." The 13 most aggressive, selected for testing, included the president of the senior class, the business manager of the college daily, the manager of track athletics, the president of the Outing Club, an officer of the Dramatic Association who was prominent in the production of student plays, and the quarterback of the football team! The 13 least aggressive men were characterized as being: "decidedly without prominence in college activities."

Moore and Gilliland were interested in developing easily administered behavioral tests of aggressiveness in the hope that a grouping of several significant tests would enable them to draw an aggressiveness profile.[3]

The assumption that seemed to underlie the selection of the tests was that the more aggressive subjects would be less prone to distraction (more in control of themselves, as it were) as they worked on a task. Thus, they were stared at, shocked, or exposed to the sight of a dead snake as they worked through a series

---

[3] Gilliland later used a modified version of the original battery (including the eye control test) in an attempt to identify successful salesmen of classified ads for a large metropolitan newspaper (Gilliland, 1926).

of mental additions. Reaction time and visual avoidance behaviors were recorded and used to compare aggressive and nonaggressive subjects.[4]

The reason for incorporating eye engagements into the behavioral battery was stated as follows: "Common sense has it that the shifty eye is generally a sign of personal weakness, if not downright dishonesty. The first test was designed with a view to bringing this element of behavior into quantitative relation with the trait aggressiveness" (Moore and Gilliland, 1921, p. 100).

The results showed that Moore and Gilliland's intuition was supported, at least with reference to the concomitance of eye control and ratings of aggressiveness. The 13 most aggressive Ss were better able to follow instructions not to look away from the experimenter, and completed their mental additions more quickly. All of the 13 aggressive Ss manifested fewer than three eye movements ($M = .46$) compared to only 23% of the nonaggressive Ss ($M = 5.54$). Compared to a control series of additions, aggressive Ss took, on the average, .7 seconds longer per series compared to an increase of 3.2 seconds per series for the less aggressive Ss. Thus, over 50 years ago, while stating that it was "hardly to be hoped for that any single test would show a point for point correspondence with the existence of the trait (of aggressiveness)," Moore and Gilliland nevertheless concluded that "the eye movement test does almost approximate such a correspondence" (p. 99).

Did these investigators of 50 years ago stumble onto a simple test of aggressive inclinations? Can you determine personal force and strength merely by counting the number of gaze aversions manifested by one instructed to look you in the eye while adding a series of numbers? Was the eye control manifested in the laboratory test an example of a general tendency to exhibit steadiness of gaze in normal social discourse? Did such steadiness more or less unconsciously affect those who made the ratings of aggressiveness? If so, perhaps one can size up the personal force and potential aggressiveness of another by virtue of his or her visual attentiveness in a state of talk—the more attentive, the more aggressive.

It seems to us that such generalization is unwise. In normal discourse one is usually not instructed to look steadily at another throughout the interaction. Whether one does or not is a matter of choice, a choice, to be sure, which is partly personal but which may also be in part dictated by both explicit and unspoken conventions concerning the appropriateness of giving or withholding visual attention. "Don't stare at the man—it's impolite" or "Look at me when I am talking to you" scolds the embarrassed or angry parent. We speak of love at first "sight" and of "losing ourselves in the pools of the beloved's eyes." "Of the special sense-organs," wrote Simmel in 1908, "the eye has a uniquely

---

[4] A word association test was also analyzed in terms of reaction time and as to how "colorful," "positive," and "definite" the responses were to stimulus words judged to be relevant to the concept of aggressiveness, e.g., "enterprise," "success," "danger," "apparent," etc.

sociological function. . . . Shame causes a person to look at the ground to avoid the glance of the other . . . not only because he is thus spared the visible evidence of the way in which the other regards his painful situation, but for the deeper reason that the lowered glance to a certain degree prevents the other from comprehending the extent of his confusion. . . . The eye cannot take unless at the same time it gives'' (Simmel, 1969, p. 358).

Let us stress Simmel's phrase: *"The eye cannot take unless at the same time it gives."* It is our belief that it is particularly useful in understanding the conventions that have grown up around eye engagements in social interaction, and is particularly relevant to the management of power relations in real life, if not in the laboratory.

To say that the eye "takes" is to say that we use our eyes to obtain information about the other. This information is useful either in gauging his reaction to our speech and/or behavior, or in using his nonverbal behaviors to better understand or to evaluate the validity of the message he provides us in words. Thus one function of looking is to obtain information from and about the speaker which cannot be derived from his words alone. Such information would seem to be relevant to our personal concerns of communication or comprehension.

To say that the eyes "give" is to suggest that the act of looking at another signals him that he has our attention. Perhaps we give it voluntarily, perhaps he has demanded it; but if we look at him—for that moment in time he has it. Thus a second function of looking would seem to be to signal the other that we accept and adhere to a norm of attention.

We suggest that while there exists in all societies a general norm of attention concerning visual behavior, in our western society, at least, the norm prescribes different amounts of visual attention for individuals who occupy different positions in a social power hierarchy. More specifically, we suggest that in any given group of interactants, the relative amount of visual attention the norm requires one to give the others is inversely related to his or her relative standing in the hierarchy of power or prestige. The higher one's standing, the less is one required to give visual attention to the others, and vice versa.[5]

A qualification is necessary here. We suggest that the above convention holds in normal discourse wherein people are talking and listening to one another, and where the situation is neither implicitly nor explicitly defined as a dominance struggle. In the laboratory test devised by Moore and Gilliland, for

[5] Perceptive novelists often anticipate the psychologists' interest in various aspects of the human condition. Long before contemporary psychologists became interested in eye engagements as regulators of social interaction (Kendon, 1967), Anton Chekhov had a Russian judge use the rule suggested above to establish his superiority over a pleading lawyer. "If an attorney had to speak to him, Pytor Dmitrich, turning a little away from him, looked with half-closed eyes at the ceiling, meaning to signify thereby that the lawyer was utterly superfluous and that he was neither recognizing him nor listening to him" (Chekhov, 1888, p. 191).

example, the subject knows that he is being mildly challenged. In such a case one is not voluntarily giving his visual attention, rather he is "emphatically instructed" to maintain a fixed gaze lest it adversely affect his score. He is, in other words, challenged to try to maintain eye contact with the experimenter—a situation in which the norm of attention as described above would not be operative.

One way to test the model described above would be to locate groups in which there exists a true hierarchy of power. If the hierarchy is one which is accepted as legitimate by the various members of the group, we could then record and compare the amounts of time during which members of the group give their visual attention to those who are superior, equal, and inferior in power to themselves. An example of such a group would be an academic departmental committee composed of a full professor who is the department chairman, two tenured associate professors, and one nontenured, recently hired assistant professor. If such a group could be observed in action we would expect the chairman to receive the most, the assistant professor the least, and the associate professors intermediate amounts of visual attention from the others. While such groups may not be difficult to find, they are, in practice, almost impossible to use for systematic data collection. Can you imagine such a committee voluntarily seated in a roomful of one-way mirrors discussing sensitive departmental problems while graduate assistants record their speech and visual interaction patterns?

With careful planning, however, realistic analogs of such groups can be simulated, and we feel that we have done so in three studies which we shall report in this chapter. The first study (Exline and Long, 1971) has already been reported in a chapter prepared for a recent meeting of Nebraska Symposium (Exline, 1972). We shall review it briefly before describing the others in greater detail.

Empirical Studies

Experiment I: Visual Attentiveness in Relation to Power Differences in Legitimate and Illegitimate Hierarchies

In this study, true power differences were created by giving one person in a dyad control over another's outcomes.[6] This person, hereafter designated HP, was instructed, unbeknownst to the person in the low power position (LP), to divide a ten-chip reward, after each of three discussion tasks, according to a schedule which gave HP more chips than LP in a 7–3, 6–4, 6–4 ratio. The chips were to be redeemed for money following the experiment, and the induction was rationalized by pointing out that in true organizations one person often had the power to determine the rewards and privileges of others.

[6] After the definition of social power by Thibaut and Kelley (1959).

Subjects were instructed separately; HP was asked not to reveal that the division of the chips was predetermined and was assured that the deception would be explained to the other upon completion of the task. The three problems were designed to encourage discussion and to provoke some disagreement. No problem had an obviously correct solution, a fact which reinforced the believability of the power induction.

After a period in which Ss read the problem and made notes, the experimenter collected the problems and left the room. A buzzer signaled the beginning of a three-minute discussion period during which time observers positioned behind a one-way mirror recorded the frequency and duration of each S's look into the line of regard of the other. Observations were concluded with the sound of the second buzzer, or after ten seconds of silence following a decision reached prior to the end of three minutes. The experimenter then returned to the discussion room to give HP chips to distribute, after which she gave them the next problem and left again.

The perceived legitimacy of the power hierarchy was varied by creating 40 working pairs, 20 of which were composed of ROTC cadets, one officer and one basic, while the other 20 were composed of students from a large gym class. ROTC cadets were in uniform and were released from a drill class for testing. In each ROTC dyad the officer was assigned the HP position. No data from pairs of acquaintances were used, such pairs being replaced in the design by pairs of unacquainted Ss.

Posttest questionnaires were administered to check upon the effectiveness of both the power and legitimacy inductions. Differences in ratings made by persons in both HP and LP positions in each legitimacy category were significant beyond .05 and .01 probability levels in directions coordinate with what would be expected from successful inductions.

On the basis of the previous discussion of the information gathering utility of, and normative expectations about visual attention, we predicted that LP would give more visual attention to the other (HP) than would HP (to LP). On the assumption that the legitimacy induction would operate most strongly upon LP (HP was, after all, a quasi-confederate) we predicted that LP in the legitimate power (ROTC) condition would give more visual attention to HP than would LP in the illegitimate power condition (Gym Class).

In summary the working hypotheses were:

Hypothesis 1: In dyads in which members occupy different power positions, LP as compared to HP will, everything else being equal, look more into the line of regard of the other.

Hypothesis 2: LP in the ROTC condition will look more into HP's line of regard than will LP in the Gym condition.

Figure 1 shows the seconds per minute in which an occupant of one power position in each legitimacy condition looked into the line of regard of the

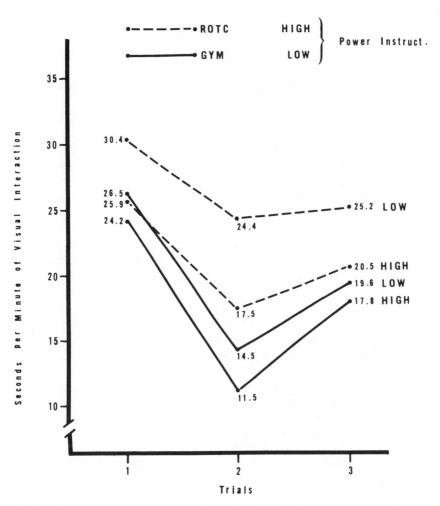

Fig. 1.   Mean seconds per minute of visual interaction of high and low power members of gym and ROTC dyads during three decision-discussion trials (N = 20 per mean). (From R. V. Exline, "Visual interaction: The glances of power and preference," in J. K. Cole (Ed.), *Nebraska Symposium on Motivation*. Copyright ©1972 by the University of Nebraska Press. Reprinted by permission.)

occupant of the other power position in each of the three tasks. There were significant main effects for trials, power position, and legitimacy conditions and interaction effects for trials by power position by legitimacy. It is clear that, over all periods and legitimacy conditions, LP gave more visual attention than did HP. The trend was established early and reached significance in the second and third trials. In overall percentage, visual attention amounted to 39.1% for LP compared to 32.6% for HP. The evidence thus supports the first hypothesis, especially since HP did not speak more than LP, indeed the reverse was true in the illegitimate condition. Thus LP did not look more because HP spoke more.

The data also support our second hypothesis in that the differences between the visual attention of HP and LP are greater in the legitimate (ROTC) power hierarchy. Furthermore while LP in the illegitimate (Gym) condition only tended to look less than LP in the legitimate (ROTC) condition during the first task, the difference reached significance on both the second and third tasks. The fact that greater overall visual attention was given in the legitimate hierarchy (40% ROTC to 31.7% for Gym dyads) is further evidence in support of the success of the legitimacy induction.

While the data appear to support the proposition that the interaction of information utility and norms of attentiveness lead to greater visual attentiveness on the part of LP, alternative explanations of the results need to be considered. It is possible that HP looked less at LP because of guilt feelings stemming from his knowledge that he, due to his quasi-confederate status, was required to treat another unfairly. It is possible that HPs' quasi-confederate status may have fostered guilt feelings which caused them to avoid looking at those they may have felt required to treat unfairly. Relevant to this suggestion was the finding that occupants of HP positions rated the distribution of chips as being less fair than did occupants of LP positions.

A second possibility concerns HPs' possible attempts to reduce the negativity of LPs' reactions to them as a consequence of the chip distribution. To receive only 3 of 10 chips in a situation in which there was no clearly objective basis on which to judge performance implies that the other has a low regard for one's contributions. Thus HP is likely to infer that LP will perceive the chip distribution as a criticism of his (LP's) performance. If HPs are intuitively aware that people do not like those who look at them while giving unfavorable feedback (Ellsworth and Carlsmith, 1968), they may wish to reduce the probability that LP will develop negative feelings toward them, not only by not looking at LP during the chip distribution, but also by reducing the amount they look at LP in discussions following unfavorable feedback. They may wish to reduce LP's possible feeling that HP enjoys his discomfort. Under those circumstances not looking may be a form of ingratiation.

The next study to be reported was designed to investigate the validity of the alternative explanations.

Experiment 2: Visual Interaction as a Consequence of Various Reward Ratios in Legitimate Power Hierarchies[7]

The possible effects of guilt and ingratiation on HPs' lesser looking in the earlier study can be investigated by adding two additional payoff conditions to a replication of the legitimate power hierarchy. In the original study HP was instructed to give himself 7 chips and the other 3 after the completion of the first task, reducing the split to a 6–4 after each of the next two tasks. In this study the self-benefiting distribution which characterized the activity of HP in the original experiment was replicated for 1/4 of the HP subjects. In addition, a second 1/4 of the HP Ss were instructed to reverse the ratios, i.e., to benefit LP in a 3–7, 4–6, 4–6 schedule (other-benefit condition), while the final 1/2 of HP Ss were instructed to divide the chips according to their "best judgment" of the relative contribution each made to the solution of the problem. The second condition (the other-benefit condition) was designed to alleviate feelings of guilt based on unfairly reducing another's rewards, while the third, labeled the free-choice condition, was added to assuage guilt that may have arisen from providing LP with false feedback. The third condition thus serves as a control for the effects of the specifically directed use of power (whether to benefit or disadvantage another) on the visual behavior of the occupant of the high power position.

In order to protect the power induction by encouraging HPs to take their power task seriously, the following instructions were given to HP in the free-choice condition:

> You may give him however many you want and keep the rest. Remember, people in leadership positions in an organization have the responsibility of not only evaluating the work of their subordinates, but of communicating these evaluations to them. This means that there are times when one must have the courage to risk unpopularity by giving negative feedback. The only way you will be able to give feedback in this situation is by how you distribute the chips. Thus if you believe that the other person's contribution to the task was less than yours, you should feel free to give him less chips than you give to yourself. Let me repeat once again that you are in control of these rewards. How you distribute them is up to your best judgment. Do you have any questions?

This instruction was designed to discourage HP from making a 50–50 split. This was done for two reasons: (1) It was felt that such a split would reduce the perception that power was realistically present in the situation. (2) To the extent that HP would benefit either himself or the other, the number of dyads falling in such conditions would be increased for the purpose of analyzing questions in addition to those of the effects of guilt and ingratiation.

We argue that the additional distribution schedules will enable us to assess the possible effects of guilt and/or ingratiation upon HP's visual attentiveness. If

[7] This section is based on an experiment carried out by the junior author as part of his master's thesis (Ellyson, 1973).

the earlier relationship found between HP and LP is replicated in the self-benefit condition but not in both of the other two conditions, then either guilt or ingratiation rather than power could explain HP's visual attention. If HP in both self and other-benefit condition, but not in the free choice condition, were to give relatively less visual attention to the other than does LP, one would suspect that the original results were either due to chance or were based on guilt or discomfort over the false feedback which characterizes both self and other-benefit conditions. Finally, if the previously found differences between HP and LP are not replicated in the self-benefit conditions, then such differences could have been due to chance rather than to power role considerations.

If, on the other hand, HP gives relatively less visual attention to LP than LP does to him in all three distribution conditions, we would suggest that the alternative explanations are untenable. In such a case the data would lend additional support to our original power role interpretation.

We have discussed our model of visual attentiveness only in terms of the total visual attention manifested by occupants of different power positions regardless of whether the interactants were speaking, listening, or mutually silent. It is necessary to bring the model into closer correspondence with reality. This can be done by recognizing that information gathering and normative signaling will combine to differentially affect the visual attentiveness of HP and LP Ss according to whether a given S is speaking or listening to another of higher or lower power.

Before deriving specific predictions concerning the relative amounts of visual attention which HP and LP give to one another as they speak and listen, we need to consider another factor relevant to the visual attention which a speaker directs to a listener—namely, the problem of information overload. A speaker must not only present his thoughts in an organized sequence, but, to the extent that he pays close visual attention to listener, he cannot avoid seeing listener's reaction to what he has just said. This increases the probability that he must process feedback while simultaneously continuing to produce cognitive material in words. It is postulated that excessive amounts of such feedback will interfere with the cognitive processes necessary to continue the flow of speech, and that inhibition of such feedback enables one to perform more efficiently as a speaker. Looking away from the listener would thus serve to reduce the amount of incoming information which a speaker must process.

The second factor, i.e., the "norm of attention," is operative in both speaking and listening roles, for conventions of courtesy would seem to require that both speaker and listener give evidence of "paying attention" to the other. Looking at another is a conventional way of indicating such attention.

Where role expectations do not require that one person in a dyad give more evidence of attention than is required of the other, these two factors (feedback inhibition and the norm of attentiveness) should systematically and differentially

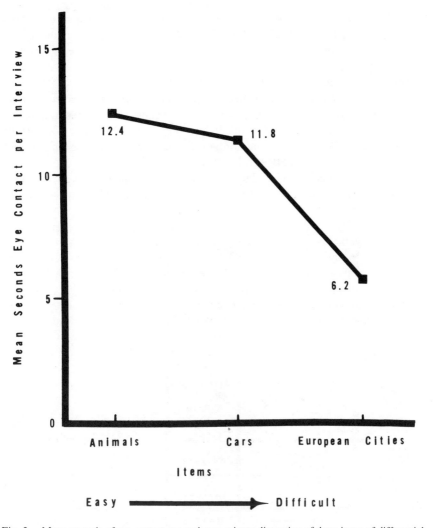

Fig. 2.   Mean seconds of eye contact per each two-minute discussion of three items of differential cognitive difficulty.

affect the looking behavior of the persons in the two roles. In other words, the norm of attention should operate equally on both speaker and listener, but the need to inhibit feedback should act mainly on the speaker. Thus, everything else being equal, each person in a dyad should look less while speaking than while listening. We suggest that the above analysis explains the consistent finding that a greater percentage of time is spent in looking while listening than in looking while speaking (Exline, 1963; Exline, Gray, & Schuette, 1965; Kendon, 1967). Further support for this suggestion is shown in Figure 2, in which we see that, as the difficulty of the cognitive theme increases, the speaker is less visually attentive to the listener (Exline and Winters, 1965).

Let us now consider how power differences in a dyad are expected to affect the influence of these factors upon visual attentiveness. We suggest that power has its major effect upon the norm of attention, particularly upon LP in the listening mode. We postulate that normative considerations require that LP give more visual attention to a HP speaker than vice versa.

The differential effects of these combined factors upon visual attentiveness in both speaking and listening roles for dyads of equal and differential power are portrayed in Figure 3.

In summary, we argue that the above model predicts the comparative ratios of looking while speaking to looking while listening for each party in a dyad. With respect to dyads in which interactants occupy positions of different power, our model suggests that the factor of feedback inhibition applies equally to all persons regardless of power position or speech mode. On the other hand, the norm of attention is postulated to operate more strongly on *S* in the listening role and requires LP to give more visual attention to a HP speaker than vice versa.

		Without Power Role Considerations:	With Power Role Considerations:	
Influence on Looking While Speaking (L S)	Feedback Inhibition	Decrease	Decrease for Both Persons	
	Norm of Attention	Increase	Increase for Both Persons	
Influence on Looking While Listening (L L)	Feedback Inhibition	Not a Factor	Not a Factor for Either Person	
	Norm of Attention	Increase	Stronger Increase on Person of Lower Power	
			LOW POWER	HIGH POWER
	Resulting Behavior :	LL>LS	LL>LS	LL≥LS

Fig. 3   A two-factor model of forces influencing the amount of visual attention manifested when speaking and listening in peer and power roles.

The hypothesis to be tested can thus be stated as follows:

Hypothesis 1: The relative amount of time LP gives his visual attention to HP when listening as compared to speaking will be greater than the relative time HP gives his visual attention to LP when listening as compared to speaking.

Procedure.   With six exceptions, the procedures used in this study exactly replicated the procedures of the original study. The exceptions are as follows: (1) Illegitimate power hierarchies were not studied; only dyads composed of an ROTC cadet officer (HP) and an ROTC basic (LP) were used. If the guilt explanation were supported in this hierarchy, it would most certainly be true for the other. (2) Two additional conditions of chip distribution were added for the reasons discussed earlier. (3) The presentation of the tasks were counterbalanced, each task being presented first, second, or third an equal number of times. In the original study tasks were presented in a fixed order. (4) An item to determine whether or not HP would report feeling guilty was added to the postexperimental questionnaire. (5) Following completion of the postexperimental questionnaire, Ss were taken to a room which they had previously not seen. Ostensibly this was done to explain the experiment while the laboratory was being used for another study. In reality it was done to provide data for an additional study designed to test an immediacy hypothesis suggested by the procedures of this study. (6) Due to a lapse of several years between the original study and the replication, the investigation was carried out in a different laboratory.

A schematic representation of the experimental arrangements is presented in Figure 4. Dimensions of the table were the same as the one used in the first study, and interactants were seated facing one another at a distance of approximately 6 feet.

Figure 5 shows representatives of each of the power positions. On the left: HP, a cadet officer; on the right: LP, an ROTC Basic.

Figure 6 represents, from left to right, the view from a visual recorder's position, and the view from the control room—the location of the speech recorder.

The tasks used in this study were identical to those used in the original study. The same pretest questionnaire was used (FIRO-B, Schutz, 1960) to provide a rationale for separating the Ss in order to accomplish the power induction. Postexperimental questionnaire items used to verify the validity of the power inductions were the same as those used in the original study. In addition a new item was added to assess the possibility that the power inductions created a feeling of guilt on the part of HP.

Visual and speech behavior were recorded on an Esterline-Angus event recorder, enabling us to analyze visual attentiveness during periods of speaking,

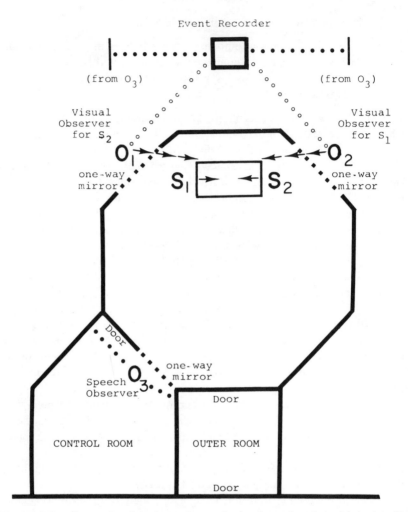

Fig. 4.   Schematic representation of arrangements for the observation of visual behavior of high power and low power subjects.

listening, and mutual silence. It also enabled us to categorize visual behavior in terms of mutual or one-way glances.

Following the completion of the final discussion task, Ss filled out a postexperimental questionnaire in different rooms, then went with E to a still different room where the purpose of the experiment was explained and one final bit of data was recorded. The final measurement was a recording of where Ss positioned themselves with reference to both E and each other. While the proxemic data was collected for a different purpose, it does provide evidence which can be used to evaluate the success of the power induction.

Results. There is no evidence to suggest that LP *S*s harbored any strong suspicions that the chip distribution, which was an integral part of the power induction, was prearranged. There is evidence to suggest that the power induction was successful and that both HP and LP perceived that a hierarchy did indeed exist.

With reference to the first point, the postexperimental questionnaire asked LP to respond to the statement: "I felt that the way I conducted the discussion had a great deal to do with the number of chips I received." The means for LPs in dyads in which HP was given a preset distribution to follow were almost identical with the means for the dyads in which HP was free to distribute the rewards as he saw fit. Both sets of means fall between the alternatives "slightly agree with the statement" and "slightly disagree with the statement." We suggest that if LPs had strongly suspected that HP had been coached, the mean responses to the item would have reflected strong or moderate disagreement with the statement. In fact, the slight disagreement noted is probably what one would expect a low-power person to feel. Does one ever believe that a superior is capable of precisely evaluating one's competence? In any event there was no differential response by LPs in the various reward conditions, and discussion

Fig. 5.   Representative occupants of high power (left) and low power (right) positions.

Fig. 6.   Views from the locations of recorders of visual behavior (left) and speech (right).

with them after the experiment provided no hints that LPs felt the rewards were predetermined.

There is positive evidence from the postexperimental questionnaire to support the conclusion that both HP and LP perceived the existence of a power hierarchy. Regardless of whether they were asked to make a free choice, to benefit themselves, or to benefit the other, HPs preferred their job in the experiment (distributing rewards) to a significantly greater degree than did LP. In addition, when asked to respond to the item: "If I were to participate in this experiment again I would prefer to have my partner's job," LPs showed significantly stronger agreement to the statement than did HPs, who disagreed with the statement. We conclude that both *S*s in the dyad would prefer to be in the high power position if the experiment were to be repeated. The preference would seem to be based on a desire to control own and other's outcomes, i.e., to have power (Thibaut & Kelley, 1959).[8]

There is also behavioral evidence, not related to visual attentiveness, which we interpret as demonstrating the impact of the power induction. In the final phase of the experiment *E* led *S*s to a previously unused room. The positioning of furniture and the order of entrance into the room was designed to enable *E* to determine the distance at which LP would seat himself from HP.

Figure 7 depicts the arrangement of the room. One chair was indicated to be reserved for *E*. This was done by hanging a laboratory coat on the back of the chair and placing a notebook, paper pad, and pen directly in front of it. HP entered the room and took a seat. In all cases but one, HP either cornered *E*'s chair at the far end of the table or sat in the seat directly opposite the marked chair. LP followed and chose a chair with full knowledge of where HP was

[8] The perception of a true power hierarchy was undoubtedly strengthened by assigning to the officer the right to distribute the rewards for both men.

seated. *E* then entered, sat in the marked chair, and unobtrusively recorded the seating arrangement.

The data indicated that the distance LP chose to sit from HP was inversely related to the degree to which he had been benefited by HP in the distribution of chips. The greater the number of chips received, the closer he sat to HP.

Data in Table I show the relationship between the chair selection and previous rewards. Four benefit conditions are listed. This was possible because the 12 officers in the free choice reward situation split evenly as to whether they benefited themselves or benefited LP in distributing the chips. All HP cadet officers in this condition benefited either themselves or LP at the end of the first task, a split which they tended to maintain over all three tasks. The bar graphs in Figure 8 clearly show how LP's choice of a seat was affected by HP's division of rewards. Chi square analysis of seating arrangements by HP–LP benefit resulted in a χ^2 of 5.04, significant at the .025 level with a phi coefficient of .458. Taken together with semantic differential ratings which showed that LPs benefited by HP evaluated them significantly more favorably ($\underline{M}$ benefit = 21.7; $\underline{M}$ no benefit = 17.8; t = 2.074, p < .05), these data demonstrate the strong impact of the power induction.

Before examining gaze direction data bearing on the power role hypothesis, let us first consider the possibility that HP's visual attentiveness in the original study was attenuated by feelings of guilt or discomfort over providing LP with false feedback and/or unfairly distributing the rewards. There are two lines of evidence which bear on this question. The direct evidence concerns HP's response to the statement: "I felt very guilty about the way I divided the chips." Responses were scaled from one "strongly disagree" to six "strongly agree." Means for the four groups of officers, i.e., instructed self-benefit, free-choice

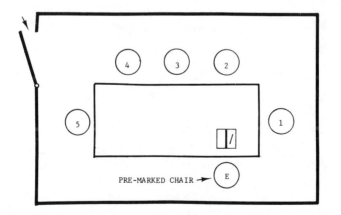

Fig. 7. Schematic representation of room arrangement used to measure distance LP chose to sit from HP in postexperiment explanation.

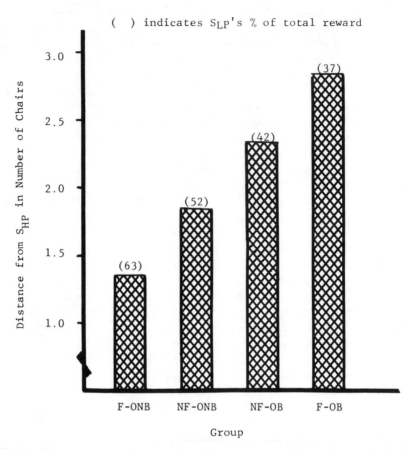

Fig. 8.   Mean distance in chair locations from HP selected by LPs differentially rewarded by HP.

self-benefit, instructed other-benefit, free-choice other-benefit, were 2.00, 2.00, 2.17, and 2.00, respectively. Thus the mean response was one of moderate disagreement with the guilt statement. There is no indication whatsoever that HPs instructed to disadvantage the other felt more guilty than those who did it freely or who benefited the other.

A second, indirect line of evidence is provided by the visual data. We suggested earlier that a guilty HP would, everything else being equal, look less at LP when instructed to benefit himself than when instructed to benefit the other, or when freely choosing to benefit either himself or LP. There is no evidence to support such a contention. A mean percent total looking time of 44.3% recorded for HP in the instructed self-benefit condition did not differ significantly from means of 43.1%, 37.6%, and 37.5% recorded for HPs who freely benefited themselves, freely benefited LP, or were instructed to benefit LP. There were no significant differences between any of these means. Indeed the trend, if any, was for HPs who benefited themselves to look more than those who benefited LP (M self-benefit = 43.7%; M LP benefit = 37.6%). Neither was there any evidence that those instructed to give false feedback looked less than those who made free choices. The mean percent looking for instructed HPs amounted to 40.9% compared to 40.3% for those given free choice.

Finally, no impressions of guilty behavior or feelings were found from observing HPs as they divided the chips, or from questioning them in the postexperimental discussion. Indeed, certain HPs appeared to relish giving LP three chips to their own seven. In summary, guilt would appear to play no role in explaining whatever differences in visual attentiveness would differentiate HP from LP in the present study, and we feel confident that, for the ROTC group at least, guilt is of little, if any, value as an explanation of the HPs' visual attentiveness in the original study reported in the Nebraska Symposium (Exline, 1972).

We are left then with the power role taking hypothesis as the favored explanation. Such an explanation would be further supported should we, some ten years later, be successful in replicating the results of the original study.

Table II shows the mean percentage of time that occupants of each power position looked at the other when speaking and when listening to him. Since no differences were found in both HPs' and LPs' behaviors across the various conditions of chip distribution, we combined the data for all HPs and for all LPs. The analysis of variance listed in Table III indicates that these data confirm our hypothesis. LPs, as predicted, looked significantly more when listening as compared to speaking. No such difference was found for HPs' look–speak vs. look–listen behavior. Figure 9 graphically portrays these patterns for total looking behavior, i.e., one-way and mutual glances combined.

In this case it can be seen that, contrary to our model, HP looks no more when listening than when speaking, while LP performs as expected. When the

Table 1. Mean Rewards Received and Chair Placements Selected by LPs Grouped as to HP's Instructions to Benefit Self or LP

Person rewarded most	Distribution of chips	LP reward % total possible		Number of chairs LP distant from HP	
		X̄	S.D.	X̄	S.D.
Self (HP)	Fixed	37	0	2.83	.67
	Free	42	4.04	2.33	.89
Other (LP)	Fixed	63	0	1.33	.51
	Free	52	3.00	1.83	1.17

data are categorized in terms of one-way looking, i.e., looking at the other when he is looking away, the patterns are more clearly as predicted (see Figure 10).

Table III shows that mutual glances occurred more often when HP spoke than when LP spoke, a finding which is significant at the .05 level. No differences were observed in the relative amount of time which each spoke during the three discussions. All in all the data strongly suggest that relative power does differentially affect the visual attentiveness of each member of the dyad.

There is a postscript to this study. Since HP subjects were all cadet officers in our University's ROTC program, we were able to obtain ratings of their leadership performance during the annual summer camp which preceded the academic year in which they cooperated as HP subjects in our laboratory study. We wondered if the amount and pattern of visual performance in the high-power

Table II.   Mean Percent of Time HP and LP Looked at the Other When Speaking and Listening to Him

Power of position	Subject activities		
	Speak $\overline{X}$	Listen $\overline{X}$	Mutual silence $\overline{X}$
High	15.00	13.90	8.48
Low	11.35	18.75	8.48

Table III.   Analysis of Variance of Mean Percent of Time Spent in Visual Interaction by High and Low Power Subjects in Various Benefit, Distribution, and Speech Conditions

Variable	df	Subject activity					
		HP Looks		LP Looks		Mutual Look	
		MS	F	MS	F	MS	F
LP benefit status (Hi–Lo)	1	.010[a]	.08	.001	.02	.089	.89
Distribution of rewards (fixed–free)	1	.090	.73	.086	1.47	.001	.01
Speaker (HP–LP–none)	2	.293	7.85*	.501	7.91*	.190	6.23[c]*
Interactions[b]	7	—	—	—	—	—	—
Error: benefit status and rewards	20	.123	—	.058		.101	
Error: speech condition	40	.037	—	.063		.030	

[a]Analysis based on arc sine transformation of all percentage data.
[b]For economy of presentation no nonsignificant interaction effects are reported.
[c]Mean percent mutual glances = 7.6, 4.6, and 3.4 respectively for H.P., L.P., and no one as speaker.
*$p < .01$

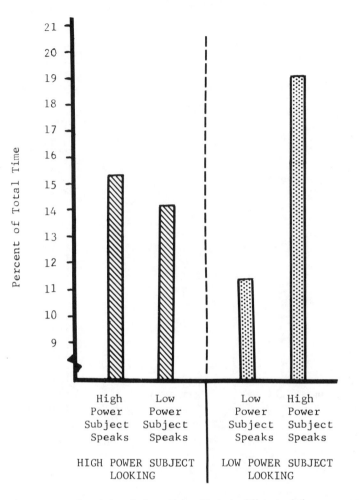

Fig. 9. Mean percent of total time during which subjects in different relative power positions looked at the other while speaking to and listening to him.

role in our laboratory study would be related to leadership performance ratings given to cadet officers by the tactical officers who observed and evaluated their activities during summer training.

Specifically, we wondered if those whose visual attentiveness in the laboratory situation best fit our model of the behavior of a person in a position of power would be those who were given superior leadership ratings in the summer

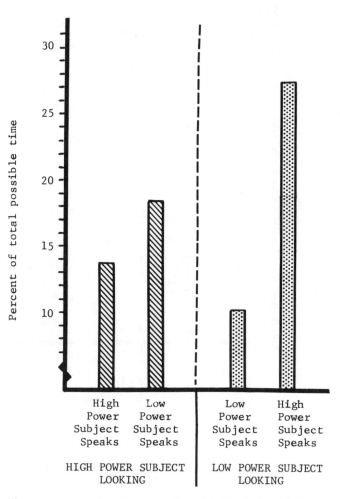

Fig. 10. Mean percent of total possible time which subject in different relative power positions spent in one-way glances at the other.

Table IV. Mean Percent of Time High and Low Leadership Rated HPs Looked at Other During Different Speech Conditions

Leadership rating	%Look–speak	% Look–listen	% Look–silence	% Look–total time
High	32	37	25	30
Low	46	60	41	48

camp. Would, that is, cadet officers who gave a relatively large amount of visual attention to a low power basic be given lower leadership ratings in summer camp than a cadet officer who gave relatively small amounts of visual attention to LP in our laboratory study? Would the officer who showed the greater ratio of look–listen to look–speak behaviors be rated as less a leader than one who showed a more balanced ratio of visual attentiveness?

Leadership performance ratings in summer camp were obtained for 22 of the 24 cadet officers who participated in the laboratory study. The ratings were made during the summer ROTC camp which preceded the semester in which the cadets participated in the laboratory experiment. Ratings were made by regular army officers, who were in daily contact with the cadets and who closely observed and rated each day the manner in which the cadets handled themselves in the various training activities and living arrangements. The specific rating in question, a leadership performance rating, was a subjective rating made at the end of the summer camp experience by army officers instructed to refer to daily leadership evaluation ratings (scale 1–7) in making their overall evaluation.

Comparison of the above rating to the cadet officers' visual behavior in the laboratory study clearly showed that the cadet officers who paid more visual attention to the low power other in the laboratory situations were those who had been given the lowest leadership ratings during the preceding summer camp. Negative rho correlations between the leadership performance rating received by the cadet officer in the field and his visual attentiveness in the laboratory when he spoke, listened, and shared a mutual silence amounted to $-.42$, $-.49$, and $-.41$, respectively. The correlation between leadership ratings and visual attention shown in the total period of the discussion reached $-.54$. All correlations were significant beyond the .05 level of probability (df 20).

Closer examination of visual attentiveness in the laboratory of cadet officers given high as compared to low leadership ratings in summer camp is instructive. Recall that in the laboratory experiment LP relative to HP looked much more while listening. Within the HP group, however, there were individual differences with respect to how closely a given HP's visual behaviors matched the performance predicted by the model. Some HP officers matched it closely, others' pattern of visual affectiveness was closer to that which the model predicted for the LP role. As was indicated earlier, the extent to which a cadet officer's visual attentiveness in the laboratory matched the HP model was directly and positively related to leadership ratings received in the summer camp.

Data in Table IV suggest not only that the 11 highest rated cadet officers engaged in less visual monitoring than did the 11 lowest rated officers, but that the greatest differences between the two groups appeared to occur with respect to visual attentiveness while listening.

Thus the visual style of the higher rated officers as compared to the lower rated officers would seem to be to give less attention to a less powerful basic when engaged in a somewhat argumentative discussion. Is this a mark of command presence? Does it signal less personal involvement with, and more detachment from, the subordinate? Does the effective officer monitor enough to keep informed but not so much as to signal undue concern with the others' approval? Our data would seem to suggest that some such mechanisms are operating.

A final point of interest concerns the 12 HP officers who in the laboratory discussion were given free choice in the distribution of rewards after each task. Six of the twelve chose to benefit the low power basic, the others rewarded themselves more than they did the basic. On the average, the six who benefited the basic rather than themselves were given higher performance ratings in summer camp; this was true with respect to every index of leadership. High-rated officers do indeed seem to look out for the men rather than themselves.

The relationship discovered between leadership ratings of HP's performance in summer camp and the amount and pattern of his visual attentiveness in his high power role during the laboratory discussion call attention to the effect of individual differences upon visual attentiveness in dyadic interactions. We suggest that personality variables related to power considerations will predictably affect the amount and patterns of visual attentiveness manifested by interactants in a dyadic discussion. The final study to be reported in the chapter will be concerned with an investigation of the above suggestion.

Interpersonal Control Orientation and Visual Attentiveness in a Dyadic Discussion[9]

The assumption on which this study is based is a simple one. We assume that the strength of one's desire to exert control over others will affect the interactants' visual attentiveness in a state of talk in a manner analogous to power role considerations. In other words, one who has a strong desire to control others (call it N dominance, aggressiveness, control-orientation, or whatever) will, everything else being equal, manifest the pattern of visual attention characteristic of the occupant of a high power position. Conversely, one with very weak

[9] Data to be described in this section represent the results of an experiment carried out by the junior author as part of his Ph.D. dissertation (Ellyson, 1974).

desires to control others will manifest the visual attention patterns characteristic of the occupant of a low power position in a hierarchial structure.

Post hoc analyses relating FIRO-B control scores (a personality measure designed to identify those who wish to control others) to speaking and listening patterns of visual attentiveness were carried out on HP and LP *S*s in the previous study. *S*s whose control scale score was high did exhibit the visual attentiveness pattern we have suggested to be characteristic of the high power role to a greater degree than did those whose control scale score was low. Put another way, there was a strong tendency for *S*s relatively high in FIRO control (expressed desire to exert control over others) to display the highest amount of intragroup visual dominance behavior—which will hereafter be referred to as VDB. VDB is defined as being inversely proportional to the ratio of look–listen to look–speak behavior.[10]

Thus control orientation is a mediating variable which, if identified, could explain a greater proportion of the variance in VDB observed in the previous studies. Assuming that the relationship between control orientation and VDB is tenable, we hypothesize that, everything else being equal, i.e., in a situation where power roles are equated and other variables are allowed to vary randomly, *Ss with high-control orientations will exhibit more VDB than will Ss of low-control orientation*.

To test the above hypothesis we first gave Schutz's FIRO-B (1958) scale to over 1,000 men enrolled in an introductory psychology course at the University of Delaware. FIRO-B is a self-report scale constructed on Guttman scaling technique. We have found it useful because it seems to control somewhat for social desirability in that it is not transparently clear to *S* as to what constitutes acceptance or rejection of the various items which compose the subscales. FIRO-B consists of three major components—inclusion, control and affectional orientations toward other people. Each major component consists of two sub-scales, i.e., behavior one exhibits toward others and behavior one desires from others. Since we were interested in differentiating *S*s as to their dominance, aggressiveness, or control orientations, we used only the control-exhibited sub-scale of FIRO-B to select subjects for our study.

From the 1,000 men originally tested we selected 16 men who described themselves as very much wanting to control others, ($\underline{M}$ Control = 7.2 on a 9-point scale) and 16 men who described themselves as little interested in such control ($\underline{M}$ Control = .5). These men were also selected so as to ensure that groups of high and low control orientations did not differ, on the average, in their

---

[10]For example, *A* looks at another 40% of the time he speaks to the other and only 30% of the time when the other speaks to him. Exactly the reverse is true for *B*. Thus *A*'s index of Visual Dominance Behavior = 30/40 or .75 whereas *B*'s VDB = 40/30 or 1.33. In this example *A* shows greater VDB than does *B*.

Table V. Mean Percent Look–Speak and Look–Listen Behaviors by Subjects Categorized as to Own and Partner's Control Orientation

Control orientation		Subjects' activities	
Own	Partner's	Look–speak	Look–listen
High	High	41.65	30.60
	Low	46.16	45.90
	Total	43.94	38.20[a]
Low	High	40.09	51.70
	Low	35.39	60.40
	Total	37.74	56.00[a]
Total by partner	High	40.87	41.15
	Low	40.78	53.15

[a]Means associated with significant effects in the analysis of variance.

desire to be controlled by others. Control-wanted orientations average 3.9 for each group of 16 men.

*S*s were assigned to one of three types of dyads according to their FIRO control scores. There were 4 H–H (high control) dyads, 4 L–L (low control) dyads, and 8 H–L (mixed dyads).

Procedures.   Procedures used in this study were similar to those in the two previous studies, the major change being the elimination of the control induction which involved distribution of rewards after each task. In addition, one of the three tasks was eliminated in order to ensure that the study could be completed in the allotted time. The same laboratory arrangements were used, and visual attention and speech were recorded in the same fashion as in previous studies.

Results.   There were no significant differences between high and low control oriented subjects in the percentage of visual attention given to the other when speaking. Mean percentages of 41.6 and 46.2 were recorded for high control *S*s talking to high and low control oriented interactants, respectively. Low control oriented *S*s looked 40.1% and 35.4% while speaking to high and low control oriented *S*s, respectively. No significant effects for control type of speaker, target, or their interaction were found.

With respect to visual attention while listening, a main effect for the control type of listener was found (Table VI). Table V shows that high control oriented *S*s looked 30.6% and 45.9%, respectively, at high and low control oriented speakers. Low control oriented listeners were visually attentive during 51.7% of high control's speech and during 60.4% of low control's speech. Thus visual attention while listening averaged to 38.2% for high control *S*s and to 56% for low control *S*s.

The best test of the hypothesis, however, can be found by analyzing the difference between look–listen and look–speak visual attention for each *S*. This difference, expressed as a ratio, was used to establish an index of visual dominance behavior, a low ratio indicating a high degree of VDB (see page 45 of this chapter). Visual dominance behavior for high control oriented Ss averaged to .89, as compared to 1.51 for low control Ss. This difference was significant at the .001 level.

The data presented in Tables VII and VIII and graphed in Figure 11 suggest that those who have strong personal inclinations to control others in their interpersonal environment tend to look more at the other when speaking than when listening to him. The opposite pattern would seem to characterize even more strongly the visual behavior of those who describe themselves as having little or no control orientation toward others. Since both of the above groups were selected so as to show equal and moderate mean orientations toward being controlled by others, the high control group is more strongly oriented toward controlling than being controlled by others, while the reverse is true for those in the low control category. Thus we composed our sample of those who (though not clearly aware of it) described themselves as being either dominant or submissive persons. On the basis of our results, it would seem that one who desires power shows it in his visual behavior. It would seem that *he who desires power "looks" as if he has it*.

Discussion

Three laboratory experiments and one correlational study of relationships between interpersonal power and visual behavior have been reported in this chapter. The first study, carried out several years before the others, suggested that the visual attention one pays to another is systematically affected by one's position in the power hierarchy. The second study confirmed the suggestion of the first by replicating the original results while simultaneously eliminating two alternative interpretations. The second study further refined our understanding of

Table VI. Analysis of Variance of Mean Percent Look–Listen Behavior of Subjects Categorized as to Own and Partner's Control Orientation

Variable	df	MS	F
Own control orientation	1	2525.83	6.58*
Partner control orientation	1	1150.80	3.00
Own × partner control	1	86.79	.23
Error	28	383.77	
Total	31		

*$p < .025$

Table VII. Mean Percent Look–Listen Minus Percent Look–Speak Behavior by Subject's Control Orientation and Control Orientation of Partner

Own control orientation	Partner's control orientation		Total
	High	*Low*	
High	−11.04	−0.26	−5.65
Low	13.19	24.99	19.09
Total	1.12	12.36	

Table VIII. Analysis of Variance for Percent Look–Listen Minus Percent Look–Speak Behavior by Subject's Control Orientation and Control Orientation of Partner

Variable	df	MS	F
Own control orientation	1	5034.55	23.76*
Partner control orientation	1	880.26	4.15
Own × partner control	1	2.11	.01
Error	28	211.93	
Total	31		

*$p < .001$

the patterning of power-related glances—power would seem to be suggested by a relatively low ratio of look–listen to look–speak behaviors. The third study suggested that a desire for power is indicated by one's pattern of visual attentiveness. Those who wish to control others will, in contrast to those who do not, manifest the same visual pattern of looking while speaking and listening to equals, as does a superior who interacts with a subordinate in a legitimate power hierarchy. Personality factors and role structures may thus combine to exaggerate a pattern of visual dominance behavior.

The correlational study suggests that the pattern we have called "Visual Dominance Behavior," viz., a relatively low index of look–listen to look–speak behavior, may be related to the assessment of one's fitness to occupy a position of power in a military setting. The military is concerned that its officers manifest "command presence." Our data suggest that one tangible element in such a presence may very well be that pattern of visual interaction we have labeled VDB.

It is likely that the military establishment is not the only type of social organization which expects those occupying leadership positions to exhibit VDB. Earlier references to Gilliland's interest in utilizing visual behavior similar to VDB to identify effective salesman (Gilliland, 1926) suggest that business organizations are also concerned with nonverbal aspects of leadership style. Efran (1968), moreover, has presented evidence to suggest that there is a general tendency, in U.S. college students at least, to give greater visual attention to one from whom evaluative feedback is expected if the perceived evaluator is of high in contrast to low status. Perhaps both students, in their behavior toward evaluators of higher status, and army tactical officers, in their evaluative assessment of the behavior of potentially high status persons, merely reflect the expectations of our society concerning visual dominance behavior to be exhibited by occupants of different status and power positions.

Persistent attention by subordinate members of a rank order toward the dominant member of a group has been identified as a feature common to

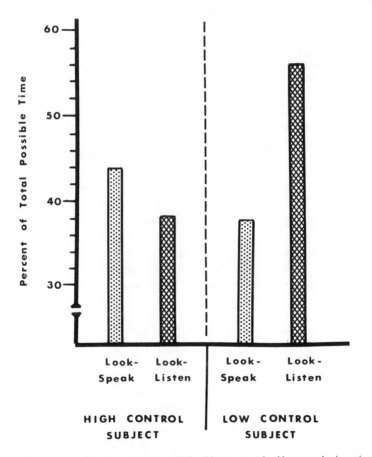

Fig. 11.   Mean percent of total possible time which subjects categorized by control orientation spent in visual attention when speaking or listening to the other.

rank-ordered behavior of subhuman primates (Chance, 1967). Chance argues that such attention tends to space the members of a rank order in ways to maximize the cohesiveness of the group, and speculates that attention is a mechanism which is basic to the cohesive organization of human groups as well as to those of subhuman primates. While we do not wish to draw an exact parallel between the visual attentiveness of man and monkey, we do suggest that, at both levels, greater visual attention of subordinates to superiors can function to facilitate less troublesome interaction. Attention assists subhuman primates to adjust their spacing so as to minimize aggression; we suggest that it enables the human to assess the intent of a superior while demonstrating acceptance of his power status.

We believe that we have demonstrated that specific differences in the relative proportion of time one looks while speaking in comparison to looking while listening to another serve to identify the acceptance of one's defined position in a known power hierarchy or to indicate the nature of one's aspiration toward power in an unstructured situation. Our predictions were based on a model which specified the effects on visual attention of the combined operation of two motives, one motive being concerned with the acceptance or inhibition of external information (feedback inhibition), the other with the signaling of the acceptance or rejection of a norm of attention.

Further research concerning the usefulness of the model is necessary: (1) It should be tested with women as well as with men. (2) We have assumed that feedback inhibition is more relevant to visual attention when one speaks than when one listens. How valid is this assumption? (3) Do the power related connotations of looking while listening, i.e., the implications of the norm of attention, change when the focus of the interaction shifts from one of mutual influence (as was the case in the laboratory studies reported in this paper) to a different basis? (4) What cultural differences exist with respect to the operation of the norm of attention within and without legitimate power hierarchies? (5) Will the manipulation of interpersonal distance à la Argyle and Dean's equilibrium theory (1965) affect the manifestation of visual dominance behavior?

We are at present investigating several of the above questions and have data which suggest that feedback inhibition, as assumed, has little effect upon visual attention when listening. There are also data which suggest that the relative amount of looking while listening shown by those more and less concerned with power, changes as a function of the extent to which the interaction permits mutual influence. Together with the completed research reported in this paper, the work in process encourages us to suggest that the study of patterns of eye engagements and avoidances promises to provide a fruitful approach to the study of power relations in face-to-face social interaction.

References

Argyle, M., & Dean, J. Eye contact, distance and affiliation. *Sociometry*, 1965, *28*, 289–304.

Chance, M. R. A. Attention structure as the basis of primate rank order. *Man*, 1967, *2*, 503–518.

Chekhov, A. "The Name-Day Party," 1888. Translated by Constance Garnett. In A. Yarmolinsky (Ed.), *The Portable Chekhov*. New York: Viking Press, 1947.

Edelman, M. S., Omark, D. R., & Freedman, D. G. *Dominance hierarchies in children*. Unpublished manuscript, Committee on Human Development, University of Chicago, 1971.

Efran, J. S. Looking for approval: Effects on visual behavior of approbation from persons differing in importance. *Journal of Personality and Social Psychology*, 1968, *10*, 21–25.

Ellsworth, P. C., & Carlsmith, J. M. Effects of eye contact and verbal content on affective response to a dyadic interaction. *Journal of Personality and Social Psychology*, 1968, *10*, 15–20.

Ellsworth, P. C., Carlsmith, J. M., & Henson, A. The stare as a stimulus to flight in human subjects: A series of field experiments. *Journal of Personality and Social Psychology*, 1972, *21*, 302–311.

Ellyson, S. L. *Visual interaction and attraction in dyads with legitimate power differences*. Unpublished master's thesis, University of Delaware, 1973.

Ellyson, S. L. *Visual behavior exhibited by males differing as to interpersonal control orientation in one- and two-way communication systems*. Unpublished dissertation, University of Delaware, 1974.

Exline, R. V. Explorations in the process of person perception: Visual interaction in relation to competition, sex, and the need for affiliation. *Journal of Personality*, 1963, *31*, 1–20.

Exline, R. V. Visual interaction: The glances of power and preference. In J. K. Cole (Ed.), *Current theory and research in motivation* (Vol. 19). Lincoln, Nebraska: University of Nebraska Press, 1972, pp. 163–206.

Exline, R., Gray, D., & Schuette, D. Visual behavior in a dyad as affected by interview content and sex of respondent. *Journal of Personality and Social Psychology*, 1965, *1*, 201–209.

Exline, R. V., & Long, B. *Visual behavior in relation to power of position in legitimate and illegitimate power hierarchies*. Unpublished manuscript, University of Delaware, 1971.

Exline, R. V., & Winters, L. C. *Effects of cognitive difficulty and cognitive style upon eye to eye contact in interviews*. Paper read at Eastern Psychological Association meetings, 1965.

Gilliland, A. R. A revision and some results with the Moore-Gilliland aggressiveness test. *Journal of Applied Psychology*, 1926, *10*, 143–150.

Hall, K. R. L., & Devore, I. Baboon social behavior. In I. Devore (Ed.), *Primate behavior: Field studies of monkeys and apes*. New York: Holt, Rinehart and Winston, 1965, pp. 53–110.

Hinde, R. A., & Rowell, T. E. Communication by posture and facial expressions in the rhesus monkey (*Macaca mulatta*). *Proceedings of the Zoological Society of London*, 1962, *138*, 1–21.

Jay, P. Field studies. In A. Schrier, H. F. Harlow, and F. Stollnitz (Eds.), *Behavior of nonhuman primates: Modern research trends*. New York: Academic Press, 1965, pp. 525–592.

Kendon, A. Some functions of gaze-direction in social interaction. *Acta Psychologica*, 1967, *26*, 22–63.

Moore, H. T., & Gilliland, A. R. The measurement of aggressiveness. *Journal of Applied Psychology*, 1921, *2*, 97–118.

Rubin, Z. Measurement of romantic love. *Journal of Personality and Social Psychology*, 1970, *16*, 265–273.

Schutz, W. C. *FIRO: A three-dimensional theory of interpersonal behavior*. New York: Holt, Rinehart, and Winston, 1958.

Simmel, G. Sociology of the senses: Visual interaction. In R. E. Park and E. W. Burgess (Eds.),

Introduction to the science of sociology. (Rev. ed.) Chicago: University of Chicago Press, 1969, 356–361.

Thayer, S. The effect of interpersonal looking duration on dominance judgments. *Journal of Social Psychology*, 1969, *79*, 285–286.

Thibaut, J. W., & Kelly, H. H. *The social psychology of groups*. New York: Wiley, 1959.

CHAPTER 3

Direct Gaze as a Social Stimulus: The Example of Aggression

Phoebe C. Ellsworth

Yale University
New Haven, Connecticut

Introduction

The study of gazes and glances, like research on other forms of nonverbal behavior, has developed without regard for traditional disciplinary lines. It has brought together ethologists, psychiatrists, anthropologists, and several subspecies of psychologists. This diversity has provided a healthy hybrid vigor, so that the study of nonverbal behavior is now flourishing even though 20 years ago it appeared to be nearly extinct. In some ways, however, the diversity has been more apparent than real; communication among investigators in different disciplines was initially facilitated by a number of shared assumptions. Paramount among these assumptions was the notion that the repertoire of nonverbal behaviors, including eye movements, constituted a set of signals, each of which had a specific and invariant meaning. Opinions diverged as to who had the capacity to read these meanings. For the ethologists, membership in the same species was considered a sufficient qualification. For the anthropologists after Darwin (1872) and the social psychologists before Tomkins (1962, 1963), Ekman (1972), and Izard (1971), membership in the same culture was regarded as necessary, and many doubted if even that was sufficient (Bruner & Taguiri, 1954). The psychiatrists and clinical psychologists tended to regard nonverbal behavior as a much more esoteric code, one which required special training and clinical insight to decipher. Most of these professionals agreed, however, that a particular look or smile or movement had a particular meaning for those who were equipped to read it.

This notion has recently been imprinted in the minds of the public by the popular press, which continues to turn out highly marketable dictionaries for translating acts and appearances into personality characteristics, dispositions, and moods. In the meantime, among the professionals, the assumption has lost generality and gained differentiation. Some nonverbal behaviors clearly function as explicit signs among conspecifics, such as the emotional facial expressions of various species of primates (Chevalier-Skolnikoff, 1973; Izard, 1971; Ekman, Friesen, & Ellsworth, 1972), although, even with these "basic" expressions, learning and context affect both sending and receiving to an increasing degree as one moves from lemur to man. Some nonverbal cues may function as signals across species, as in predator–prey relationships (Ratner, this volume) or in interactions between look-alike species such as man and monkey (Exline & Yellin, 1969). Some nonverbal behaviors are shared within cultures or subcultures and may have no meaning for other groups, or they may have a different meaning, as in the case of the first two fingers extended to form a V, which once stood for victory. Other nonverbal behaviors may have reliable diagnostic significance for psychologists, although here the evidence is much less clear. Finally, there remain a great many nonverbal behaviors which do not have an invariant significance, but which may nonetheless be influential stimuli in social interactions. The "meaning" of these behaviors changes from one situation to another and from one interpersonal relationship to another.

The term "meaning" is itself multiply meaningful. It may refer to an actual correlation between a gesture and an identifiable internal state. In a communicative context it may refer to the sender's intention to communicate a specific meaning, to the receiver's attribution of a meaning to the behavior, or to a generally shared wordlike meaning understood by both the sender and the receiver. The correlation of nonverbal behavior with inner states is the object of much current research (Izard, 1972; Ekman, 1973), but has not yet been studied very much in the context of an ongoing social interaction. As Wiener and his colleagues (1972) point out, studies of shared meaning, involving a code which satisfies the criteria of communication in the narrow sense of the term, are extremely rare. Nor are there many studies of the sender's intentional use of nonverbal signals to convey a meaning, except for role-playing studies outside the context of face-to-face social interactions. We do not often think of nonverbal cues as intentional. It may be that middle-class Anglo-American culture neither recognizes nor encourages the deliberate use of nonverbal channels to enrich the verbal message, but prefers to regard nonverbal behaviors as unintentional manifestations of one's cultural background or one's state of mind. This point has been argued cogently in another context by Gross (1975), who points out that "social-gestural behavior is rarely scrutinized as a vehicle for the intentional articulation and communication of symbolically implicative meaning." By implication, he also makes the corollary observation that people who *can* control their nonverbal channels, such as actors and conmen, are considered specialists in an art too difficult to be practiced by the general populace. It is notable that the one major article which systematically considers nonverbal behavior as a social skill (Argyle & Kendon, 1967) is almost always cited with reference to particular findings in its literature review, almost never with reference to the theoretical framework.

Most studies that have dealt with the meaning of nonverbal behavior in social interaction have concentrated on the meanings inferred by an observer of the behavior. Similarly, in this discussion, the "meaning" which changes when the same cue occurs in different contexts refers to the observer's reaction to the cue and his interpretation of it, since as yet we have very little information about other types of social meaning.

Eye movements belong to the category of behaviors which have variable significance.[1] Direct gaze and gaze avoidance each cover a broad category of meanings, with the situation, the relationship, and the personal histories of the interactants supplying the particulars. The responses and interpretations elicited by a look are neither automatic nor invariant. Instead, these cues provide a flexible contributing factor in social interaction, combining with other factors to produce a behavioral response or an attribution.

Limitations to the Interpretation of the Gaze

Although glances and gazes do not have specific sign-referent meanings for the observer, they are not completely neutral stimuli which depend entirely on contextual cues for their interpretation. A gaze is not as ambiguous as a Rorschach blot is supposed to be, in that a person faced with another's gaze is not free to choose from the whole range of possible interpretations, unconstrained by any intrinsic stimulus properties. The eyes may not be the "windows of the soul," allowing a clear and accurate view of the mental furnishings and activities within, but neither are they mirrors, merely reflecting the perceiver and his environment. A direct gaze elicits certain broad classes of response, while precluding others. Similarly, gaze aversion suggests certain interpretations to the perceiver, but not others, and these interpretations are different from those elicited by a direct gaze. Thus while the exact meaning of a visual behavior will vary with the context, the behavior itself will narrow the range of variation, resulting in certain general consistencies of response and interpretation.

---

[1] Note that this paper does not deal with the regulatory function of eye movement (cf. Argyle & Kendon, 1967; Ellsworth & Ludwig, 1972; Wiener *et al.*, 1972; Duncan & Niederehe, 1974), by which the procedural give-and-take of a conversation is guided. It is doubtful that these movements affect the participants' emotional responses or provoke attributions unless they depart markedly from the normal expected usage.

At our present state of knowledge, we can be fairly confident of three such limitations on the range of interpretation of visual behavior, which are a function of the behavior itself. A direct gaze is *salient*; it is *arousing*; and it is *involving*. Gaze aversion is generally none of these things. This list is not very long, and it is not intended to be exhaustive; other major differentiating factors may emerge from future research, and configural categories more subtle than the direct gaze/gaze aversion dichotomy will almost certainly come to have predictive value. But at the present time these three properties are rather well established; others remain in the realm of speculation.

Salience.   To begin with, a direct gaze is a salient element in the environment. Unlike many nonverbal behaviors having a potential cue value which is rarely realized, such as foot movements, changes in pupil size, and subtle facial or postural changes, a direct gaze has a high probability of being noticed. For a behavior that involves no noise and little movement, it has a remarkable capacity to draw attention to itself even at a distance. Most people can remember occasions when they have emerged from their thoughts during a subway ride, a solitary meal in a restaurant, or a park bench meditation and looked up, only to find themselves looking straight into someone else's eyes. While the eerie sensation evoked may suggest magic rays or John Donne's "eye-beames," a more conservative explanation is that the direct gaze was a salient stimulus in peripheral vision or in a just-previous semiconscious scanning of the surroundings, and that the person did not "just happen" to look up at that time, but looked up in response to the gaze. People often use a direct gaze to attract another person's attention in situations where noise or gesticulation are inappropriate. The fact that we expect others to be responsive to our gaze is illustrated by our exasperation when dealing with people who have learned immunity to the effects of a stare, such as waiters.

Neither these anecdotal observations nor the tempting arguments based on the plausible evolutionary significance of a perpetual sensitivity to direct gaze can be construed as hard evidence. While there are a few studies of the development of responsiveness to gazelike configurations in infants, research directly concerned with the salience of the gaze for adult humans is lacking. Indirect evidence is provided by postexperimental interviews in which investigators have asked subjects in high and low eye contact conditions to guess which condition they had been in. Most experimenters report that subjects could easily make the discrimination, and even in studies where subjects' reports were relatively inaccurate (Argyle & Williams, 1969), the effect of the different gaze conditions on other perceptions indicates that at some level they were noticed. The literature on human beings' ability to discriminate differences in gaze direction is well summarized by Vine (1971).

Of course the ability to discriminate is rather faint evidence for the perceptual salience of the gaze. More to the point, perhaps, is a study in which subjects were shown photographs of groups of people, some of whom were gazing directly at the camera, while others were not. In one version, after the pictures had been removed subjects were asked to describe the people they remembered. In another version, subjects were later shown individual photographs of the people in the groups and asked to point out the ones they had seen before. In both versions, the individuals who had been looking directly into the camera in the group shots were more often remembered than those who were not (Ellsworth, unpublished data).

Thus, by salience we mean that when a direct gaze occurs in a situation it is likely to be noticed, to serve as a stimulus. Thus it is more likely than many other nonverbal behaviors to elicit some kind of response, including attempts to attribute meaning. The first limitation on the range of interpretations elicited by a direct gaze, then, is simply the proposition that some kind of interpretation is more likely than no interpretation. This is probably not the case for an averted gaze, which can easily go unnoticed unless the perceiver is already involved in a face-to-face conversation with a person who persistently avoids his gaze.

Arousal. If a gaze is likely to be a stimulus, it is also likely to be an arousing stimulus; it is not affectively neutral. Whether it is the direct gaze itself or eye *contact* that is arousing is difficult to say, since at the moment when the perceiver looks up and sees someone gazing directly at him, both occur simultaneously. On the basis of our own research on staring (Ellsworth, Carlsmith, & Henson, 1972) and a recent study by Bond and Komai (1974), we would guess that the arousal stems largely from the perception that one is being looked at.

Evidence for the arousing effects of the gaze comes from two recent studies in which physiological responses were measured. In one (Kleinke & Pohlen, 1971), some subjects in a prisoner's dilemma game were paired with a partner who gazed at them steadily, while others were paired with a partner who looked away from them. Subjects were free to look at their partners or not. Kleinke and Pohlen found that subjects in the direct gaze condition had significantly higher heart rates than subjects in the averted gaze condition. Using a within-subjects design, Nichols and Champness (1971) asked subjects to look at another person who sometimes met their gaze and sometimes looked away. They found that subjects' GSR increased when their partners looked at them and decreased during periods of averted gaze.

If the salience of a direct gaze increases the probability that it will be noticed, the arousal produced indicates to the perceiver that it is worth noticing and worth interpreting. The arousing properties of the gaze provide a partial link between the study of visual behavior and certain areas of basic theory in experimental social psychology, particularly the line of theory that began with Festinger's (1954) social comparison theory, grew through Schachter's (1964) theory of the determinants of emotional state, and developed into attribution theory (Jones, Kanouse, Kelley, Nisbett, Valins, & Weiner, 1971). Schachter argues that a state of physiological arousal creates a need in the individual "to understand and label his bodily feelings" (1964, p. 52), and that the individual will seek an explanatory stimulus in his environment when none is self-evident. In Schachter's research (Schachter & Singer, 1962), the arousal was produced by an injection of epinephrine, mislabeled so that subjects were unaware of the arousing stimulus and had to search their environment for possible explanations. If the arousal is produced by a gaze, the eliciting stimulus is obvious, but in order to define his own arousal, the perceiver may first need to interpret the gaze itself and the gazer's intentions. Since the gaze is arousing, the range of possible interpretations is narrowed to include only those which are affectively significant; a certain range of neutral interpretations is ruled out.

Whether this arousal is seen as pleasant or aversive depends upon a variety of contextual factors. If the situation is a pleasant one, eye contact often makes it more pleasant. If the situation is somewhat unpleasant to begin with, the extra arousal created by the gaze will also be regarded as aversive (Ellsworth & Carlsmith, 1968, 1973), except for special cases where a person feels a particular need for social contact as a means of reducing unpleasant uncertainty (Ellsworth, Hoyt, Friedman, & Perlick, 1974). In any situation, direct gaze which is too frequent or too prolonged may produce levels of arousal that are extreme enough to be perceived as aversive in themselves (Ellsworth *et al.*, 1972; Ellsworth & Ross, in press). The definition of "inappropriately" high levels of gaze depends on the situation and the relationship. Thus the gaze itself is open to a range of contextually-determined interpretations, but these interpretations are limited to those which are affectively or evaluatively significant.

Gaze aversion will not generally have these arousing properties, and in some situations withdrawal of the gaze may serve to reduce arousal. Of course, there are exceptional situations in which gaze aversion may be arousing, most notably situations in which a person wants to establish or maintain social contact, and his interactant, by looking away, is perceived as refusing him. Clearly the individual's goals in the situation are one of the important determinants of his reactions to the other's visual behavior.

Involvement. The possible interpretations placed on the arousal produced by a direct gaze will be more limited than the possible interpretations of the arousal produced by an injection of epinephrine. When a gaze is the stimulus, the interpretation of the consequent arousal must include either attributions of the other person's orientation toward oneself or assessments of the state of the relationship, or both. Argyle and Kendon (1967) suggest that "in the mutual look the participants express their involvement with each other" (p. 70). Similarly, Tomkins (1963) argues that the amount of actual eye contact in interactions is low because of the powerful sense of interpersonal involvement which results when two people see each other's feeling simultaneously.

Returning to the meaning of the gaze for the recipient, we would argue that a person interprets another's direct gaze as an indication of the level or type of interpersonal involvement intended by the other, or as an indication of the state of the relationship at that moment. That involvement is central to the interpretation of a direct gaze is demonstrated by the literature on eye contact and attraction. Sometimes a direct gaze leads to increased liking, sometimes to the reverse, but it almost always leads to a consciousness of the level of involvement or intensity of interpersonal relations, a question or perception about the other person's intention with regard to the relationship, and a reaction to these cognitions. As Ellsworth and Ludwig (1972) argue, the arousal produced by a direct gaze "is probably not so general as to be easily attributed to *any* stimulus that happens to be present. . . . We believe that an interpersonal cause will be sought. While interpersonal attraction is not implied, interpersonal *involvement* is, and the subject's interpretation of the arousal will almost always be focused on his relationship with the other person" (p. 397). An averted gaze may often be seen as an attempt to reduce the level of involvement or to avoid confrontation.

Again, the type of involvement inferred will depend on the situation and the relationship, and its desirability will depend on the perceiver's goals. In the early stages of a romance, when infinite involvement still seems like a delightful state of affairs, people will welcome an amount of gazing that would seem intolerable under any other circumstances. In the frozen silence following an argument, even a fleeting glance may be enough to bring about a resumption of open hostilities. In these situations, interpretations will be immediate and confident. In situations where the gaze does not suggest a clear interpretation, the unexplained arousal and ambiguous involvement implied may be aversive in themselves.

Visual Behavior and Social Interaction

Following this line of thinking, the study of visual behavior in social interaction is not linked to any special topical area in social psychology, such as aggression or attraction. Instead, it is linked to the general line of research and theory on person perception and suggests a set of processes that may operate in any kind of face-to-face interaction. A direct gaze assures that a person will perceive himself to be *in* a social situation, and its arousing properties guarantee a certain level of concern about how to interpret the relationship and how to respond. The arousal probably also increases the likelihood that the inferences drawn about the other person and the relationship will be affectively loaded cognitions, rather than detached and impersonal judgments. Thus the limitations suggested here for the interpretation of a direct gaze—its existence as a stimulus, its arousing effects, and its tendency to focus attention on the relationship and the level of involvement—all serve to sensitize the person to other social psychological variables that may affect his perception and his behavior. When a person is gazed at, he cares about the situation. The link to Schachter's (1964) theory is obvious, suggesting that the individual who is gazed at will be highly motivated to make explanatory attributions. Moving to another line of theory, that of Zajonc (1965), one might speculate that these attributions may be stereotyped, as familiar responses are more likely to be produced in conditions of high arousal.

Within these limitations, however, the particular interpretation of the gaze varies with the context, and the response to the gaze varies with the interpretation. Thus in human beings the "aggressive" properties of the gaze are situationally determined. In the following pages we shall examine a number of studies of potentially aggressive situations, as an illustration of the variety of responses elicited by a direct gaze in different contexts. In these studies, we deliberately chose visual behaviors that appear to have fairly explicit meanings for nonhuman primates: the stare characteristic of threat and the downcast gaze of appeasement. It was felt that if these gestures had context-dependent effects for humans, the evidence that the interpretation of visual behavior in general was context dependent would be stronger than if we had chosen some arbitrary behavior, such as a glance upward and to the right.

The Stare

A steady, direct gaze is perhaps the most common component of threat displays in nonhuman primates, eliciting fight, flight, or appeasement, depending on the status relationship of the animals involved (van Hooff, 1967; Chevalier-Skolnikoff, 1973). According to the formulation presented in the Introduction, we would expect the stare to be noticed, to be arousing, and to be suggestive of an interpersonal involvement between the starer and the target. We would not expect the target necessarily to conclude that the stare was a threat; instead, we would expect the target to interpret the type of involvement implied in the light of other contextual factors.

In our first set of experiments (Ellsworth *et al.*, 1972), the context was deliberately ambiguous; we provided the target with no cues which he might use to interpret the meaning of the stare. We predicted that in this kind of ambiguous situation, the arousal produced by the stare would be extremely unsettling, and the person stared at would be motivated to escape.

Staring and Avoidance

Procedure. In order to increase generality and impact, these studies were carried out in a field setting. The subjects were drivers stopped at a red light, and the experimenter was a bystander waiting on the corner of the sidewalk nearest to the subject's car. Since the street was a one-way street and the car was in the lane nearest to the experimenter, the eye-to-eye distance between subject and experimenter was quite small, usually between 4 and 5 feet.

When a car pulled up to the intersection in the appropriate lane, the experimenter assigned the driver at random to either the *stare condition* or the *no stare condition*. In the stare condition, the experimenter raised his head and looked at the driver, keeping a completely neutral expression,[2] and continued to look at the driver until the light changed and the driver took off. In the no stare condition, the experimenter glanced up to make a quick estimate of the driver's age and sex, looked away, and did not look back at the driver at any time. This glance was the typical brief noncommittal glance characteristic of Goffman's "civil inattention" (Goffman, 1963).

When the light changed, an observer with a stopwatch measured the length of time taken by drivers to cross the intersection. This measure was assumed to be an indication of the subjects' motivation to avoid the experimenter, and it was predicted that subjects who were stared at would cross the intersection faster than those who were not.

Results. The prediction was strongly confirmed: people who were stared at did cross the intersection faster. These results were replicated with the experimenter on a motor scooter or on the street corner, with subjects who were drivers or pedestrians, and with both sexes of experimenter and subject. Eleven different experimenters all succeeded in producing the effect.

Discussion. Now let us examine this experiment in terms of the factors outlined in the Introduction.

In regard to the *salience* of the stare, the experimenters were quite sure that almost all subjects noticed them when they were staring, even though they made no noise and did nothing else to draw attention to themselves. For purposes of data analysis it was assumed that all subjects noticed the gaze; if a substantial number had not, the differences between groups would have been greatly attenuated. Thus the basic results of the experiment are one indication of the salience of the stare. Observational data support this conclusion. Most drivers looked up at the starer within a few seconds of their arrival at the stoplight, thus supporting our assumption that if a pair of direct-gazing eyes is present in the environment, even if only in peripheral vision, they will attract the subject's attention.

That the stare was *arousing* is also indicated by the results of the experiment: the subjects' precipitous departure from the staring experimenter's presence. Again, observational data support this interpretation. Subjects who were stared at fidgeted, changed the stations on their car radios, revved their engines,

---

[2] The neutral expression was based on photographs used for Ekman, Friesen, & Tomkins's Facial Affect Scoring Technique (1971), which the author had helped to develop.

struck up conversations with their passengers, and frequently glanced back at the experimenter, hastily withdrawing their gaze when they met his eyes.

In their interpretation of this research, the authors also assumed that the stare was *involving*, that it functioned as a demand for some sort of interpersonal response. If there had been some obvious appropriate response, the subject could have discharged the tension aroused by the persistent, ever-salient eyes by performing that response. But there wasn't. The situation was quite ambiguous and provided the subject with no clear cues that might guide his interpretation of the stare or his choice of an appropriate response. Thus he was involved in an interpersonal encounter with the starer, willy-nilly; his tension was aroused still further by his lack of a response suited to the occasion; and he was motivated to escape from this uncomfortable situation as soon as possible.

The results are compatible with this formulation. They are also compatible with other formulations. One could argue that they provide good evidence for the proposition that the stare has a single meaning, functioning as an aggressive threat signal in man as it does in other primates, and automatically triggering a tendency to flight.

If our formulation were true, we should be able to show that when an appropriate response is available, people who are stared at will not flee from the starer, but rather will perform that response, even if it involves actually approaching the starer.

Staring and Approach

In a follow-up study (Ellsworth & Langer, in press), the situation was modeled on those typical of bystander intervention research, in which the response called for involves approaching the victim and offering assistance. When the nature of the victim's plight and the remedy required was clear, it was predicted that a victim who stared at a potential helper would elicit approach and assistance. The more ambiguous the victim's predicament, the less likely staring would be to elicit helpful behavior; as the appropriate response becomes doubtful, the tendency to flee becomes stronger.

This study was carried out in a shopping mall. All subjects were accosted by a breathless young woman carrying a suitcase. In the *clear condition*, the girl said, "Listen, there's a girl back there . . . who looks like she's lost a contact lens and needs some help. I can't stop because I'm going to miss a train." In the *ambiguous condition*, she said, "Listen, there's a girl back there . . . who looks like she's not feeling well and needs some help. I can't stop because I'm going to miss a train." In both conditions the girl gestured toward the "victim" to make sure the subject knew who she was, and then hurried on.

Upon looking around, the subject saw another girl, half crouching and leaning against a wall about 25 feet away. This girl was either looking at the ground or staring directly at the subject.

Again, we would argue that the stare was salient, arousing, and involving, but the meaning of the involvement was either clear or ambiguous. The response to the lens-loser is clear: one helps to search for the lens. The response to a person who "looks like she's not feeling well" is much less clear: it may involve making a phone call, it may involve more extensive help, or it may be an embarrassing mistake on the part of the first girl. When the subject asks herself, "What does this girl want from me?", she has no ready answer. In this situation, we predicted that the stare would again elicit avoidance, while in the clear condition it would elicit approach.

An observer noted how many subjects in each of the four conditions approached the starer, and how many hurried on without approaching. The results of this study are presented in Table I.

Using the arc-sine transformation for differences among ratios (Langer & Abelson, 1972), we find that there is no main effect for staring. The interaction of staring with situational ambiguity is of borderline significance ($z = 1.60; p = .06$). Using more sensitive indices, which include time taken to approach and degree of hesitation, this effect is stronger. These results indicate that the stare has no intrinsic effect; instead, the effect depends on the context. When the response is obvious and the nature of the implied involvement is clear, people do not run away from the starer but approach and help. In fact, they are somewhat more likely to approach a person who is staring than a person who is not staring. When the response and the implications of the involvement are ambiguous, people are more likely to avoid the whole situation, as they did in the earlier studies.

The approach effect has been demonstrated in other contexts as well. For example, if a woman carrying a load of packages stands on a street corner and stares at a pedestrian who is waiting to cross, the pedestrian will cross faster than a pedestrian who is not stared at. But if she drops a package and stares, the person stared at is likely to approach, pick up the package, and hand it to her. The fallen package provides an explanation for the involving stare and suggests a clear response. This finding has been replicated independently by Gordon Bear (personal communication, 1974).

The absence of main effects for the stare in these studies demonstrates that staring is not necessarily perceived as a threatening signal and does not automatically elicit flight. In the right context, a stare can increase the possibility of a familiar, helpful approach. Again, it is unlikely that the interpretation of the stare

Table I. Percentage of Subjects Helping

Condition	Clear	Ambiguous
Stare	83%	25%
No stare	58%	42%

$n = 12$ in each condition.

is completely dependent on context, although context clearly plays an important role. The stare is probably not perceived as a sign of indifference in any context, for example, unless the starer is perceived as blind, psychotic, or otherwise unaware that he is staring. In ordinary circumstances, the stare is arousing and signals involvement; the context determines the type of involvement implied, from which an appropriate response may be inferred.

What about the situation where no helpful contextual information is provided, as in the first set of staring experiments? We have argued that the resultant uncertainty may be the stimulus to flight. It is also possible, however, that when no contradictory contextual information is provided, the stare is perceived as potentially hostile. Either because of faint stirrings of our primate nerves or because the stare appears to be an intentional disregard for strong cultural norms, people may more readily label a stare as hostile than as friendly, fearful, interested, or anything else. This label, as we have seen, can easily be overruled by additional contextual information, so it may not be an important determinant of behavior, but it may be the most probable attribution in the ambiguous situation. Our data do not allow us to distinguish between these two possibilities.

The Complexities of the "Appeasement" Gesture

In nonhuman primates the stare is the visual behavior which is most consistent in its effects across species and across situations. We have given examples of situations where human subjects are the victims of potentially threatening stares, and have shown that whether or not the stare is threatening depends on the context. Another type of visual behavior which is quite consistent both in appearance and in consequences across other primate species is gaze aversion or "facing away." This pattern usually occurs when the animal is attacked, especially when flight is impossible, and it usually succeeds in preventing or curtailing the attack (van Hooff, 1967).

In the research to which we now turn (Ellsworth & Carlsmith, 1973), the subject was the aggressor, and the visual behavior of his victim was varied. Two types of visual signals were used: a direct gaze, and gaze aversion. One-third of the victims consistently met their attacker's gaze at the initiation of each attack, one-third consistently averted their gaze, and one-third varied these two behaviors in a random sequence.

Procedure. Believing that they were participating in an experiment designed to compare the effects of noise with other stressors, a subject and a confederate engaged in two interactions, during each of which one of them was authorized to administer stressful stimuli to the other. During the first interaction, the confederate motivated the subject to friendliness or aggression by delivering either more or less than the amount of white noise recommended by the experimenter and by behaving in a generally hostile manner. Thus one aspect of the context that was varied was the nature of the subject's prior interaction with the confederate.

In the second interaction the subject was allowed to deliver electric shocks to the confederate, preceding each shock with a warning. At each warning signal the confederate either established eye contact, looked downward, or varied these two behaviors according to a predetermined random schedule. The subject could deliver shocks at will during the 5-minute interaction, but he had to precede each shock with a warning.

The design of the experiment was thus a 2 × 3 factorial, with presence versus absence of aggression aroused against the future victim and with three different types of visual behavior from the victim during the aggressive encounter. The two random sequence conditions constituted a within-subjects design with the same variables (Look/No Look; Anger Aroused/No Anger Aroused) as the between-subjects design represented by the other four conditions. This consistency or variability of the victim's behavior created another contextual factor which might affect the aggressor's response to the gaze. A gaze that is simply one of an unbroken series of gazes might evoke quite a different response from a gaze occurring in a sequence that also includes gaze aversion.

The Positive–Negative Treatment. The positive–negative treatment began as soon as the subject and the confederate met. If the subject was in the *positive condition*, the confederate smiled at him, responded favorably to anything he said and, in the case of taciturn subjects, initiated a conversation, making sure to defer to the subject and to agree with him at all times. When asked to deliver loud bursts of white noise to the subject, the confederate gave only one or two bursts per minute, despite the experimenter's instructions to aim for the 4–6 range. He also gave an impression of concern and consideration for the subject throughout the administration of stressful stimuli.

In the *negative condition*, upon meeting the subject, the confederate looked him over in a critical manner and turned away. If the subject attempted to initiate a conversation, the confederate responded with cold, noncommittal monosyllables. He behaved in an insolent manner to the young and rather nervous female experimenter and to the subject himself during the administration of white noise. He also delivered eight to ten bursts of white noise during each of the five 1-minute trials, thus arrogantly exceeding the number recommended by the experimenter. Verbal measures taken at the end of the interaction indicated that subjects in the negative condition were significantly angrier than those in the positive condition.

After filling out these scales and receiving further instructions, subjects moved into the second stress interaction. This time the subject was allowed to deliver shocks to the confederate *ad libitum* for a 5-minute period. He was asked, however, to provide a warning before each shock by pressing a buzzer. While he was not required to follow each warning with a shock ("false alarms" were permitted), he was required to precede each shock with a warning ("surprise shocks" were not permitted).

Eye Contact Manipulation. In the *direct gaze condition*, when the buzzer sounded, the confederate-victim looked up at the subject and continued to look until the shock was delivered (or the subject signaled that no shock was forthcoming). In the *gaze aversion condition*, the victim glanced up at the subject for a fraction of a second when the buzzer sounded and then looked down. In the within-subjects design, these behaviors were varied in a random sequence; each time the buzzer sounded, the victim either looked or averted his gaze, in no predictable order. The victim's facial expressions were generally neutral or characterized by mild concentration. Detailed descriptions of these procedures and precautions against experimenter bias can be found in Ellsworth & Carlsmith (1973).

Results. Since subjects had a chance to decide whether to deliver low, medium, or high shock, an index measure of aggression was used in which shocks were weighted for intensity. These are the scores that are reported in Table II. In general, they parallel the results for simple frequency scores.

Here again it is clear that the direct gaze has no consistent effect on behavior. In the first place, direct gaze had minimal influence on the subjects who were not angry. The levels of shock for the nonangered subjects were low and fairly consistent, ranging from 16.6 to 19.8. The amount of shock delivered in these conditions probably represents a baseline level defined by the demand characteristics of the experiment; the subject delivered a certain number of shocks required by his role as "good subject", and this number was unaffected by the victim's behavior.

Once the subject was angry, however, the victim's behavior did affect the amount of aggression expressed, but here again the effect of direct gaze was dependent on situational factors. In the between-subjects design, where the victim's behavior was perfectly consistent, the direct gaze inhibited aggression. The amount of shock delivered by subjects in the *negative/direct gaze condition*

Table II.   Mean Frequency of Shock (Weighted Means)

Condition	Direct gaze	Averted gaze	Total
Between-subjects design			
Positive	16.6	16.9	
Negative	19.9	30.5	
Within-subjects design			
Positive	11.8	8.0	19.8
Negative	14.4	13.0	27.4

$n = 10$ in each of the six Between-subjects conditions.

was not significantly different from the amount delivered by nonangered subjects but was significantly different from the amount delivered by subjects in the *negative/gaze aversion condition*. The amount of shock delivered by angered subjects to victims whose visual behavior was variable ($\bar{x} = 27.4$) did not differ significantly from the amount delivered to the victim who always looked away ($\bar{x} = 30.5$). The similarity of these two means suggests that the difference in amount of aggression expressed toward the constantly gazing victim and the victim who constantly averts his gaze represents an inhibition of aggression towards the victim who looks, rather than an enhancement of aggression against the victim who looks away.

When the victim sometimes looked at the aggressor and sometimes averted his gaze downward (the within-subjects design), the picture changed dramatically. In this situation the victim received significantly more shock when he gazed at the subject than when he looked away, and this result held regardless of whether or not the subject had been previously antagonized by his future victim. Apparently, eye contact is an effective inhibitor of aggression only if it is consistent.

Discussion. No theory that attributes a simple triggering effect to direct gaze can account for these effects. One source of information useful for understanding the behavioral data is the subject's interpretations of the meaning of the direct gaze. These are highly consistent in some ways, highly variable in others. While subjects were not asked to report on the amount of direct gaze specifically, they were asked to report on certain of the victim's nonverbal behaviors, including "eye and brow movements." Almost all subjects in the conditions involving direct gaze (either consistent or variable) answered this question by referring to the victim's tendency to look at them before each shock. This was the only behavior mentioned, and subjects were extremely emphatic in their reports, thus reconfirming our initial postulate about the salience of direct gaze. In addition, 50% to 100% of the subjects in each of these conditions (the lower figures coming from the positive conditions) spontaneously commented on the aversiveness of being looked at in this situation, suggesting that the eye contact was arousing and, in this kind of unpleasant situation, negatively arousing. No subjects reported that the direct gaze was pleasant. Beyond this high agreement, interpretations also suggested various types of interpersonal involvement ("he's challenging me," "he's afraid of me," etc.), but there was no consistency in the type of involvement suggested.

Given this high level of agreement about the aversive nature of the direct gaze, we may assume that the subjects were motivated to avoid it. What could they do? Two rather different alternatives existed. First, since the victim only looked up when the warning notice was given, the subject could avoid the direct gaze by pressing the warning buzzer and consequently the shock button less often. With this strategy, the victim's gaze is a punishment which comes to control the subject's behavior. Second, the subject can use the shock to administer punishments of his own, shocking the victim whenever he looks at the subject. The phrase "whenever he looks," however, implies that the subject has a sense of the variability of the victim's behavior—if the victim always looks, the subject cannot administer differential punishment. This variability, of course, is characteristic only of the within-subjects design, and this is exactly where direct gaze elicits more shock than gaze aversion.

Turning to the situation where the victim's behavior is constant, it is clear that the punishment strategy will not work. Thus the only means left to the subject for avoiding the eye contact is to avoid eliciting it in the first place—to decrease the frequency of shock. Actually, it was not immediately clear to the subjects in the constant-gaze condition that the punishment strategy was doomed to failure. The temporal sequencing of shock across the 5-minute period for angered subjects in the constant-gaze condition indicates that they probably tried the punishment alternative first. During the first minute they deliver more shocks than other groups. However, unlike any other subjects their rate of shocking declines from minute to minute until during the fifth minute they are giving almost as little shock as the lowest group (the nonangered Direct Gaze group). Thus when punishment proved ineffective, subjects chose the avoidance alternative, and the result was the low overall level of shock found in the constant look condition.

The consistencies that we have suggested for the direct gaze emerged again in this research: the gaze was salient, arousing, and involving. Most subjects also spontaneously pointed out that it was aversive, and we might add as a fourth principle that unless the general nature of the interaction is pleasant (or likely to be pleasant, as in the "some enchanted evening" gaze), the arousal produced by the direct gaze will be experienced as aversive. This hypothesis may simply be part of a more general formulation about arousal: only if an arousing situation is pleasant or comfortably explicable (as in the lost-lens situation) will arousal be experienced as pleasant. One might also hypothesize that the amount of direct gaze that is tolerable is a direct function of the subject's sense of well-being (positive affect plus sense of certainty about the situation) in his present environment. These feelings will also therefore affect the subject's feelings about the situational equilibrium, in Argyle and Dean's (1965) sense.

This experiment also places severe limitations on the consistency of response to a direct gaze, however. Subjects' specific interpretations of the meaning of the gaze varied widely, and the contextual factor of temporal sequencing of the gaze had a major effect on the subject's responses. A gaze which was embedded in a series consisting of nothing but gazes elicited quite different behavior from a gaze which was embedded in a series of behaviors which also included gaze aversion. Had the situation been slightly different, so that subjects could not have avoided the direct gaze by refusing to initiate further interaction, the results would have been still different. In a study of this sort, in which subjects were confronted with two victims and asked to choose between them on each of a fixed number of trials, subjects gave more shock to the victim who consistently looked at them than to the victim who constantly looked down. When subjects were not angry with the victims, visual behavior again had no effect on aggression. When one victim's behavior was constant and the other's was variable, new contextual factors and new interpretations came into play (Manzolati & Ellsworth, in preparation).

Discussion and Speculations

Taken together, these studies provide fairly strong support for the proposition that the meaning of a look is not intrinsic to the look but derives in large measure from the context. Thus a stare is not just a threatening signal that triggers flight, and a downcast gaze is much more complicated than a simple appeasement gesture. However, this flexibility of interpretation across contexts does not imply that visual behaviors are unimportant social stimuli. On the contrary, within each social context studied, the direct gaze had powerful and fairly consistent effects, effects which differed from those of gaze aversion. It was, as we have argued, a salient, arousing, and involving stimulus, a stimulus which demanded a response. If no appropriate response could be found, the person who was gazed at tried to escape from the demand by fleeing from the situation.

Human aggression is rarely provoked by an automatic triggering stimulus, short of physical attack. Even a direct insult may provoke chuckling rather than bristling if it is delivered in the right tone of voice. Aggression is controlled by a person's perception of the situation, his experience with similar situations, his state of arousal, and his perception of the consequences of aggression. The visual behavior of the potential opponent can certainly contribute to aggression, but not because of any simple triggering effect. A direct gaze can raise the level of arousal; it may, due to its salience, cause a person to be picked out of a crowd by a drunk with a chip on his shoulder; it may provoke pangs of conscience. Since an aggressive encounter is typically an unpleasant situation, a direct gaze will typically be seen as aversive within this context. Finer interpretations will depend on specific situational factors.

Since we have relied so heavily on these other situational factors in our analysis, it may be useful to suggest what some of these factors might be. Little work has been done in these areas; it is here that the collaboration between those who study nonverbal behavior and those who study social interaction from a more general theoretical point of view may prove most fruitful. We have argued that a gaze will be noticed, that it will be an arousing and involving stimulus in social interaction. As such, it may serve as a lightning rod for other motivations aroused in the interaction, eliciting behaviors that might otherwise have lain dormant, provoking interpretations, and creating a truly social relationship, however brief, even within the often sterile and artificial settings used by experimental social psychologists.

What follows is largely speculation. It is an attempt to outline some broad categories of factors that might modify the interpretation of visual behavior in social interaction. It is not intended to be exhaustive, any more than the salient/arousing/involving categorization of gaze properties was meant to be. It is intended as a first tentative attempt at order.

Factors Affecting the Interpretation of Visual Behavior

Contextual Factors.   The context of a gaze may be as small as the face in which it is set, or as large and amorphous as the ''affective tone'' of the situation. The face, as a context, may often have a meaning which is quite specific, unlike the gaze itself. Relatively intense expressions of single emotions do have meanings which can be accurately judged by members of the species (Izard, 1971; Ekman, 1973). Some of these emotions, such as fear, anger, surprise, and interest, include a direct gaze as a component. Thus when the eyes look out of one of these contexts, the meaning of their gaze will not be free to vary as we have suggested. The gaze will suggest something beyond mere involvement; a particular type of emotional involvement will be implied. Similarly, the averted gaze of shame or sorrow or disgust will be given a particular interpretation, rather than a general one. In ordinary conversations, however, these clear and obvious facial expressions may be rather rare. While other, less archetypical facial configurations may also provide contexts in which the meaning of the gaze is reliably interpreted, as yet we have little relevant data. Our guess is that they will limit the range of interpretations possible, without being definitive.

Between the face and the atmosphere of the situation lies a huge range of factors—posture, status relationships, degree of acquaintance, purpose, setting and formality of the interaction, cultural factors, and so on, and so on. Few of these have received much empirical attention in relation to visual behavior, with the exception of Birdwhistell's observations of subcultural differences (1970), explorations of status relationships by Mehrabian (1969) and Exline (this volume), and Rubin's research on romance (1970).

At a much more general level, it appears that the primary evaluative response to a direct gaze is made on the basis of the general emotional tone of the interaction. The same gaze will create positive feelings if the content of the gazer's conversation is favorable to the other person, and negative feelings if the content is unfavorable (Ellsworth & Carlsmith, 1968; Scherwitz & Helmreich,

1973). In the aggressive interaction described before, most subjects spontaneously remarked on the unpleasantness of the gaze. Thus to some extent the gaze serves as an intensifier and a point of focus for feelings aroused by the general situation, much like a magnifying glass.

Properties of the Behavior Itself: Timing and Contingency. Any behavior that is salient, and evokes a strong positive or negative response, may act as a reinforcer. Thus in the aggression study described earlier, the aversive gaze that invariably followed the warning signal served as a negative reinforcer, so that gradually the frequency of warning and hence of shock decreased. This was an effect of the timing and consistency of the gaze. In another study (Ellsworth & Ross, in press) direct gaze that was contingent on personally revealing statements affected the level of the speaker's intimacy as much as steady direct gaze, even though the amount of time spent gazing in the contingent condition was much less. Similarly, gaze aversion contingent upon intimate statements was as effective as continuous gaze aversion in modifying the speaker's self-disclosure. Thus the contingency of direct gaze is at least as important as the overall amount.

We have argued previously that perception of the visual behavior as homogeneous or variable has other profound effects on its interpretation. When a person perceives another's unpleasant behavior as variable, he sees it as potentially responsive to situational factors and his own influence. The social situation is seen as more interactive, in that the perceiver can attempt to control the unpleasant behavior by means of his own reinforcements. When the behavior is completely homogeneous, on the other hand, it is by definition immune to interactional attempts to modify it. The perceiver can only choose to put up with it or avoid the interaction. If he cannot avoid the interaction, he may retaliate against the other person anyway, perhaps out of sheer frustration, even though he does not feel that he has any chance of modifying the aversive behavior (Manzolati & Ellsworth, in preparation). Similarly, variable behavior that is pleasant may elicit charming and winsome actions designed to increase the frequency of the pleasant behavior, while constant pleasant behavior will not call forth such efforts. When the perceiver attempts to make attributions about the other on the basis of homogeneous behavior, he will not see himself or the rest of the environment as playing much of a role in affecting that behavior, but will tend to see it as a reflection of the other's underlying character.

Timing may be important in another way. If there are moments within the sequence of phrases and silences during a conversation when interactants are more likely to look for feedback, a visual behavior which occurs at this time may well be more influential, and more likely to elicit attributions, than the same behavior occurring at some other time during the verbal flow. This possibility is discussed by Ellsworth and Ludwig (1972).

Perceiver's Motivation and Set. As suggested by Argyle and Kendon (1967), the goals of the interactants may also affect their susceptibility to the influence of visual behavior and their interpretation of its meaning. In an interaction that is emotionally significant, participants may respond to many more nonverbal movements and make many more attributions. Thus in the control group of the aggression study, when no aggression was aroused and the level of shock was primarily a reflection of baseline demand characteristics, the victim's visual behavior had little or no effect. Once the subjects were angry and emotionally involved in the situation, the visual behavior became an important influence on their behavior. The same hyperawareness of subtle cues that occurs when a fight is in the offing is also characteristic of the early tentative stages of a love affair, when every look and gesture becomes significant.

The perceiver's level of uncertainty may also affect his tendency to look for cues and make interpretations, by increasing his motivation to understand what is going on. Hence, people may be much more sensitive to visual behavior and other nonverbal cues from potentially important strangers than to those emitted by definitely important but familiar friends. In a comfortable stable relationship, a person may feel that there is nothing to explain, and so neglect to seek or notice subtle cues.

Another cognitive set which may affect attention to different types of nonverbal cues and their interpretation is the person's perception of who is being evaluated in the interaction. Argyle and Williams (1969) have found that one person in a face-to-face interaction typically feels like an observer, while his partner feels observed. Ludwig and Ellsworth (1974) found that subjects who felt observed or evaluated assigned greater meaning to differences in the other person's visual behaviors than did subjects who felt that they were doing the evaluating in the interaction. This study also raised the intriguing possibility that subjects may interpret their own behavior and motivations on the basis of the nonverbal signals they receive from others.

The perceiver's cognitive set may also include assumptions about the amount of direct gaze that is appropriate for the interaction. Argyle and Dean (1965) have suggested that participants strive to maintain an equilibrium level of intimacy, keeping intensifying cues such as eye contact and proximity within the bounds set by their notions of appropriateness, and compensating for excesses in one channel by reducing the intimacy or immediacy of another channel. Thus conflicting notions of appropriateness should lead to a considerable amount of nonverbal negotiation, while levels acceptable to both parties should result in fairly stable rates of the various contact behaviors. Definitions of the appropriate level of intimacy may be affected by cultural background, status and role, and sex (Ellsworth & Ross, in press). Thus the same visual behavior will not be regarded as appropriate by all persons in all contexts, and reactions and interpretations of the behavior will vary accordingly.

Summary

The direct gaze is a salient, arousing, and involving stimulus in social interaction, but within these limits, particular directions or durations of the gaze do not have intrinsic meaning. Instead, they are interpreted in the light of other situational and contextual factors. In the case of aggression, a gaze which is threatening in a neutral or ambiguous situation can become unthreatening or even encouraging if an appropriate explanation is provided. The effects of a victim's gaze will vary depending on the consistency of his behavior, the aggressor's emotional attitude toward him, and the presence and behavior of other potential victims.

Despite this variability in interpretation, the gaze is an important stimulus in social interaction because it is a stimulus that is highly likely to be noticed and to elicit a social interpretation. While the specific interpretation may depend on the surrounding behaviors, the timing of the visual behavior, the relationship, the behavior of others, and the person's motivations and goals in the interaction, the gaze will elicit some sort of response and some sort of interpretation. While the gaze is not a specific sign, it is generally significant.

References

Argyle, M., & Dean, J. Eye contact, distance, and affiliation. *Sociometry, 1965, 28,* 289–304.

Argyle, M., & Kendon, A. The experimental analysis of social performances. In L. Berkowitz (Ed.), *Advances in Experimental Social Psychology* (Vol. 3. New York: Academic Press, 1967, pp. 55–99.

Argyle, M., & Williams, M. Observer or observed? A reversible perspective in person perception. *Sociometry, 1969,32,* 396–412.

Birdwhistell, R. L. *Kinesics and Context.* Philadelphia: University of Pennsylvania Press, 1970.

Bond, M. H., & Komai, H. The effects of types of gazing and their variation on Japanese nonverbal behavior and person perception. Unpublished manuscript, Kwansei Gakuin University, Nishinomiya, Japan, 1974.

Bruner, J. S., & Taguiri, R. The perception of people. In G. Lindzey (Ed.), *Handbook of Social Psychology* (Vol. II). Reading, Mass.: Addison-Wesley, 1954, pp. 634–654.

Chevalier, Skolnikoff, S. Facial expression of emotion in nonhuman primates. In P. Ekman (Ed.), *Darwin and Facial Expression.* New York: Academic Press, 1973, pp. 11–89.

Darwin, C. *The Expression of the Emotions in Man and Animals.* London: John Murray, 1872. Chicago: University of Chicago Press (current ed.), 1965.

Donne, J. *The extasie,* 1633.

Duncan, S., Jr., & Niederehe, G. On signaling that it's your turn to speak. *Journal of Experimental Social Psychology,* 1974, *10,* 234–254.

Ekman, P. Universals and cultural differences in facial expressions of emotion. In J. K. Cole (Ed.), *Nebraska Symposium on Motivation, 1971.* Lincoln: University of Nebraska Press, 1972.

Ekman, P. *Darwin and Facial Expression*. New York: Academic Press, 1973.

Ekman, P., Friesen, W. V., & Tomkins, S. S. Facial affect scoring technique: a first validity study. *Semiotica*, 1971, *3*, 37–38.

Ekman, P., Friesen, W. V., & Ellsworth, P. *Emotion in the Human Face*. New York: Pergamon, 1972.

Ellsworth, P. C., & Carlsmith, J. M. Effects of eye contact and verbal content on affective response to a dyadic interaction. *Journal of Personality and Social Psychology*, 1968, *10*, 15–20.

Ellsworth, P. C., Carlsmith, J. M., & Henson, A. The stare as a stimulus to flight in human subjects: A series of field experiments. *Journal of Personality and Social Psychology*, 1972, *21*, 302–311.

Ellsworth, P. C., & Ludwig, L. M. Visual behavior in social interaction. *Journal of Communication*, 1972, *22*, 365–403.

Ellsworth, P. C., & Carlsmith, J. M. Eye contact and gaze aversion in an aggressive encounter. *Journal of Personality and Social Psychology*, 1973, *28*, 280–292.

Ellsworth, P. C., & Ross, L. D. Eye contact and intimacy. *Journal of Experimental Social Psychology*, in press.

Ellsworth, P. C., & Langer, E. J. Staring and approach: An interpretation of the stare as a nonspecific activator. *Journal of Personality and Social Psychology*, in press.

Ellsworth, P. C., Hoyt, M. F., Friedman, H., & Perlick, D. Eye contact, liking, and the desire for social comparison. Unpublished manuscript, 1974.

Exline, R. V., & Yellin, A. Eye contact as a sign between man and monkey. *Symposium on nonverbal communication, Nineteenth International Congress of Psychology*, London, 1969.

Festinger, L. A theory of social comparison processes. *Human Relations*, 1954, *7*, 114–140.

Goffman, E. *Behavior in Public Places*. Glencoe, Ill.: The Free Press of Glencoe, 1963.

Gross, L. The price of progress: Modes of communication, art, and education. In J. Cohen (Ed.), *Obstacles to Communication*. UNESCO, 1975.

Izard, C. E. *The Face of Emotion*. New York: Appleton-Century-Crofts, 1971.

Izard, C. E. *Patterns of Emotions: A New Analysis for Anxiety and Depression*. New York: Academic Press, 1972.

Jones E. E., Kanouse, D. R., Kelley, H. H., Nisbett, R. E., Valins, S., & Weiner, B. *Attribution: Perceiving the Causes of Behavior*. Morristown, N. J.: General Learning Press, 1971.

Kleinke, C. L., & Pohlen, P. D. Affective and emotional responses as a function of other person's gaze and cooperativeness in a two-person game. *Journal of Personality and Social Psychology*, 1971, *17*, 308–313.

Langer, E. J., & Abelson, R. P. The semantics of asking a favor: How to succeed in getting help without really dying. *Journal of Personality and Social Psychology*, 1972, *24*, 26–33.

Ludwig, L. M., & Ellsworth, P. C. Some effects of observation set on the interpretation of nonverbal cues. Unpublished manuscript, 1974.

Manzolati, J., & Ellsworth, P. Aggression against two victims with differing visual behavior. Unpublished manuscript, Stanford University, in preparation.

Mehrabian, A. Significance of posture and position in the communication of attitude and status relationships. *Psychological Bulletin*, 1969, *71*, 359–372.

Nichols, K. A., & Champness, B. G. Eye gaze and the GSR. *Journal of Experimental Social Psychology*, 1971, *7*, 623–626.

Rubin, Z. Measurement of romantic love. *Journal of Personality and Social Psychology*, 1970, *16*, 265–273.

Schachter, S. The interaction of cognitive and physiological determinants of emotional state. In L. Berkowitz (Ed.) *Advances in Experimental Social Psychology* (Vol. I). New York: Academic Press, 1964, pp. 49–80.

Schachter, S., & Singer, J. E. Cognitive, social & physiological determinants of emotional state. *Psychological Review*, 1962, *69*, 379–399.

Scherwitz, L., & Helmreich, R. Interactive effects of eye contact and verbal content on interpersonal attraction in dyads. *Journal of Personality and Social Psychology*, 1973, *25*, 6–14.

Tomkins, S. S. *Affect, Imagery, Consciousness.* Vol. I: *The Positive Affects.* New York: Springer, 1962.

Tomkins, S. S. *Affect, Imagery, Consciousness.* Vol. II: *The Negative Affects.* New York: Springer, 1963.

van Hooff, J. A. R. A. M. The facial displays of the catarrhine monkeys and apes. In D. Morris (Ed.), *Primate Ethology.* Chicago: Aldine, 1967.

Vine, I. Judgement of direction of gaze: An interpretation of discrepant results. *British Journal of Social and Clinical Psychology*, 1971, *10*, 320–331.

Wiener, M., Devoe, S., Rubinow, S., & Geller, J. Nonverbal behavior and nonverbal communication. *Psychological Review*, 1972, *79*, 185–214.

Zajonc, R. B. Social facilitation. *Science*, 1965, *149*, 269–274.

CHAPTER 4

Patterns of Emotions and Emotion Communication in "Hostility" and Aggression[1]

Carroll E. Izard

Vanderbilt University[2]
Nashville, Tennessee

The behavioral sciences have an uncommonly difficult problem delineating and defining some of their more important concepts. One of the reasons for this is that behavioral science often has to deal with terms that have a variety of meanings both in the dictionary and in common usage. Typically, behavioral scientists do not discover or invent things that can be given a new and unambiguous name. A few decades ago in the biological sciences a substance was discovered and given the name penicillin. Since that time, a host of antibiotics have been developed and given special names, and each name symbolizes a particular set of biochemical properties. Many of these special names, like penicillin, are now in common usage. Thus the vocabulary of other sciences moves from the realm of science to common usage. There are few, if any, parallels in the behavioral sciences. In the behavioral sciences the reverse is most often the case. Terms go from common usage to behavioral science. This inevitably causes problems. It is difficult to deal scientifically with a term whose meaning may vary even from individual to individual.

[1] The research on the effects of bilateral sectioning of the facial nerve in rhesus monkeys, reported herein, was supported by Grant # HD00973 from the National Institute of Child Health and Human Development.
[2] The author also serves as a senior scientist in The John F. Kennedy Center for Research on Education and Human Development, George Peabody College for Teachers.

The concept that is the subject of this book is a prime example of the terminological problem. The concept of aggression in its various forms has many meanings. Aggressiveness can be considered as a characteristic of the all-American hero—extroverted, self-assertive, and eminently successful. But aggressiveness may also be used to characterize the ugly American—cruel, combative, and destructive. Aggressiveness can be viewed as a mechanism essential for the defense of personal integrity, family, community, or country, or as the fatal step toward the destruction or dehumanizing of both the actor and the victim.

Regrettably, this acknowledgment of a very complex problem for the students of aggression will not be followed by a set of answers that will satisfy everyone. However, I shall define aggression and some related terms as they will be used in this chapter. It is probably not fruitful in the long run to attempt to invent a new term for aggression since its relationship to the old one would probably create confusion as it moved from science to common usage. Perhaps a more fruitful approach would be to use common terms but restrict their meanings as appropriate for the particular theoretical framework and experimentation to be done. It is with this attitude that the following definitions are offered.

1. *Emotion (Fundamental, Discrete)*. An emotion is a complex phenomenon having neurophysiological, behavioral-expressive, and experiential components. The intraindividual process whereby these components interact to produce the emotion is an evolutionary-biogenetic phenomenon. For example, in the human being the expression of anger and the experiential phenomenon of anger are innate, pancultural, universal phenomena.

2. *Patterns of Emotions*. A pattern of emotions is a combination of two or more fundamental emotions which under particular conditions tend to occur together (either simultaneously or in alternating sequence) and to interact in such a way that all of the emotions in the pattern have some motivational impact on the organism and its behavior.

3. *Drives*. A drive is a motivational state brought about by tissue change or tissue deficit. I refer to the common phenomena of hunger, thirst, fatigue, etc. The motivational intensity of all the drives, except pain, is cyclical in nature. Two of the drives, pain and sex, have some of the characteristics of emotions.

4. *Affect*. Affect is a general nonspecific term that includes all the foregoing motivational states and processes. Thus, the affective domain includes the fundamental emotions, patterns of emotions, and drives. The affective domain also embraces all states or processes in which one of the affects is linked with or interacting with perception or cognition.

5. *Emotion–Emotion Interaction*. An emotion-emotion interaction is the amplification, attenuation, or inhibition of one emotion by another.

6. *Emotion–Drive Interaction*. These are motivational states characterized by the amplification, attenuation, or inhibition of drive by emotion or vice versa.

7. *Affect–Cognition Interaction.* Affects typically interact with and influence perceptual and cognitive processes. On the other hand, cognition often plays a role in the activation and regulation of affect.

8. *Affective–Cognitive Orientation.* Frequent interaction of a particular affect or pattern of affects with a particular set of ideas may produce an affective—cognitive orientation which then functions as a characteristic of the individual or personality trait.

9. *Behavior.* Behavior is distinguished from affective states and processes. Thus emotions and drives are not considered as behavior but as the experiential phenomena that produce behavior or behavioral tendencies. Behavior consists of various forms of action, verbal or physical, typically action that is a function of the whole organism.

10. *Affect Expression.* Affect expression occupies a middle ground between an experiential/motivational state and behavior. For example, the patterning of the striate muscles of the face in the form of anger expression is part of an experiential/motivational process and a form of behavior. However, the more essential properties of a facial, vocal, gestural, or postural expression that is integral to the emotion process are motivational not behavioral.

While I think it is useful to draw these distinctions between affective processes, affect expression, and behavior, it is recognized that maintaining these distinctions will be difficult. While these statements distinguish between subjective experience and behavior and thus narrow the meaning of the latter, our definition of behavior is still rather broad. It includes perceptual and cognitive processes (perception, imaging, thinking, remembering, planning, speaking), as well as manipulatory and locomotor activity.

11. *Hostility.* Hostility is a complex affective concept. It consists of a variable set of interacting emotions and drives. The emotions most prominent in the pattern of hostility are anger, disgust, and contempt. Hostility also involves drive states–cognition and various affect interactions. Hostility has both experiential and expressive components. The affects in hostility influence perceptual processes and tend to foster cognitive processes consonant with the underlying affect. The characteristics of hostility will be discussed in greater detail in later sections of the chapter.

12. *Aggression.* Within the theoretical framework underlying the foregoing definitions, aggression is defined as hostile behavior. Thus aggression is a physical act instigated and maintained in part by one or more of the emotions in the hostility pattern and intended to harm the object. The term "physical act" includes speech as well as all other physical actions. The harm may be psychological or biological, a blow to the body, or to the self-concept. Thus the hurt caused by aggression may be from genuine pain, negative emotions, or both. In general, aggression follows from the hostility affects and the associated imagery and ideas. However, aggressive action can influence the ongoing

hostility. Thus hostility is considered as the complex motivational condition and aggression the subsequent behavior. Although this discussion will have more to say about aggression, its central concern is with hostility and with the affects and patterns of affects that constitute it.

The conceptual framework outlined by these definitions indicates that we do not communicate aggression nonverbally. Affect expression communicates anger, disgust, contempt, or hostility.

Affect, Communication, and Consciousness

Since this symposium is focusing on nonverbal communication and aggression, one could reasonably question the relevance of a discussion dealing mainly with intraindividual processes. Two things make intraindividual processes relevant to the topic of communication and aggression.

First, there are two broad classes of communication: intraindividual communication and interindividual or social communication. The emotion process illustrates this very well. In the emotion process that goes on within the individual, the facial activity that produces an anger expression communicates both to the individual (actor) and to the perceiver (other, observing individual). In fact, it is the feedback signals from the proprioceptors and cutaneous receptors in the face that provide the sensory data for an emotion experience. This emotion experience has very definite communicative (as well as experiential/motivational) value for the individual (actor). At the same time, the anger expression communicates a specific message to any and all observing individuals capable of recognizing the pattern. Among primates (including human primates) the evidence is very strong that recognition is possible for all members of the species at birth or within the few weeks required for the maturation and normal exercise of the essential mechanisms.

Second, what is communicated to other individuals (social communication) is in large measure a function of intraindividual communication, or the affective states and processes in consciousness. As an emotion increases in intensity, the more likely it is to exercise control over conscious processes and to communicate social signals that tend to dominate awareness. In general, the higher our level of awareness of a given emotion or affect, the more likely it is to be communicated socially or, at least, to influence social communication.

The affects, particularly the emotions, organize and control the self, consciousness, and subjective experience by means of intraindividual communication. Much of this intraindividual communication is nonverbal. It consists in large measure of the subtle languages of the body and of nonverbal imagery generated by the integrative activity of the neocortex. The affects control or influence others by means of the social signals, most importantly emotion communication. The role of the affects in organizing consciousness has important implications for the form and content of nonverbal communication.

In brief, differential affect theory conceptualizes the organization of consciousness as follows. Sensations from both interocepters and exterocepters provide the basis for consciousness. Consciousness at its most elementary level is awareness of sensation. (Calling this level of consciousness elementary is not intended to detract from its significance or desirability. This level of consciousness is one of the goals of some forms of meditation.) Emotion (affect) is the most fundamental organization of sensation that has meaning (and that has specific experiential/motivational properties). The very basic sensory-cortical process that produces affect from sensation lays the groundwork for all perceptual and cognitive processes in consciousness. Thus the affects are the organizing principles in consciousness. Affect is a component of consciousness which consists of awareness of "pure sensation." Such a basic level of consciousness obtains in adults only in very unusual circumstances, such as in a highly disciplined practice of meditation. Generally, consciousness is characterized by affect and, most importantly in human beings, by emotion. And the emotions in consciousness influence all perception, cognition, and behavior, including the socially communicative behavior associated with sociality and prosocial behavior and with hostility and aggression.

Patterns of Affects in Anger, Disgust, Contempt, and Hostility

In order to understand the arguments and data of this section, it is necessary to distinguish between the concept of emotion situation and emotion experience. Discrete emotion has already been defined, and one of its components is a particular and specific subjective experience. It has also been recognized that the activation of a specific emotion in the laboratory by means of a standard stimulus (or prescribed stimulus situation) is very nearly impossible. What usually obtains in experimental studies as well as in everyday life are situations that elicit a pattern or combination of two or more emotions. Often a single discrete emotion is dominant in experience, but often two or more are present simultaneously or in alternating sequence in such a way as to have some influence upon experience and behavior.

In a series of investigations of "anxiety" and "depression" and the discrete emotions associated with these complex phenomena, subjects were asked to imagine or visualize a particular emotion situation and to continue imaging the scene while completing the Differential Emotions Scale (Izard, Dougherty,

Bloxom & Kotsch, 1974). For example, they were asked to visualize a guilt situation, but this did not mean that we expected them to visualize a situation that elicited only guilt. It was recognized that subjects asked to visualize a guilt situation would probably visualize a situation of sufficient complexity that it would elicit not only guilt but a number of related emotions. Thus a guilt situation may be one that elicits a high degree of guilt and a moderate degree of fear, distress, disgust, and shyness. However, the fact that a realistic guilt situation elicits a pattern of emotions does not alter the fact that each of these emotions in the guilt situation has a specific experiential quality.

In the earlier research, "anxiety" and "depression" were defined as patterns of emotions and feelings (Izard, 1972). A number of empirical studies showed that the profile of emotions was essentially the same in both imagined and real-life emotion situations. The data supported the notion that the concepts of "anxiety" and "depression" were not useful as scientific concepts unless the user was careful to delineate the pattern of emotions and feelings involved in these multidimensional concepts.

In "anxiety" the key emotion was fear but several other emotions, including distress and guilt, were substantially elevated. It should be noted, however, that the profile of emotions obtained when subjects were imaging or visualizing an "anxiety" situation was substantially different from that obtained when subjects visualized a fear situation. Similarly, in "depression" the key emotion was distress, but a number of other emotions, including anger, disgust, contempt, fear, and guilt, were substantially elevated. As in the case of "anxiety" and fear, the profile of emotions obtained when subjects visualized a "depression" situation was clearly distinct from the one obtained when subjects visualized a distress situation. However, the similarity of the profiles of distress and "depression" were greater than was the case for fear and "anxiety."

Studies paralleling those for "anxiety" and "depression" have now been completed for "hostility." The profiles of emotions in visualized "hostility," anger, disgust, and contempt situations are presented in Table I. These results differ in some ways from those obtained in the studies of "anxiety" and "depression" situations. While both "anxiety" and "depression" situations had emotion profiles that were distinct from that of any of the fundamental emotions, this was not the case for "hostility." The profiles of emotions for "hostility" and anger were virtually identical. Further, except for the expected difference for the key emotion (the one named in a given visualization instruction) the profiles for disgust and contempt were very similar in shape to those for "hostility" and anger.

Of the four profiles, that for contempt is the most deviant from the others. If we take the sum of the mean scores for anger, disgust, and contempt as a general index of the intensity of "hostility," then the contempt situation elicited the lowest amount of "hostility." The largest part of the difference is accounted for by the fact that the contempt situation elicited substantially less anger than the

Table I. Profiles of Emotions in Visualized Hostility, Anger, Disgust, and Contempt Situations[a]

Emotion	Situation			
	Hostility $N = 213$	Anger $N = 30$	Disgust $N = 33$	Contempt $N = 37$
Anger	12.46	12.53	10.39	9.86
Contempt	10.28	10.60	9.88	10.49
Disgust	10.05	10.97	10.70	9.19
Distress	8.99	9.33	8.97	7.78
Interest	8.58	8.93	7.79	8.68
Surprise	7.66	7.87	7.09	6.62
Fear	5.62	5.97	5.27	4.89
Guilt	5.42	6.33	5.33	5.00
Shyness	4.64	4.57	4.61	4.08
Joy	3.43	3.80	3.70	5.16

[a]Scores derived from the Differential Emotions Scale; maximum score is 15, minimum score is 3 (Izard et al., in preparation).

"hostility" or anger situations and slightly less than the disgust situation. The contempt profile differs in some other ways. First, the amount of distress elicited in the contempt situation is substantially lower than that for the other three. The amount of fear in the contempt situation is substantially less than that in the "hostility" and anger situations and somewhat less than that of disgust. There is also slightly less guilt and shyness in the contempt situation than in the others. The direction of the difference is reversed in the case of joy, which is highest in the contempt situation. Virtually no joy is reported in the hostility, anger, or disgust situations, but the mean in contempt is well above the absolute minimum of 3.00.

One might conclude from this that the situations that elicit contempt are less likely to result in aggression than those that elicit anger and disgust. If this conclusion is correct, contempt is the most benign of the three emotions in the hostility triad. However, if we look again at the profile of emotions in contempt, there are some factors that militate against this conclusion. The contempt situation elicited the least amount of distress, guilt, and fear, three emotions that might serve to inhibit aggression. Further, the contempt situation is somehow more enjoyable, and presumably the concomitant experience and subsequent behavior are more tolerable.

It is no accident that we speak of the "heat of anger"; the flushed face of the angry individual feels and looks hot. Aggression that occurs in anger is more likely to be a direct result of relatively intense emotion in an individual whose energy has been highly mobilized. On the contrary, contempt can be considered the "cool" emotion in the "hostility" triad. It seems reasonable that it is the contempt situation in which the "cold-blooded" aggressor operates, since contempt is a distancing and devaluing emotion. This description also has validity in the language of common usage, as indicated by such phrases as "murder in cold blood," or "cold-blooded killer."

One possible factor contributing to the similarity of the "hostility" and anger profiles was the instruction to visualize a situation of intense hostility. In a follow-up study the term "intense" was omitted and several drive and affective–cognitive scales replaced six of the emotion scales that were not considered especially important in the hostility profile. The results are presented in Table II. The rank order of emotion means, disregarding the other scales, is very similar to that for hostility and anger in Table I. Apparently the term "intense" had no special effect in the instructions of the previous study. In fact, the second study showed a somewhat higher "hostility" (anger/disgust/contempt) index. As in the first study, females had substantially higher scores on distress than did males. Table II shows that drive states and affective-cognitive orientations are part of the hostility pattern. As expected, vigor, egotism, and skepticism were substantially elevated and tranquility and sex were depressed. (In a few individual profiles sex was elevated. These subjects described hostility situations involving a person of the opposite sex.) The data of Table II show that "hostility" is a complex pattern of emotions, drives, and affective–cognitive orientations.

The foregoing analysis supports the notion that there are a variety of emotion profiles that involve enough "hostility" to increase the likelihood of aggression. Awareness of the similarities and differences among these situations and their emotion profiles may increase our understanding of the motivations underlying or accompanying aggressive acts.

Table II. Profile of Affects in a Visualized Hostility Situation[a]

Scale	Mean
Anger	13.34
Contempt	12.73
Disgust	11.48
Distress	8.57
Vigor	9.48
Skepticism	8.27
Egotism	7.16
Fear	6.05
Sociality	5.14
Guilt	5.09
Sex	3.64
Tranquility	3.66

[a]Scores derived from the Differential Affects Scale; maximum score is 15, minimum score is 3 (Izard et al., in preparation).

The rank ordering of emotion means in the "hostility" situation was identical for males and females. However, females reported slightly higher scores in anger, disgust, and contempt, but they exceeded the males even more in distress and surprise. The greater mean in distress suggests that the hostility situation elicits in the female an emotion which could tend to inhibit aggressive acts. The relatively greater surprise may mean that it is more unusual and hence a bit astonishing for the female to find herself experiencing (or admitting) intense hostility feelings.

Intraindividual Emotion Communication in Hostility

In primates facial expression is central in intraindividual emotion communication just as it is in interindividual communication. Facial expression—patterning of the facial muscles into the expression of a discrete emotion—initiates a neural message to the brain. Everyone can readily agree that muscle contractions result in the firing of sensory nerves that conduct messages to the cortex. However, investigators have not always agreed on the precise function of these sensory messages from the face. Most investigators agree that they are somehow related to emotion, but they differ as to how they are related. Darwin (1904), who laid the foundation for the study of facial expression over a century ago, maintained that facial expression could serve as a regulator of emotion: "The free expression of outward signs of an emotion intensifies it. On the other hand, the repression, as far as possible, of all outward signs, softens our emotion" (p. 22). In the early statement of his feedback principle James (1890) indicated that the sensory messages from striate muscles of the face and body together with feedback from visceral organs were the cause of the subjective experience of emotion. When James's theory merged with Lange's, the emphasis was placed on the feedback from visceral organs, and the famous research of Cannon and Bard demonstrating the presence of emotion expression in viscerally denervated animals dealt a serious blow to the feedback principle.

F. H. Allport (1924) gave new life to the feedback principle by specifying that the important sensory messages for the emotion process came from the propriocepters in voluntary striped muscle, not from the smooth muscles of the viscera. He argued cogently that it was sensory messages from the somatic system that enables the individual to distinguish one emotion from the other.

More recently Tomkins (1962), Gellhorn (1964), and Izard (1971) have made detailed theoretical arguments for the causal role of proprioceptive feedback from the face in the subjective experience of emotion. In the theory presented by Tomkins and Izard, an emotion consists of three interrelated components: neural activity of the brain and nervous system, striate muscle or facial-postural activity, and subjective experience. Each of these components has sufficient autonomy to be dissociated from the others under certain conditions but the three components are characteristically interactive and interdependent in the emotion process.

The neural component of emotion has several aspects. Initially, there is an emotion-specific neural message that is generated by activity that may begin either in the receptors or in the neocortex. From the cortex, the neural message is discharged downward to subcortical centers, particularly the hypothalamus, which initiates the message that causes the emotion expression in facial and postural muscles. The expression constitutes the second component and the principal source of information both to the subject having the emotion and to anyone observing the expression. The proprioceptive and cutaneous impulses provided by the expressive component of emotion is transmitted via the Vth cranial (trigeminal) nerve to the association areas of the cortex, the structure responsible for the integration of all elements of the emotion process, and it is this integrative activity in the cortex that generates the subjective experience (third component) of emotion.

The foregoing model of emotion leads to a number of questions. First, can emotion-specific facial expression occur without the corresponding subjective experience of the emotion? Conversely, can the subjective experience of emotion occur without facial expression? Or, stated more in terms of the theme of this book, can there be emotion without emotion communication? I have discussed these not altogether simple questions in detail elsewhere (Izard, Kidd, Kotsch, and Izard, 1974), and all of that discussion is not quite relevant to our present purposes. I shall say in summary that while there are theoretically explicable exceptions to the foregoing emotion model, the model is considered to be descriptive of emotion as it usually occurs.

The foregoing model of emotions suggests another important question: Can voluntary or simulated facial expression be used to initiate or inhibit emotion experience? This question has been pursued in a series of empirical studies. I shall summarize these and give most attention to the ones that relate to the emotion of anger, since it is a key emotion in "hostility."

In the first study addressing itself to this question, Laird (1974) "asked subjects to contract and relax various facial muscles until, without their awareness, they were in a smile or frown position." After the subjects' facial muscles were manipulated into an expression, a photograph of KKK rallies or of children playing was projected for 15 seconds on a screen in front of the subjects. Subjects then reported their emotion on the Mood Adjective Checklist (MACL)(Nowlis, 1965).

Laird indicated that his subjects reported feeling "angrier" when "frowning" and "happier" when "smiling." This summary statement was misleading or at least incomplete. He had no basis for inferring that both manipulations were effective, since his design did not permit the evaluation of the separate effects of the two expression manipulations. The data from our own laboratory showed that the anger expression is effective in this context but not the joy expression, as simulated in these manipulations.

Although Laird acknowledged that his data were explicable in terms of our sensory-feedback or interactive components model (outlined earlier), he preferred to explain his findings in terms of attribution theory. More specifically, his reasoning was guided by Bem's (1972) self-perception theory, a version of attribution theory that emphasizes the role of self-observation. The anger experience in the "frown" condition was explained as follows: "It is as if the subjects said to themselves, 'I am frowning . . . and I don't have any nonemotional reasons for frowning, so I must be angry.'" Although he admitted that this was a metaphorical, not a literal, description of events, he emphasized the interpretive role of the subject ("perceiver") in the activation of the experience of anger. In effect he maintained that the subject had to *interpret* (cognize about?) the proprioceptive and cutaneous impulses from the face in order to give himself the signal to experience anger. I have discussed several problems with this reasoning elsewhere (Izard *et al.*, in preparation). Perhaps the chief weakness of his explanation is that it implies that the relationship between anger experience and anger expression is learned, yet extensive cross-cultural data strongly support the thesis that it is innate—a product of evolutionary-genetic processes (Ekman, Friesen, & Ellsworth, 1972; Izard, 1971).

In order to see if Laird's findings would hold for females and with certain desired procedural changes, the present investigators conducted a pilot study with 48 female undergraduates, 24 manipulated subjects, and 24 yoked controls. The methods were like those described by Laird (1974), except for some modifications of the instructions regarding the expressions, the omission of the second independent variable (pictures of KKK rallies or of children playing), and the substitution of the Differential Emotions Scale (DES) (Izard, 1972) for the Mood Adjective Checklist (MACL) (Nowlis, 1965). We also added a non-manipulated (no expression) condition. Despite the different sex of subjects, changes in instructions, omission of the pictures, and a different response measure, our results were similar to Laird's. As anticipated, the anger expression was effective in inducing emotion (or at least self-report of emotion) while the joy expression was not.

In the second study, 24 male and 24 female undergraduate volunteer subjects were scheduled in pairs, one member of the pair being randomly designated as the experimental subject and the other as a yoked control ("observer"). The subjects could see the experimenter but not each other. The experimental subject was asked to follow all instructions regarding muscle contraction and the yoked control was asked to ignore them. Five factors (joy, anger, distress, shyness, vigor) of the DES were used to assess the subjective experience of the subjects. They completed the DES following the general instructions in order to familiarize them with the test and then used it after each facial expression condition during the experiment. The facial muscles of each experimental subject were manipulated so as to display a joy, anger, and neutral condition. The order of the facial patterns was balanced. Each facial pattern was executed for two 10-second intervals with a brief rest in between. Then the pattern was fixed for a third time and the subject was instructed to hold the pattern while completing the abbreviated DES. Scores for each DES factor were subjected to a 2 (sex of subject) × 3 (expression conditions) analysis of variance.

The means and standard deviations for the experimental and control subjects for each of the five DES factors are shown in Table III. The results were generally as predicted. For the control subjects, neither sex of subject nor expression condition was significant for any of the DES factors. However, the analyses for the experimental subjects revealed the effectiveness of the induced anger expression. The subjects who were manipulated into an anger expression not only reported a significantly higher anger experience than was present in the other two emotion conditions or in their matched controls, they also reported significantly lower joy experience than was present in either of the other two conditions or in the matched controls.

The scores on the shyness scale revealed an interesting sex difference in this experiment. The facial muscle manipulations elicited a significant increase in shyness in the male subjects but not in the females.

As was the case in Laird's study, our postexperimental inquiry showed that only a few subjects "caught on" and indicated that they knew that the experi-

Table III. Emotion-Experience (DES) Means and Standard Deviations (in Parentheses) for the Emotion-Expression Conditions[a]

	Expression					
	Anger		Smile		Neutral	
	Experimental	Control	Experimental	Control	Experimental	Control
Anger	8.08	5.17	5.42	5.29	4.33	5.04
	(3.29)	(3.00)	(2.78)	(2.87)	(2.02)	(2.89)
Enjoyment	5.42	8.13	7.71	7.71	7.63	7.96
	(2.80)	(3.30)	(2.64)	(3.16)	(3.09)	(3.03)
Vigor	5.54	8.71	7.58	8.63	7.50	8.50
	(2.18)	(3.17)	(2.18)	(2.94)	(2.45)	(3.40)
Shame/shyness	5.21	4.08	5.29	3.88	4.46	3.83
	(2.29)	(1.38)	(2.69)	(1.27)	(2.61)	(.98)
Distress	5.96	5.50	5.00	5.42	4.88	5.25
	(2.73)	(2.96)	(2.53)	(2.72)	(2.44)	(2.79)

[a]From Izard *et al.*, in preparation.

menter was manipulating their faces into an angry or joyful expression. These subjects were replaced. We had some doubt about the effectiveness of our postexperimental inquiry, but as Laird found, the informal reports of our subjects after the experiment suggested that the anger experience following the anger expression manipulation was genuine.

The foregoing experiments left two questions unanswered. First, since the anger expression creates more tension in facial muscles than the smile expression, is our effect due simply to intense muscle tension? Second, can the expression effect be produced by imagery, by having subjects listen to the facial manipulation instructions and visualize the various movements without actually performing them? Kotsch and Izard (in preparation) designed a study to answer these questions.

We again used the yoked control, but this time we instructed the control subjects to listen to each instruction carefully and to visualize each of the movements made by the experimental subject without actually making them. Each subject participated in four facial expression conditions: (a) a partial anger expression (frown only); (b) mild anger using muscles in both the eye and mouth region but with only a mild degree of tension; (c) an intense anger expression made by putting a high degree of tension in all of the muscles involved in the anger expression; and (d) an intense nonemotional expression. The latter expression consisted of having the subject pull the upper and lower lip tightly against the teeth and squint very hard.

We assumed that contractions of the facial muscles involved in the anger expression would elicit the experience of anger and result in the self-report of anger on the DES. We also assumed that imaging the movements of the muscles involved in anger expression would activate a mild experience of anger and result in some change in DES anger scores. We predicted that the intense nonemotion contraction would not activate anger or change DES anger scores.

The results confirmed our first two predictions but failed to confirm the third. Both imaging the muscle movements involved in the intense anger expression and the active contraction of these muscles resulted in significant increases in the anger experience, as measured by the DES (see Figure 1). According to differential emotion theory, imaging the muscle movements involved in the anger expression could elicit the anger experience in either or both of two fashions. First, imaging the movements could actually result in minor or micromomentary expression, feedback from which could activate the anger experience. Second, imaging the movements could result in a proprioceptive image or a memory of what it feels like to have the anger expression, and this proprioceptive image of the anger expression could activate the anger experience. As expected, the anger experience reported from imaging the muscle movements of the intense anger expression was milder than that activated by mild anger expression, which in turn was significantly less than that elicited by the intense anger expression.

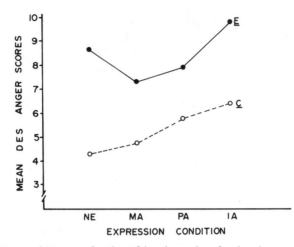

Fig. 1. Anger experience as a function of imaging and performing the movements of facial expressions. (From Kotsch & Izard, in preparation.)

A fourth experiment replicated the second, substituting distress for anger and adding cheek muscle movements to the joy expression, while videotaping the subjects' expressive movements. The results were complicated by the fact that the distress expression and the more complete joy expression proved very difficult for the subjects. Trained judges frequently rated the attempted distress expressions as anger and the joy expression as contempt. There were significant expression effects for both manipulations, but as might be expected from the judges' ratings of the expressions, they were not emotion-specific. The attempted distress expression elicited DES self-reports of increased distress and anger experience, and the attempted joy expression elicited more anger than the neutral condition.

The correlation of the ratings of videotaped expressions and the DES scores has not been completed, but the data suggest that much more training in facial-muscle control will be necessary before subjects can be manipulated into an adequate emotion expression and used to test for the effect of manipulated facial expression on emotion experience. As it now stands, it is not clear as to how much the increased anger experience reported in all the foregoing studies was due to a genuine anger expression and how much simply to facial muscle tension or the nuisance value of the manipulation. This potentially important line of research will have to contend with other complex problems. For example, is it possible to give people adequate training in facial muscle control without their catching on to the manipulation? Second, if, as Wilson (1929) proposed, voluntary and involuntary expressions involve different neural pathways, will the feedback from manipulated and naturally occurring expressions provide the same sensory data or be integrated in the same way in the cortex?

Emotion Expression, Interindividual Emotion Communication, and Aggression

How does the expression of anger or hostility affect the perceiver? What is the relationship between anger expression and aggressive acts? More generally, how does emotion communication influence both prosocial and agonistic behavior? These questions suggest several lines of investigation. We have pursued two of them: (a) voluntary manipulation of facial expression in aggressive encounters in human subjects, and (b) the reduction of emotion communication via sectioning of the seventh cranial (facial) nerve in socially living rhesus macaque monkeys. In the first study with the human subjects, Savitsky, Izard, Kotsch, and Christy (1974) designed a study to investigate how the aggressor's response was influenced by the victim's facial expression. Before describing this study, I shall review some of the previous studies concerned with influencing or regulating the aggressive behavior of subjects.

In many of the laboratory studies of aggression with human subjects, the subject has been isolated from the recipient, a person who may or may not be present in another room. This procedure limits considerably the generalizability of the results, but regardless of their value they do not represent the model we are interested in here. I am focusing on aggression in face-to-face encounters. A study of Zimbardo (1969) showed that the physical presence of the victim influenced the behavior of the aggressor. It has been disappointing that so few investigators have followed the implication of Zimbardo's finding and hence there are relatively few studies that have examined the effects of the victim's communication on the aggressor. Some of the studies that have developed this area have focused on the effects of eye contact or interocular responses and these are presented by Ellsworth and Exline in the present volume.

Aside from the work on eye contact the bulk of the work on the effect of the victim's communication on subsequent aggression has come from ethology. Ethological studies have shown that expressive behavior often eliminates or reduces overt aggression in coral reef fish (Rasa 1969), elephant seals (Le Boeuf & Peterson, 1969), and baboons (Kummer, 1968).

Both expressions of threat and expressions of submission or appeasement have been judged as effective in influencing agonistic behavior among nonhuman primates. In rhesus macaque monkeys submissive expressions range from the fear grimace to presenting the rump as in sexual invitations. These expressive communications have been judged as effective in inhibiting aggressive behavior (Hinde & Rowell, 1962). The effect of a threat expression may vary considerably with the status of the animal and the situation. A high status animal in his own territory will frequently succeed in avoiding fights by means of threat displays. But a territorial intruder or low status animal may provoke fighting with a threat expression. Morris (1967) suggested that people can avoid the attack of a potential aggressor by displaying fear and humility and by avoiding threatening expressions.

Morris's inference was based primarily on observations of nonhuman animals. Most theories of human aggression have not addressed the question of the effect of the victim's threat expression on the occurrence of subsequent aggression. Predicting the effect of the victim's expression is not at all easy. Undoubtedly there are some variables in human subjects that correspond in some way to status and territory among nonhuman primates, but it is much easier to determine a dominance hierarchy among a group of socially living rhesus macaque monkeys than it is to assess the status of a human subject who walks into the laboratory. The equations for predicting the effect of expression on subsequent aggression are always multivariate and both organismic and environmental variables are involved. A couple of examples will illustrate the complexity of the problem of prediction. If an aggressor is not particularly angry or ego-involved in the encounter, the anger expression of the potential victim may signal a counterattack that the aggressor would choose to avoid. In this case the threat expression would decrease or avoid further aggression. On the other hand if the potential aggressor sees himself as a winner, the anger expression of the potential victim may provoke greater aggressive behavior. In summary, hostile communication (via affect expression) tends to change the threshold of aggression, but the direction of the change may vary with social status, territorial prerogatives, and other ecological factors.

The ethically controversial studies of Milgram (1963, 1964, 1965) showed that the aggressive responses made by subjects in response to the request of an "authority" was significantly influenced by the victim's presence and proximity. Immediacy was varied from a condition in which there was no visual or vocal contact (remote condition) to a condition in which the subject forced the victim's hand onto the shock plate (touch-proximity condition). Immediacy proved to be a potent deterrent of aggression. The percentage of subjects who obeyed the experimenter and continued to give shocks to the maximum (labeled "danger severe shock") in spite of screams of pain and urgent protests from the victim varied from 66% in the remote condition to 30% to the touch-proximity condition. Thus while immediacy made a large difference in the subject's willingness to aggress on comand, 30% of subjects recruited from the community represent a rather sizeable segment who were apparently willing to risk executing a subject because an authority (experimenter) told them to do so. The reduction in aggressive responses as a result of the immediacy of the victim is consonant with Zimbardo's (1969) concept of individuation as a deterrent of aggression and with the contention of ethologists (e.g., Ardrey, 1966; Lorenz, 1966) that wars are more likely because our vast weapon technology makes it possible to kill at great distances.

Other studies have attempted to assess the effect of the victim's nonverbal communication but the results of these studies are not consistent. Wheeler and Caggiula (1966), Feshbach, Stiles, and Bitner (1967), and Hartman (1969) found that a victim's indication of pain was followed by an increase in shock aggression. In the latter two studies the subject had previously been insulted. On the other hand, Buss (1966a,b) and Barron (1971a,b) have found that pain cues from the victim reduced the subject's aggressive responses. One of the reasons for the inconsistency in the results of these studies may have been the failure to specify the emotional state of the subject, the relative status of experimenters and subjects, and the precise nature of the nonverbal cues emitted by the victim. In many cases, the nonverbal cues were simply described as grunts and groans, without any indication as to the specificity of such communications. Barron's study, which showed a sharp reduction in aggressive responses as a result of pain cues, represents an exception. Subjects observed a "pain meter" to see the effect their shock was having on the victim. While Barron's feedback was specific it had the disadvantage of removing the victim from the possibility of face-to-face encounter with the aggressor.

The Savitsky et al. study communicated well-defined expressions of specific emotions to an aggressor via a confederate victim's face. Half the subjects (aggressors) were insulted by a confederate victim and the other half were treated neutrally and not insulted. Then subjects were assigned to a victim who expressed facially either fear, anger, joy, or a neutral countenance following the delivery of shock by the subjects. We hypothesized that the victim's expression of discrete emotions would significantly influence the subject's aggression. We had a number of specific expectations based on the assumption that our insult manipulation would arouse anger in the subjects, but as it did not, our results are interesting only insofar as the facial expression manipulation is concerned. The DES was used to assess the emotional state of the subjects during the experiment, and the subjects also completed a DES to describe the emotions of the victim. In addition the subjects completed a first impression rating scale as an additional description of the victim.

The subject's task was to teach the victim a paired-word list and to administer shock for incorrect responses for the purpose of facilitating learning. He was told that the best level of shock varied from person to person and that he was free to use his judgment in the matter. Each subject was exposed to a victim with a cheerful expression, an angry expression, a joyful expression, or an emotionally nonspecific or neutral expression. The subject's DES ratings of the victims showed that facial expressions were clearly perceived and differentiated.

Two of the emotion-specific facial expressions did significantly influence the aggression of the subjects. Subjects who were exposed to a smiling victim gave a consistently higher level of shocks. Apparently subjects in this group perceived their victim as not being harmed and as enjoying the task. It is reasonable to assume that the victim's apparent enjoyment elicited some enjoyment in the subjects (Tomkins, 1962). For these subjects, the learning task and the administration of shock may have taken on the character of a game. Since the victim appeared to enjoy the penalities (shock), the subject enjoyed delivering them, and consequently there was an increase in shock for this condition. It is possible that some subjects were also motivated to increase shock in order to get the subject to be more serious about the task. Interestingly, the smile in our study had an effect similar to the aversive glance in Ellsworth's study (Chapter 3, this volume).

Subjects exposed to the anger expression decreased their aggressive responses. The decrease in shock aggression on the part of the subjects may have been motivated by anticipation of subsequent retaliation or an embarrassing confrontation with the victim. The victim's anger expression may also have threatened the subject and acted directly as an inhibitor of aggression.

Since our analysis of the subjects self-reported emotion scores suggested that they were not anger-aroused we made the assumption that our results are descriptive of the category of aggression that has been termed instrumental aggression. The subjects were using the shock as a means of facilitating learning and apparently did not perceive themselves as hurting or harming the victims.

Studies of Rhesus Monkeys with Sectioned Facial Nerves

The series of studies on the effects of bilateral sectioning of the facial nerve in rhesus monkeys was based on two related assumptions. First, it was assumed that in monkeys as in human beings, facial expression is a component of the emotion process and that reduction or elimination of this component would alter the emotional responsiveness of the animal. Second, it was assumed that reduction in this important realm of social communication would result in some deterioration of the social life of the group. More specifically it was predicted that there would be a decrease in prosocial behavior and an increase in agonistic behavior.

The subjects for the first study were four male and eight female feral-reared rhesus monkeys (*Macaca mulatta*) about 3½ to 4 years of age. The experimental (*E*) colony, two males and four females, were acquired first. The two males and four females that constituted the control (*C*) colony were acquired after the observations of the *E* colony were completed. The living area for the group was a 2.41 m × 2.41 m × 3.66 m cage that contained two perches and a tire swing.

It is well known that primate investigators are plagued by individual differences among rhesus monkeys and the necessity of using relatively small numbers of these expensive subjects, but we had one problem that may have been unusual. One of the females in the control colony was continually sexually receptive, a monkey nymphomaniac, if you please, and her attachment to the dominant male and her apparent jealousy created considerable uproar in the colony. Despite these and other differences which I have discussed in detail elsewhere (Izard, Walker, Cobb, & Meier, in preparation), we thought we could make some comparisons between the two groups.

Perhaps the greatest emphasis should be placed on the results of the longitudinal study within the experimental group itself. Analyses of variance showed that the reduction in emotion communication by sectioning of the facial nerve did produce a decrease in prosocial behavior and an increase in agonistic behavior. This effect was sustained over a 3-year period and until the colony was disbanded. The data are presented graphically in Figure 2.

For the comparisons of the E and C groups each of the behavior categories was subjected to an analysis of variance. The analysis for play behavior showed that while the E group decreased significantly over time, play in the control group increased significantly. Grooming showed no significant change over time in the control group, but the decrease in this important prosocial activity in the experimental group was highly significant.

Threat behavior increased significantly in the experimental colony and in contrast it decreased significantly in the control colony. However, both groups showed significant increases in displacement and attack. E. W. Menzel, Jr.

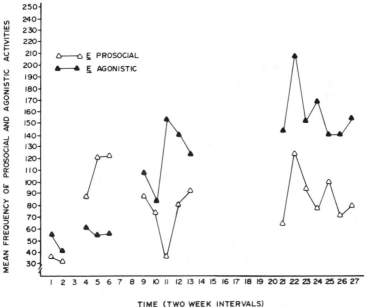

Fig. 2. Prosocial and agonistic activities in young adult rhesus macaques with sectioned facial nerves.

(personal communication) and Miller (Chapter 6, this volume) have reported that aggression is typically far more frequent in the confines of a communal cage than in the wild. Nevertheless, we can speculate that there would have been less agonistic behavior in our C group without the nymphomaniac. Despite the increase in agonistic behavior in the control group, the increase in prosocial behavior was equally great or greater (see Figure 3).

In summary, there was a marked difference between the E and C groups in the ratio of prosocial and agonistic behavior. Judging from the two groups we worked with, this was due primarily to the suppression of the prosocial activities of play and grooming in the E colony.

Studies of Mother–Infant and Peer Interactions in a Playpen Apparatus

After all of the adults in the E colony had been operated, two of the females gave birth to male infants within about 6 weeks of each other. These infants lived in the colony for about the first 10 or 11 months of their lives and until the colony was disbanded. Then each of these infants was placed with his mother in an individual cage for about 6 weeks. At this time these two mother–infant dyads became the subjects for an experiment focusing on mother–infant and peer interactions.

The apparatus in which the study was conducted is similar to the playpen setting described by Hanson (1962, 1966). Individual home cages were attached to the corners of a large common play area 1.5 m × 1.5 m × .8 m. Infants could escape through a small door into the common play area but mothers were confined to the individual cage. Mothers could be in visual and vocal contact with their infants at all times but could not reach their infants physically once they were an arm's length into the playpen.

A mother–infant behavior scale was designed to record the individual activities and the social behavior involved in the mother–infant and peer interactions. The scale covered 50 different types of response or activities, grouped into ten major categories. The scale was designed for an observation period of 40 twenty-second intervals; each response or action of the mother and infants that occurred during each 20-second epoch were recorded.

There were 3 weeks of preoperative observations followed by 9 weeks of postoperative observation. Then the second infant was operated and an additional 3 weeks of postoperative observations were obtained.

Each of the major categories of behavior were subjected to an analysis of variance, in which blocks of time before and after the operation of each yearling were treated as "between factors." The analyses were designed to give us the short-term effects of the first operation, the long-term effects of the first operation, and the short-term effects of the second operation. First, let's summarize the immediate effects of the first operation. Facial communication, which actu-

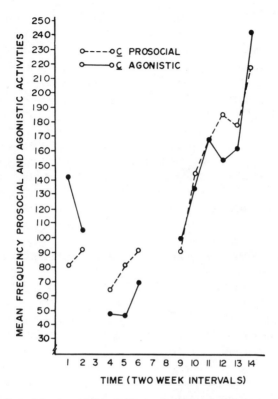

Fig. 3.   Prosocial and agonistic activities in normal young adult rhesus macaques.

ally consisted primarily of threat expressions on the part of the mothers increased in the operative family while that of the other family decreased. Vocal behavior decreased significantly in the group as a whole. The family with the operated yearling showed a significantly greater decrease in grooming than did the other family. Physical aggression mean scores (hitting, pushing, fighting, biting) tended to increase after the operation, with the mothers increasing significantly more than the yearlings. There was a significant decrease in ventral–ventral contact for both families following the first operation. The pre- and post-operative means were 53.17 and 21.50, respectively. The decrease was greater for the operated family than for the nonoperated family.

The long-term effects of the first operation showed that facial behavior, of which 70% was threat expressions, tended to increase more for the mothers than for the yearlings. The mothers decreased their vocal behavior significantly more than the yearlings. In the category of grooming the dyad with the operated yearling groomed significantly more than the other dyad, although both families showed some increase. Another long-term effect of the operation was a decrease in the amount of ventral–ventral contact, with the family with the operated yearling showing the greater decrease. There was a general decrease in body contact and a significant increase in the frequency with which the yearlings moved away from the mothers and out into the playpen. (Part of the change in the distance measures may have been due to the fact that the mother of the operated yearling gave birth to an infant a few days before the end of the long-term postoperative period.)

The additional effects of the second operation included a decrease in vocal behavior for the entire group, with family one decreasing more than family two. The yearlings, however, showed significantly more vocal behavior during this period than did the mothers. The most significant change following the second operation was a dramatic decrease in social play (rough and tumble play). The mean score for play decreased from 36.64 prior to the second operation to 19.58.

At the conclusion of this experiment the two operated infants were separated from their mothers and placed in the communal cage described earlier, with four normal males and two normal females of approximately the same age. Systematic observations were made on these eight juveniles for 16 weeks. The central aim of this study (Walker & Wilcoxon, in preparation) was to determine the effects of high and low population densities on the various categories of behavior. Density was increased by halving the number of animals in the group every other 4-week period in the 16-week study. When separated the two subgroups of four animals each occupied equal-sized cages separated by a concrete wall. The density was increased simply by rejoining the two smaller groups in one of the cages. The data showed that the operated animals differed substantially from all other juveniles in both prosocial and agonistic behavior categories. The operates showed a greater average increase in social grooming in the two high-density periods than any of the other pairs except the females in the second high-density period. In all except the first of the four periods, the operated animals showed substantially less social play than did any of the normal males, and in the last two 4-week periods they showed less social play than both males and females. Most of the animals tended to show some decrease in activity play in the high density condition, but the decrease of the operated pair was much sharper than that for any other pair.

The data in the agonistic behavior categories showed rather clearly that the operated animals had the lowest status in the dominance hierarchy. Their status was even lower than the two females, one of whom was younger than both of the operates. Unlike the other six juveniles, neither of the operates displayed a single threat expression during the entire 16 weeks of observations. However, they were the target of threat expressions more often than any of the normal males and about the same number of times as the females. The operated males never displaced any of the other juveniles during the course of the study. The operated showed the least amount of physical aggression, less even than the two females.

On the contrary, the operated were attacked about as often as were the females and much more often than any of the normal males.

The low level of social play among the operated juveniles was consistent with all the other studies, but their level of social grooming and attack appears to be a bit contradictory, at least to the data from the operated adult group. Actually, grooming was an infrequent behavior in the juvenile study and a change in frequency of one or two per week would result in a 50% or 100% change. Thus the finding on grooming could be a chance phenomenon. The difference in physical attack between the juveniles and the adult experimental group may be a function of the age difference and the confounding of status and operation in the juveniles. Most of the agonistic behavior in the playpen study was due to the mothers, not the yearlings. Generally, aggression is infrequent among infant and juvenile monkeys and apes (E. W. Menzel, personal communication). However, the fact that the low status animals in both the juvenile and adult experimental colony exhibited relatively infrequent agonistic behavior and the overall level of aggression in these groups strongly suggested that the operation did not directly increase aggressive behavior in the operated animals.

Another playpen study is now under way; two feral-reared mothers and their second-born laboratory infants are the subjects. In this study the infants were operated when they were 2 weeks of age. After the infants had reached 21 and 24 weeks of age, respectively, they had not yet engaged in social play. One of the infants did not leave the home cage until she was 9 weeks of age. At 21 weeks of age the male infant was still spending a great deal of time in the mother–infant ventral–ventral position, and his social and exploratory behavior was not unlike that of a monkey approximately 4 to 6 weeks of age. The usual rather sharp decrease in mother–infant body contact at around 6 to 8 weeks of age did not occur in these operated infants.

In general, the study of the mother–infant dyads and the juveniles corroborated the findings from the study of the socially living young-adult groups and supported our basic hypothesis. In all of the studies there tended to be some deterioration in the social life of the operated animals. The most substantial change appears to be the decrease in prosocial behavior which, of course, results in a change in the ratio of prosocial and agonistic behavior.

Summary

Bigelow (1972) suggested that the principal function of the brain was self-control and that the principal function of the nervous system as a whole was communication. He also maintained that all intelligent behavior, including self-control, communication, and cooperation is inextricably bound up with emotional states.

In this chapter, I have proposed that the affects are the organizing principles in consciousness. Except for sensation, they are the most fundamental events in awareness. They are prior to perception and cognition, which they influence continually. In human beings the emotions are the primary motivational system. The empirical studies reported in this chapter have supported the proposition that both intraindividual and interindividual emotion communication (e.g., facial expression) influence the experiential phenomena of anger, disgust, contempt, and "hostility," as well as physical acts of aggression. Surgical reduction of expressive behavior (bilateral sectioning of facial nerve) in rhesus monkeys leads to a deterioration in social life, particularly to a suppression of prosocial behavior and to a change in the ratio of prosocial and agonistic activity. It is suggested that self-control, including the control of aggression, is achieved by intraindividual and interindividual emotion communication.

References

Allport, F. H. *Social psychology*. Cambridge: Houghton Mifflin, 1924.

Ardrey, R. *The territorial imperative*. New York: Dell, 1966.

Barron, R. A. Magnitude of victim's pain cues and level of prior anger arousal as determinants of adult aggressive behavior. *Journal of Personality and Social Psychology*, 1971, *17*, 236–243. (a)

Barron, R. A. Exposure to an aggressive model and apparent probability of retaliation from the victim as determinants of aggressive behavior. *Journal of Experimental and Social Psychology*, 1971, 7. (b)

Bem, D. J. Self-perception theory. In L. Berkowitz (Ed.), *Advances in Experimental Psychology* (Vol. 6). New York: Academic Press, 1972.

Bigelow, R. The evolution of cooperation, aggression, and self-control. In J. K. Cole (Ed.), *Nebraska Symposium on Motivation*. Lincoln: University of Nebraska Press, 1972.

Buss, A. H. The effect of harm on subsequent aggression. *Journal of Experimental Research in Personality*, 1966, *1*, 249–255. (a)

Buss, A. H. Instrumentality of aggression, feedback and frustration as determinants of physical aggression. *Journal of Personality and Social Psychology*, 1966, *3*, 153–162. (b)

Darwin, C. *The expression of the emotions in man and animals*. London: John Murray, 1904.

Dumas, G. *La vie affective*. Paris: Presses Universitaires de France, 1948.

Ekman, P., Friesen, W. V., & Ellsworth, P. *Emotions in the human face*. New York: Pergamon, 1972.

Feshbach, S., Stiles, W. G., & Bitner, E. The reinforcing effect of witnessing aggression. *Journal of Experimental Research in Personality*, 1967, *2*, 133–139.

Gellhorn, E. Motion and emotion: The role of proprioception in the physiology and pathology of the emotions. *Psychological Review*, 1964, *71*, 6, 456–472.

Hansen, E. W. The development of maternal and infant behavior in the rhesus monkey. Unpublished doctoral dissertation, University of Wisconsin, 1962.

Hansen, E. W. The development of maternal and infant behavior in the rhesus monkey. *Behaviour*, 1966, *27*, 107–149.

Hartman, D. P. Influence of symbolically modeled instrumental aggression and pain cues on aggressive behavior. *Journal of Personality and Social Psychology*, 1969, *11*, 280–288.

Hinde, R. A., & Rowell, T. E. Communication by postures and facial expression in the rhesus monkey (*Macaca mulatta*). *Proceedings of the Zoological Society* (London), 1962, *138*, 1–21.

Izard, C. E. *The face of emotion*. New York: Appleton-Century-Crofts, 1971.

Izard, C. E. *Patterns of emotions: A new analysis of anxiety and depression*. New York: Academic Press, 1972.

Izard, C. E., Dougherty, F. E., Bloxom, B. M., & Kotsch, W. E. *The differential emotion scale: a method of measuring the subjective experience of discrete emotions*. Unpublished ms., Department of Psychology, Vanderbilt University, 1974.

Izard, C. E., Kotsch, W. E., Kidd, R. F., & Izard, C. E., Jr. The facial expression of anger as an activator of the subjective experience of anger, in preparation.

Izard, C. E., & Tomkins, S. S. Affect and behavior: Anxiety as a negative affect. In C. D. Spielberger (Ed.), *Anxiety and behavior*. New York: Academic Press, 1966, pp. 81–125.

Izard, C. E., Walker, K., Cobb, C. A. Jr., & Meier, G. W. Prosocial and agonistic behavior in rhesus monkeys with surgically sectioned facial nerves. In preparation.

James W. *The principles of psychology*. New York: Holt, 1890.

Kotsch, W. E., & Izard, C. E. A further analysis of the effect of anger expression on anger experience. In preparation.

Kummer, H. *Social organization of hamadrya baboon*. Chicago: University of Chicago Press, 1968.

Laird, J. E. Self-attribution of emotion: The effects of expressive behavior on the quality of emotional experience. *Journal of Personality and Social Psychology*, 1974, *29*, 475–486.

LeBoeuf, B. J., & Peterson, R. S. Social status and mating activity in elephant seals. *Science*, 1969, *163*, 91–93.

Lorenz, K. *On aggression*. New York: Harcourt, Brace, & World, 1966.

Milgram, S. Behavioral study of obedience. *Journal of Abnormal and Social Psychology*, 1963, *67*, 371–378.

Milgram, S. Group pressure and action against a person. *Journal of Abnormal and Social Psychology*, 1964, *69*, 137–143.

Milgram, S. Some conditions of obedience and disobedience to authority. *Human Relations*, 1965, *18* (1), 53–75.

Morris, D. *The naked ape*. New York: Dell, 1967.

Nowlis, V. Research with the Mood Adjective Checklist. In S. S. Tomkins,& C. E. Izard (Eds.), *Affect, cognition, and personality*. New York: Springer, 1965, pp. 352–389.

Rasa, O. A. E. Territoriality and the establishment of dominance by means of visual cues in *pomacentrus jenkinsi* (*Pices: Pomacentridae*). *Zeitschrift fur Tierpsychologie*, 1969, *26*, 825–845. (Cited by R. N. Johnson, *Aggression in man and animals*. Philadelphia: W. B. Saunders, 1972.)

Savitsky, J. C., Izard, C. E., Kotsch, W. E., & Christy, L. Aggressor's response to the victim's facial expression of emotion. *Journal of Experimental Personality*, 1974, *7*, 346–357.

Schachter, S. *Emotion obesity and crime*. New York: Academic Press, 1971.

Tomkins, S. *Affect imagery consciousness* (Vol. 1). New York: Springer, 1962.

Walker, K. E., & Wilcoxon, H. C. The effect of a change in social density on the behavior of juvenile rhesus monkeys (*Macaca mulatta*). In preparation.

Wheeler, L., & Caggiula, A. R. The contagion of aggression. *Journal of Experimental and Social Psychology*, 1966, *2*, 1–10.

Zimbardo, P. G. *The human choice: Individuation, reason, and order versus deindividuation, impulse, and chaos*. Unpublished manuscript, Stanford University, 1969.

CHAPTER 5

Communication and Aggression in a Group of Young Chimpanzees[1]

E. W. Menzel, Jr.[2]

State University of New York
Stony Brook, New York

After considering the matter for 24 years, the United Nations today finally came up with a definition of the word "aggression."

A ripple of properly subdued excitement ran through the meeting chamber when the Committee on the Definition of Aggression agreed on a hazy three-page definition of the concept, which has been a diplomatic hot potato since the Versailles peace conference of 1919.

The New York Times
- April 13, 1974

Descriptions of a social event may proceed in either of two basically different ways: We may attend to the physical parameters of the event, or we may attend to the meaning or functional significance of the event for an observer. The term "aggression" is a clear example of the latter type of description. It is a judgment which has an imperfect and only partially known correspondence to the spatio-temporal "facts" of physical science. Furthermore, the functional significance of the same event might be judged very differently by different observers. Even a panel of physicists does not always agree on how to describe an event. But it would be even more foolhardy to hope for perfect agreement between the judgments of (a) the initiator of an attack, invasion, intrusion, provocation, or fight; (b) the recipient of that act; (c) a judge from the same social community;

[1]Data collection was supported by NIH grant FR-00164 to the Delta Regional Primate Research Center and writing was supported by NSF grants BO-38791 and GU-3850 to the State University of New York at Stony Brook.

[2]I thank Palmer Midgett, Jr., for his assistance with the research.

(d) a panel of judges from other societies of the same species; and (e) the behavioral scientist who tries to describe aggressive events as if he were a total outsider watching creatures from a different planet. In many cases, even a judge cannot easily decide who was the initiator or what were the hostilities.

The point of view from which I shall approach the problem of aggression should therefore be admitted from the start to be that of a biologically oriented "outsider." From this perspective, the common denominator of aggressive behaviors is that they are all means by which animals coordinate and regulate their societies and compete for the requisites of survival, reproduction, and whatever else makes life tolerable (Brown & Orians, 1970; Lorenz, 1966; Tinbergen, 1968). Since the same thing may be said about almost any behavior, however, it is necessary to be somewhat more specific. In Carpenter's (1964) words, the equilibrium in the relationships between individuals is the net resultant of two different types of forces—centripetal forces, or those which bring individuals closer together either figuratively or literally; and centrifugal forces, or those which cause individuals to avoid, attack, or disperse from each other (see also Marler, 1968; Mowrer, 1960; McBride, 1964). In talking about aggression we are obviously concerned most with the centrifugal aspect of coordination. At least initially, I see no point in trying to be much more precise than this, or in trying to completely separate aggressive from nonaggressive components of coordination.

According to some biologists, there seems to be no clear boundary line between aggressive behavior in general and "communication of aggression" in particular (Altmann, 1967; Bastian & Bermant, 1973). However, there are certainly quantitative continua along which we may distinguish these phenomena. Communication implies a greater degree of socially conventionalized competition (Wynne-Edwards, 1962)—a greater sharing of common rules for goal-directed activities. The less these rules are predictable from Newtonian physics, and from other species of animals, and from other social groups of the same species, the more interesting or convincing they become to a student of "communication" per se. Thus both overt aggression and communication of aggression involve a correlation between the actions of individuals, an "exchange of information" (in the most general sense of that term), and a "centrifugal" end effect. But they may differ enormously in the amount of energy expenditure required to produce the same effect, in the degree to which there can be apparent "action at a distance," and in the complexity of their respective mechanical "wiring diagrams." A mother primate who gets her infant to shut up by scolding it vocally and a big male who gets his rival to go to the bottom of a cliff by glaring and pointing are obviously of more interest than individuals who achieve the same end effects by clamping a hand over the infant's mouth or pushing the rival off a ledge. In this respect, the distinction between overt aggression and communication of aggression is at least as straightforward and objective as the distinction between an unconditional stimulus and a conditional stimulus (Pavlov, 1927)—and by this I do not imply that all communication systems are learned. As Mackay (1969) shows, it is possible even from a mechanical point of view to distinguish between rigorous and nonrigorous definitions of communication—provided we ask the right mechanical questions.

The topic of primate communication itself has been approached in at least three different, complementary ways. First, many investigators, especially psychologists and linguists, take human language as a model system and ask to what extent animals can be trained to use such a system (Fouts, 1972; Gardner & Gardner, 1971; Premack, 1971; Rumbaugh, Gill, & von Glaserfeld, 1973), or to what extent their "natural" communication systems display the same logical properties or so-called design features (Hockett, 1960; Altmann, 1967; Thorpe, 1972). This of course presupposes that we know what human language is—a matter on which I share Dr. Sarles's (this volume) skepticism.

The second approach is more characteristic of Lorenzian ethologists. These investigators focus their attention on selected classes of species-specific individual behaviors—gestures, postures, facial expressions, vocalizations, and so on—and ask how each particular class of behavior serves to regulate and control the behavior of other individuals and their access to resources (e.g., Marler, 1965; 1968). The reasoning here is analogous to that of structuralistic psychology, in that one attempts first of all to catalogue all possible elements of a system and then sets out to examine how each of the various elements is associated with the others and with environmental events.

The third approach is best illustrated by the work of von Frisch on bees (1955) and by some of Carpenter's writings (1964). It consists of focusing one's attention on group-level or populational-level coordinations as such and then gradually dissecting this gestalt to determine what sorts of rules, cues, and information processing systems are involved. How is it that when one bee finds a supply of food and flies off, presumably to its hive, we soon see many bees arriving at the same food supply? How is it that each monkey in a social group tends to move variously as morsels of food and potential dangers are perceived at a distance (and hence the group might be expected to disperse, somewhat as molecules of gas diffuse)—and yet the "group as a whole" never completely loses its integrity, and individuals rarely get lost from each other?

As Ashby (1970) puts it, any such coordination presupposes a certain minimum quantity of information flowing between the parts of a system. Given the facts of coordination, we may estimate rather precisely the minimum quantity of information that is necessary, and we may do so independently of any more precise knowledge of the behavior of the individuals involved. We may also be able to surmise, from these facts of coordination, that the animals *are* communicating long before we know *how* they are doing it or what role any particular species-specific behavior plays in the process.

I myself favor the last approach to communication. In this chapter I shall therefore try to do three things. First, I shall try to demonstrate how the phenomenon of group coordination may be rendered just as observable as any molar behavior on the part of a single individual. Second, I shall examine some of the "codes" and "rules" which determine how chimpanzees coordinate their actions with respect to each other and to strangers and food supplies. Third, I shall consider some of the cues they utilize in these processes. Most of my experiments bear only indirectly on fighting and ethological displays as such. However, here I must stress that, at least in well-established groups of primates, neither fighting nor stereotyped, ritualized displays of aggression occur very frequently in pure form. As Hall (1968) and Tinbergen (1968) point out, these behaviors are components of a larger adaptive system in which behaviors such as "knowing when to stay out of trouble" play just as important a part as aggression. It is not in any one particular cue or means to group goals, but in their ability to achieve a relatively constant end effect for the "group as a whole" by a wide variety of interchangable means, that primates might have the edge over so-called "lower" species.

Coordination as a Directly Observable Phenomenon

When I was first starting to observe monkeys in the wild, I asked an experienced field observer what operational criteria he used in calling "that bunch of individuals over there" a social group and in talking about such things as group coordination. Having at that time a strong bent for sticking to the momentarily observable details of individual behavior, I was not very pleased by his answer. He replied, in effect, "I call the monkeys a group because they act like a group, and if you can't see the same thing you don't have your eyes open!"

Although it is clearly possible to be more analytical than this about what sorts of cues one is utilizing, I have come to suspect that in a more basic sense my advisor's naive realism was correct. By insisting on focusing attention on the elements which comprise a group, I had fragmented the gestalt which might otherwise have been directly perceptible, and then I was concerned about how the gestalt could be constructed from these pieces. The only trick to visualizing a group as a whole directly, or in perceiving a larger coordination as such, is to either figuratively or literally view the larger scene from overhead and ask how the animals move with respect to each other and the environment over appreciable periods of time. If it is impossible to perceive the larger temporal patternings here, one can watch the animals when they are more active than usual, or use some device such as time-lapse photography.

Ordinarily we see too much irrelevant detail, even in a movie. It therefore helps considerably if some of the details are ignored initially—for example, by treating animals and the environmental goals to which they travel as if they were mere points on a map. Once one has learned to see the motions of these points with respect to each other, additional details can be added, as one desires. Thus, for example, in studying group travel one might initially look only at how the "whole mass of monkeys" (or the spatial centroid of the group) moves with respect to the environment; next, one can also look at how each individual moves with respect to this group centroid; and next, one can also look at the movement of each body part with respect to a given individual's center of gravity—which is the level of analysis at which Lorenzian ethologists claim to be working. There are certainly other ways in which the total number of mechanical degrees of freedom may be partitioned. But the preceding scheme clearly emphasizes the facts that: (a) various levels of analysis of physical motion are independent of each other; (b) only if all possible independent levels of analysis are taken together simultaneously can we derive an exhaustive description of physical motion; and (c) any level is as objective and amenable to scientific study as any other—thus the choice of which level to study first depends on what theoretical problems one puts first. If one's interest is in the actions of a group as a whole with respect to another group, but all of one's empirical data are concerned solely with how several individuals' body parts move with respect to each individual's center of gravity, one's claim to being a scientific authority on intergroup behavior must rest on something other than one's own empirical data.

The foregoing argument can be illustrated with a simple experiment. Four young chimpanzees, who have lived together for more than a year and who seem, intuitively speaking, to form a very compatible and stable social group, are placed in a small holding cage which opens into a 1-acre outdoor test enclosure. A human being who is instructed to act (on alternate days) either as a "friendly person" or as a "mean stranger" (Hebb, 1949; Mason, 1965) then enters the enclosure. He stands for several minutes at one end of the enclosure and then walks back and forth across the length of the enclosure, traveling at an average rate of 30 feet per minute. In his role as friendly person he is instructed to do nothing to distress the chimpanzees and to reciprocate gently if they initiate play. In his role as mean stranger he wears a mask (which, control tests suggest, makes it unlikely that he can be recognized by the chimpanzees) and carries a hollow plastic baseball bat. He is instructed not to chase any chimpanzees but to whack them over the head if they get within striking distance.

Our interest is, of course, in how the group of animals will organize itself in dealing with these two classes of social stimuli. I would have much preferred to use a radio-controllable chimpanzee or some other less anthropocentric form of ethological model (Tinbergen, 1951), but after wasting a considerable amount of taxpayers' money on such schemes, I reverted to the most accessible and reliably operating form of chimpanzee dummy, namely, people.

When the test person is stationed at one end of the enclosure, the door of the release cage is opened and the chimpanzees are turned loose to do whatever they choose. The test lasts for 30 minutes, and then the chimpanzees are transported back to their home cage. The next test using the same social stimuli is presented 48 hours later, and altogether we conducted 10 tests with the friendly person and 15 with the mean stranger.

In a few sessions the behavior of the chimpanzees was filmed. Usually, however, we employed a recording method analogous to snapshot photography. As an interval timer sounded a loud click each 60 seconds, an observer on an observation tower indicated the position of each animal on a scale map of the enclosure (to about the nearest 10 feet) and recorded what they were doing, and with whom or what. More extensive qualitative notes were made after the session, both by the observer and by the test person.

To see that the chimpanzees are coordinating their behaviors and moving as a cohesive group, and to see that this group as a whole is in turn adjusting its behavior to that of the test person, it is necessary only to consider the gross spatial data. These data could be completely represented in a single easily visualizable picture if we made a large 3-dimensional graph showing the position of each individual's center of gravity in the 2-dimensional field at each recorded instant in time. Figure 1 is, however, sufficient for our present purposes. For two sessions with each test person, it shows the positions of the test person and each animal on the long dimension of the enclosure at 1-minute intervals. In constructing this figure all we have done is to remove enough detail from a series of time-sample photographs that we can collapse the remaining maplike detail of primary interest into a single frame that permits the viewer to integrate the information he might otherwise not be able to integrate. In other words, the figure is still very close to the raw data, and, with practice, one can easily learn to directly perceive the same things in data maps, a movie, or even a natural event as it occurs "out there."

What, more specifically, might a sufficiently trained observer see? From the information available in Figure 1 alone we could see at least the following (and tests of statistical significance would show these conclusions to be quite warranted statistically).

At any given instant in time, the animals seem to be much closer to each other than one might expect of objects that were placed about the field at random.

Over more extended periods of time, the animals appear to move as a unit in close association with each other. That is, their distances from each other at any particular time are very small relative to each animal's travels across the period of, say, a half hour; and given the position of any one animal, one can closely predict the position of the others.

Not only is there coordination within the group (by the above criterion), but also the movement of the whole mass, or the group's centroid, is coordinated with the movement of the test person. Since the travel of the test persons was specified a priori before the experiment and proceeded without regard to what the chimpanzees were doing, we might say the test persons were controlling the group's travels, rather than vice versa.

The degree of control exerted by each test person is definitely greater on the first day of the test than on later days.

The mean stranger is given a wider berth than the friendly person.

However, it is principally by looking at the lower limit of spacing that we can distinguish between the animals' reactions to the two test persons. Taking a broader view, it is clear that the predominant behavior toward the aggressive stranger is positive in valence, rather than negative or zero. Not only the data of Figure 1 but also our qualitative data and intuitive judgments at the time of the test strongly suggest that (except in their narrow physical sense) the terms

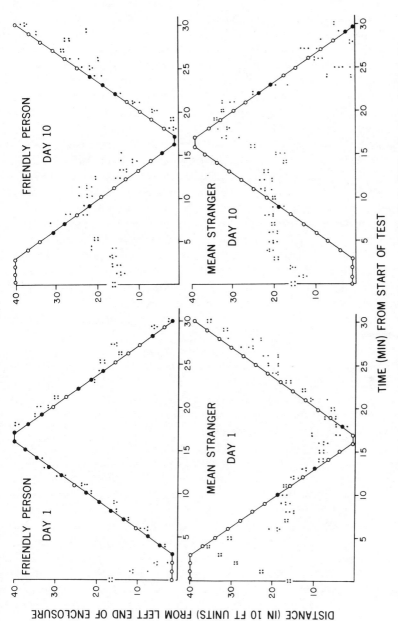

Fig. 1. Response of a group of four young chimpanzees to a moving test person. Circles indicate the test person's position at each 1-minute interval and each dot represents one chimpanzee. If a circle is filled, one or more chimpanzees are in the same spatial area as the test person.

approach and avoidance are purely relativistic concepts, dependent upon the observer's scale of observation and the scope of his attention. The question of whether the animals are really attracted to the test persons or are avoiding them, or are aggressive or in a state of psychological conflict, etc., seems less informative than the more generic question of what is the equilibrium point toward which coordinative relations tend, and what is the range of permissible values around this point (i.e., the lower limit, at which the animals try to increase distance; and the upper limit, at which animals try to follow again or reduce distance), and how do these values change according to the circumstances of the test.

For a finer grained and more obviously psychological picture of what was going on in this test we would of course have to consider also the more molecular reactions of the animals—how they initially indulged in vigorous play with the friendly person, and whimpered when he got too far away, and seldom threatened him or clung to each other, and then subsequently (on later days) seemed to satiate in play and followed less closely; and how, with the mean stranger, they initially approached with piloerection, pulled back a group member who got too close and clung to him, hooted and stamped their feet and threw sticks and screamed and ran away when hit—only to whimper and follow when the stranger moved off—and eventually adapted to the point where (after several days) they no longer seemed cautious, and sometimes seemed to actually solicit getting hit with the bat and to reciprocate with rough play and a panting vocalization analogous to laughter. I shall omit a detailed account of such data, partly because of space limitations, and partly because the data are more pertinent to questions regarding individual behavior than to the molar fact of group coordination. They supplement and complement the data we have already presented and help to explain how and why animals move together, but the molar facts of group coordination can be perceived independently of individual behavior at the ethological level of analysis.

It might be mentioned that the sorts of results obtained in the present test were not peculiar to the chimpanzees' reactions to human beings. Indeed, almost any strange being (including strange chimpanzees) or a highly dominant group member or even certain classes of novel inanimate objects usually evoked the same approach and following behavior at a macroscopic level of analysis and the same avoidance and mock-threat behavior at short distances that was seen with the mean stranger. The same thing may be seen in any group of wild primates. Spatial adjustments between any two individuals seem to have their near limits and their far limits, their minima and maxima. Highly dominant adult males are, for example, usually given a berth of a few feet, and if this personal space is breached without some displays of appeasement on the part of the subordinate, the latter might get threatened or bitten. If, however, the same aggressive male moves out a considerable distance, it becomes quite clear that he might be a principal determiner of group behavior and highly attractive in a more macroscopic sense, for suddenly the whole group starts to follow. The amount of time two animals spend in friendly (or hostile) physical contacts with each other might, indeed, sometimes tell one relatively little about how strongly they are attracted to or repelled by each other. Thus, for example, I have had a few pairs of chimpanzees who virtually never groomed or played with each other and who were seldom seen in any sort of physical contact, and yet, the two animals were seldom more than 30 feet apart, defended each other in fights, and showed a much higher positive association (both statistically and otherwise) with each other than they showed with any other animal. They had, incidentally, been raised together from infancy.

Communication about Objects

How is the observed coordination among animals and their organized group response toward an object possible? In the preceding sort of test it sometimes seemed as if the chimpanzees were not merely exchanging signals with each other and with the test person, but were also in a sense communicating with each other about the test person. For example, one chimpanzee might orient toward the mean stranger (when he was a considerable distance away), stamp his feet in a display of threat or bluff, glance back and forth between the test person and his companions, and then tap a companion on the shoulder, take a few steps, and look back again—and at this the whole group would either set out together to give the test person another hard time, or the most timid member of the group (Shadow) would start to whimper and try to pull the others in some other direction—for example, toward a favorite climbing tree. Often a human observer could predict, from the exchanges between animals and their common response to the environment, the precise destination of a long travel sequence and the nature of the behavior that the group as a whole would engage in once it got there. This gave us reason to suspect that the chimpanzees themselves could make the same deductions from each other's behavior. However, it is almost an article of faith in the current literature on human language and animal behavior that without symbolic language animals cannot communicate about objects and events. Also, it is conceivable (as long as the objects are visible to all) that instead of exchanging information with each other, the coordination among animals is produced simply by their common response to the same external (nonsocial) variables. Therefore a more rigorous type of test was necessary.

First, the group is locked inside a release cage from which they cannot see what is going on in the enclosure. Next, an experimenter enters the field and hides a test object at a randomly designated location, never using the same location twice over a series of trials. Then one previously selected member of the group is taken from the release cage, carried over to the object, shown the object, and returned to the group. The experimenter leaves the field, ascends the observation tower, and pulls a cable which opens the release cage door and turns the animals loose to respond as they choose. With this delayed response procedure the group as a whole has no cues as to what object (if any) is out there or where it is, other than cues provided by the leader's memory and his behavior. (Control tests were of course done to verify that variables such as odor or inadvertent behavior on the part of the observers were not sufficient to explain group performance. If we gave no animal the information, the group very seldom went to the object directly or responded differentially according to the nature of the object.)

The results of such tests were very clearcut (Menzel, 1971, 1973). Any individual was capable of rallying the whole group to respond in fairly organized fashion to objects about which he alone knew. Ordinarily, the informed animal led the group to the hidden object, and if they were slow to follow he used a variety of devices (including visual glances, grimacing, extending a hand toward a companion, tapping the companion on the shoulder and presenting his back, etc.) to recruit a following. He very seldom set off to the object alone, and in this sense performance was clearly a cooperative performance; i.e., the leader was as dependent on the group for getting to the object as they were dependent on him for knowing where to go.

Not only did the group continue to travel together as a cohesive unit on the basis of cues from a single leader, but also the animals whom we had provided with no cues seemed to know approximately where the object was, and what sort of object it was, long before the leader reached the spot where it had been hidden. Thus, for example, if we had shown the leader food, other animals often ran ahead of him, glanced back at him periodically, as if to determine his trajectory, and then dove for any likely-looking hiding place which lay ahead on this path and searched it manually in exactly the same fashion as they searched around the leader if he had missed a food pile by a few feet. By any objective criteria of predictive behavior (Krushinskii, 1960; Rosenblueth, Wiener, & Bigelow, 1943) and expectancy (Tinklepaugh, 1928), the behavior of the followers can be so described.

If the hidden object were a snake, stuffed alligator, or other strange form which was likely to induce caution or aggression, the whole group often emerged from the release cage showing piloerection, staring in the direction of the object, and staying close to a companion. As with the mean stranger in tests described in the preceding section, the group as a whole approached the test object. As they grew closer they appeared more and more cautious. Sometimes the leader would not approach any closer than 30 feet, and the others still seemed to know just about where the object was hidden. And instead of searching the hiding place manually (as they did with food), they "mobbed" that spot by hooting, tree shaking, threat displays, throwing grass, sticks, or earth, hitting with a stick, or slapping with a hand and jumping back. Usually the leader performed one such response first, but in some cases a follower was the first. The same behavior occurred whether we left the object in the enclosure or removed it completely after having shown it to the leader; thus cues from the object itself may be excluded.

On the basis of many such tests, I would hypothesize that the discrimination of negative (caution- or aggression-inducing) from positive classes of objects was based principally on cues such as the leader's piloerection, vocalization, locomotor deceleration and increase in caution as he approached and stared at a particular locus, and tendency to circle the locus or approach it from overhead via some vertical structure. The approximate location of either class of object (positive or negative) was in turn probably predicted from the leader's direction of travel, postural pointing, and visual orientation, or indeed any molar behavior (e.g., stick throwing) that was aimed toward some particular locus.

Is such behavior really communication? With Dr. Sarles (this volume) I believe that the very question reveals a human chauvinism which equates real communication with what we think people do —i.e., it equates communication with words and sentences produced either verbally or with stylized manual gestures rather than some other form of response. What, however, is a sentence or a word? As Olson (1970) puts it, "Words do not 'mean' referents or stand for referents, they have a use—they specify perceived events relative to a set of alternatives; they provide information" (p. 263). "[It] is impossible to specify the meaning of a word or a sentence unambiguously unless one knows the context and hence the set of alternative referents being entertained by the listener" (p. 260). There is no good reason other than theoretical convenience to suppose that the use of words (let alone the use of a particular modality of response) is based on processes that are somehow distinct from those that underlie other forms of information processing.

I am certainly not arguing that there are no differences between chimpanzee and human communication systems. However, both systems do serve to coordinate group life, to provide information regarding the environment, and to furnish a basis for response to events that are displaced in space or time from the signaler.

The "Group Split Threshold"

Thus far we have considered situations in which the members of a group respond in the same way at the same time to the same goal objects and seem to operate as a cohesive and cooperative unit against the rest of the world. Now let us consider another part of the story, namely, competition within the group. The problem facing any primate group is not only to stay close enough together to keep from getting lost or becoming unable to defend each other, but also to range widely enough that everyone can obtain food and whatever other resources are necessary for survival. This could in some cases be accomplished by everyone sticking together and simply traveling farther in a given day. But such a solution would entail a far greater consumption of energy on the part of everyone than would alternative solutions, and it might give rise to intragroup fighting over each piece of food as it comes along. One alternative solution is for individuals to disperse themselves just widely enough at any given instant to avoid potentially direct competition with each other. If the animals are coordinating their movements with respect to each other on a moment-to-moment basis, and if indeed their momentary distances from each other are not random but a sort of balancing of all social forces (positive and negative) that are currently operative, one might indeed expect to find fairly clear threshold distances beyond which the animals will not separate.

A simple extension of our previous test procedures supports this assumption. While a group of six chimpanzees is locked in the release cage, we put out two goal objects. In this case the goal objects are pieces of food, impaled on two stakes and positioned in such a way that they are both clearly visible from the door of the release cage. The stakes are equidistant from the release cage but they lie in opposite directions, so that the group will have to split (i.e., travel in two opposed directions simultaneously) to get both foods simultaneously. The animals can, of course, choose whether to do this or to travel together first to one goal and then to the next or to perish from indecision like Buridan's ass did when confronted with two bales of hay. The distance between the two stakes varies from 40 to 400 feet, using the up-and-down method of limits. In other words, if the group splits on a given trial, we move the stakes 10 feet farther apart on the next trial, and if they do not split, we move the stakes 10 feet closer on the next trial. The "group split threshold" is defined as the average of the two distance values between which the change in group response occurred. If one or more animals is at least 10 feet to the left of the release cage exactly 30 seconds after the release cage door is opened and if one or more animals is at least 10 feet to the right of the release cage at the same time, the group is scored as "splitting." (This measure agreed very closely with intuitive judgments on the trial as a whole, made by an independent observer.)

If the two foods were relatively close together, the group split with little or no hesitation and it was each chimp for himself. As the foods were moved farther and farther apart, the animals started to look back and forth between the two goals and at each other. They vacillated, hesitated, and milled about, and tapped their favorite companions on the shoulder and presented their backs for tandem walking (a pattern characteristically used if the animals were cautious or moving on a long trek; it consisted of animals walking with synchronized steps, one animal walking to the rear of the other and holding him around the waist). If the companion would not follow, the leader whimpered. No one would travel alone if this meant getting more than about 50 feet from at least one companion, and in this sense food getting was clearly a cooperative venture.

At intermediate distances, two parties of chimps eventually split from each other, the members of each party sticking close together. At still longer distances, however, there was no splitting at all. The whole group pulled this way and that and finally wound up going as a unit, first to one goal and then to the other one. On a given test day, the exact distances at which these changes in group behavior occurred were quite reliable from one trial to the next—unless there were some disturbance in the area (e.g., an airplane passing overhead), in which case the distance threshold suddenly shrank. Figure 2 shows the probability of group splitting as a function of the distance between the two foods. These are pooled data for all trials.

Perhaps the most striking fact was that the chimpanzees did not have to walk all the way to their upper limits of tolerable spacing and then come back: it was as if they anticipated before the outset of a long trek that if they proceeded to one currently present distant goal, and if the others went in the opposite direction, they would get too far apart. Thus the group decision as to whether or not to split was almost always made directly in front of the release cage, in an area no larger than 10 feet. Also, the animals seemed to be much less disturbed if the group spread out a considerable distance along a single direction of march than if it started to travel in two directions simultaneously: it was as if distance and direction were independently effective parameters of spacing, and the directional parameter was the more important.

The reasons for group cohesiveness and strong following tendencies in juvenile chimpanzees are fairly obvious, but the reasons for the same animals to sometimes split from each other are equally obvious. If the animals traveled together, a single individual (Libi) got most of the food. Her closest companion, Bido, followed her faithfully anyway, but the other animals did not. It was they (and, in particular, Belle) who initiated the practice of splitting and eventually caused the group to split at longer and longer distances. On the first days of the test the split threshold was only about 70 feet. However, as Figure 3 shows, it

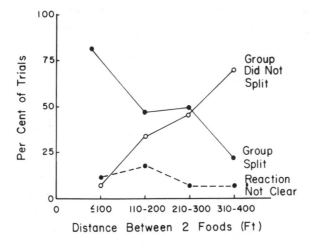

Fig. 2. The probability of the group's traveling in two directions simultaneously (i.e., splitting), as a function of the distance between two foods.

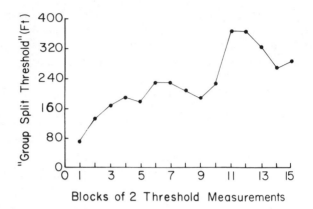

Fig. 3.   Effects of practice upon the maximum distance at which the group would still split.

increased very rapidly to 300 feet or more. We had never before seen such extreme spacings in this group. On trials in which the group split, Libi and Belle each obtained about 40% of the food, and the other 4 chimps (primarily Polly) the remaining 20%.

Occasionally a fight erupted over food. However, this happened only when two animals had been racing for the same piece of food and reached it almost simultaneously. Most often the contest was settled at a distance, by letting the dominant animal or the one who happened to have the biggest lead go ahead. If an animal (even the most subordinate) actually had his food in hand and was sitting quietly eating it (instead of trying to run away with it), he was almost never directly challenged for the food. Instead, the others would snuggle up to him and watch him eat, possibly trying to beg a share by whimpering and extending their hand or lips to his mouth. In some cases, also, a loser engaged the winner in play, and then (when the winner put some food down or was not watching closely) made a sneaky grab for the food.

The Unique Role of Food in Controlling Dispersion

Although chimpanzees—at least captive chimpanzees—will attend to almost any change in their environment and approach and compete for many classes of objects, not all objects are of equal biological significance, and the manner in which and the degree to which any given object disrupts a group's momentary equilibrium might accordingly be expected to depend upon what it is. Indeed, my observations suggested that with juvenile chimpanzees there was probably no class of object that would produce the extreme dispersals of animals in space that we had seen with food—and we had tried just about every class of object we could get our hands on. Perhaps, as ecologists tell us, the distribution of food is the most important single variable in determining the population in a given area at a given time.

To illustrate the effects of different classes of objects upon intragroup patterns of spacing and competition, I compared food with novel objects. Since the chimpanzees would play with the latter for hours and compete for them vigorously (indeed, in this group many more fights occurred over toys than occurred over any other class of object, including food), it is safe to say that they were highly attracted to them.

The procedure is essentially the same as in the last test. While the chimps are in the release cage, an experimenter positions one stake 70 feet to the left and another stake 70 feet to the right of the release cage. The distance between the two stakes (140 feet) is short enough that, with food, the group would be expected to split on essentially every trial. On each stake we put an identical object or set of objects. However, these might be either (a) a piece of food, (b) a novel object (a new set of objects is used for each such trial), (c) both a piece of food and a novel object, or (d) nothing. Each trial continues for several minutes. With this procedure we can assess the degree to which either class of object facilitates group dispersal or inhibits it, and how long it takes the group to return to its normal spacing arrangements after first being perturbed by the test stimulus.

The animals traveled almost as rapidly toward the novel objects as toward food: if one ignores the direction of travel and looks only at how far each animal had gone from the release cage in the first 30 seconds of the trial, one finds only small differences between the first three conditions, and all conditions produced more travel than the "no object or food" control condition (condition d). In other respects, also, the animals appeared quite eager for either class of object.

However, the two classes of objects produced very different effects upon group dispersal patterns. In their initial travel to the two stakes, the group split on 22/24 trials for food only (condition a), 5/24 trials for object only (condition b), 22/24 trials for food plus object (condition c), and 0/24 trials for the empty stake (condition d). Clearly, food was the principal facilitator of dispersal, and novel objects did not inhibit dispersal but did relatively little to facilitate it.

In all conditions, group dispersal was a temporary phenomenon. Once the chimpanzees secured the spatially separated goals and had consumed the food, they shortly commenced to come back together again, until they reached the equilibrium spacing arrangements seen under routine conditions. Figure 4 shows how this process of dispersing-then-regrouping proceeded. Presumably, sociologically centripetal and centrifugal factors are balanced in such a way as to produce spacing arrangements that are the best possible at any particular instant in time with respect to all relevant stimuli, but when several such factors cannot be balanced simultaneously, a temporal or sequential priority is assigned to each course of action. With some classes of goals (food), the group at first splits and goes in two directions simultaneously, and then, later, "socially cohesive

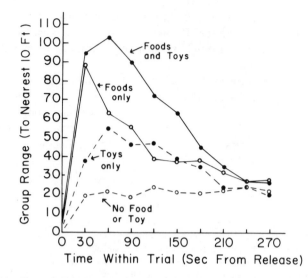

Fig. 4. Group dispersal-then-reaggregation in going for different classes of goals. The goals were 140 feet apart, so a group range of more than half that distance usually reflects a group split.

forces'' apparently pull the animals back together again. With other classes of objects, the group travels together as a unit, going first to one object and then to the next. In either of these two solutions, it takes almost the same amount of time to have done with the disturbance and settle down once more, but the former solution is much more likely to distribute a resource equitably among group members and to eliminate fighting—at least over resources which are rapidly consumed and cannot be passed from one animal to the next.

Communication about Objects and Its Effect on Group Splitting

In the preceding test the two goal objects were visible to all animals at the start of a trial, which is certainly not representative of all the situations a group of primates would face in their everyday foragings. In some cases, undoubtedly, only one or two animals know what is out there, and the rest of the group must decide what to do on the basis of cues from these leaders. Will they still split if the (leader's) goals are food, and not split if the (leader's) goals are some other class of object? If so, the evidence for communication about objects is even clearer than before.

Two objects are carefully hidden in the enclosure for a new variation on our basic delayed response procedure. A previously selected leader is taken from the release cage, shown one object, and returned to the release cage; then another leader is similarly shown the other object and returned to the release cage; then the experimenters leave the enclosure and open the release cage door. Over a long series of trials all possible (6) pairs of four leaders are tested several times on each of 4 conditions: (a) Both see equivalent piles of fruit, (b) both see the same type of novel object, (c) A sees fruit and B sees a novel object, (d) B sees novel object and A sees fruit. With this procedure there is no possible way in which one leader can guess what the other has seen, except through cues from him. For the group to respond appropriately, the animals must pool the information from the two leaders.

The results were almost the same as one would expect had the goal objects been visible at the time of group response. (However, it must be mentioned that this test was conducted almost two years after the preceding one, and some of the leaders were different, so direct statistical comparisons between the two tests are not warranted.) If both leaders had been shown fruit, the group split on 20/24 trials; if both had been shown novel objects, the group split on 9/24 trials; and if one had been shown fruit and the other had been shown a novel object, the group split on 21/48 trials, and 84% of the time (excluding ties) the group majority went with the leader who was traveling to the food. Both the effects of the two classes of objects of group splitting and the group's preference for going first to food are statistically significant; however, the novel objects were almost always approached and manipulated vigorously after the food had been consumed, and more fights occurred over them than over food.

Amount and Distribution of Food as Determiners of Dispersion

Another way to state our problem is as follows: "Competition" and "cooperation" are two sides of the same coin of coordination, and almost any statement about competition can be translated into a statement about cooperation, and vice versa. Biologically speaking, there is just as much competition within a group as between strangers, but the rules become more subtle and shared by all, and they are less apt to entail bloodshed and useless expenditure of energy. In other words, societies (almost by definition) develop *conventionalized* forms of competition over resources (Wynne-Edwards, 1962). The conventions provide relatively orderly and efficient (cooperative?) means of determining who will get what, and when.

The best known such convention in animal societies is a stable dominance order. Dominance orders can be seen in almost any vertebrate society, including societies of monkeys and apes. Other things being equal, certain individuals (usually the largest and strongest) can characteristically drive other individuals from a common goal object, and once their physical superiority becomes known, there are few further serious contests for priority. The subordinate animal usually gives way at the first sign from the dominant, and the more skilled the two animals become at reading the situation and each other's intent, the more subtle and displaced in space/time their signals of dominance and subordination become. Distal signaling largely replaces fighting and takes on rules of its own.

This, however, is less than half of the whole story, for it is seldom that everything other than the intrinsic superiority of one individual versus another is equal. Thus, for example, one animal may have the backing of a relative who outranks his opponent—which completely changes the picture (Kawai, 1958; Sade, 1965). Or the subordinate may already have the goal object in hand, in which case he is much less apt to be challenged for it. It is as if the animals have rules of some sort regarding who possesses a given piece of food, or an infant, or a receptive female, or a momentary resting place, or a larger territory, and the complementary dominance rules operate only when neither animal possesses the object in question (Kummer, 1973). Or, still further, primates may simply be skilled enough at predicting each other's moves and assessing the lay of the land that (by dispersing themselves appropriately ahead of time) they can ordinarily stay out of situations which would give rise to a contest or the need for obvious displays of dominance or subordination. No scientist would predict that the stronger animal would invariably get food if the food were thrown exactly between two animals who sit 100 yards apart. Nor would one necessarily expect that the usually dominant animal would get food if the two animals were only 10 yards apart but the food were thrown right into the subordinate's lap. The spatial extent of a given animal's sphere of influence could no doubt be measured fairly precisely, and for any particular pair of animals one animal would be expected to have a larger sphere of influence than the other—but at least in a free-field situation there would always be some distance at which priority of access would pass from A to B. Similarly, animals probably differ greatly in how generalized (across many classes of objects and situations) their priority of access to incentives is, but no individual has first priority with all classes of objects and in all situations.

In sum, to create a fair test of dominance, we as experimenters usually control or eliminate all variables other than the one in which we are interested; thus we take the control of these variables away from the animals themselves. But it is the free selection of these variables, as well as dominance per se, which ordinarily determines priority of access to a particular goal and the distribution of animals relative to resources in general.

The question, then, is how well the members of a group can perceive the overall situation and regulate their positions with respect to each other and to desirable objects such as food. In further experiments with my group of young chimpanzees, I looked more closely at this question.

Instead of providing only a single goal on either side of the enclosure and examining whether or not the group will split into two parties, the situation is made more complex. Six stakes are arranged along a semicircle about 70 feet away from the release cage; 3 stakes lie to the left and 3 stakes lie to the right of the release cage. Then, over a series of trials, we randomly put food on either (a) none,

(b) 1, (c) 2, or (d) 3 stakes on each side. (The rewards on each side are always equal.) How well can the group perceive these variations in food supply, and to what degree can the six animals work out an efficient group technique for going to and dividing up the food?

As Figure 5 shows, the more food there was on each side of the cage, the greater the dispersion of the group. The differences between each pair of conditions is statistically significant. On the average, half of the animals went to the left and half went to the right. However, with multiple foods a unique group travel pattern arose: we may call it a "hierarchical group split" pattern (see Figure 6). Here the group of six chimpanzees first split into two parties at the door of the cage, each animal usually going with his preferred companion and forgetting less preferred companions. Then, as each of these parties got closer to the food stakes it in turn subdivided. Still later, after the food was gone, everyone gradually started to regroup—as in Figure 4. Only one animal (the smallest one, Bandit) did not join in the races for food, and he often went over later and managed to beg some from the others. Since he performed very effectively as a leader when he alone knew where a hidden food pile lay, we may infer that his failure to run was due to the social competition rather than to lack of food motivation per se.

Under conditions where only one piece of food was available in each direction, Libi and Belle usually led splinter parties in opposite directions from each other and got the food. As the food supply was increased, however, each animal (other than Bandit) came to get an almost equal share of the food—for each animal watched the others and took care to go to a food stake which was not covered by a more dominant or faster-running animal. Practically no fighting and few obvious ethological displays of aggression or subordination were seen in the process.

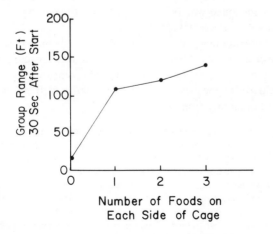

Fig. 5.   Group dispersion 30 seconds after the start of a trial, as a function of the amount of food on each side of the enclosure.

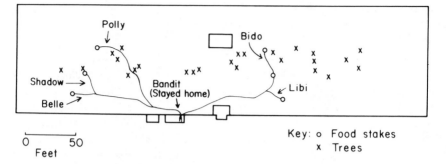

Fig. 6. A typical trial on the condition involving 3 food stakes on each side of the field, showing the hierarchical group-split pattern.

Table I shows the results for the condition on which there were 3 foods on each side of the cage. It would appear that each animal had priority of access at one or more positions in the field—as if the group as a whole worked out an equitable distribution of food by carving up the field into territories. Other data suggest that this solution took time. Over the several days of the test, the group came increasingly to fan out in all directions simultaneously from the door of the release cage (each animal going straight to his stake unless it was already covered by another animal): there was a statistically highly significant increase from one day to the next in the dispersion of the group exactly 30 seconds after the start of a trial, and this was not attributable to a simple increase in running speed on the part of each animal. Furthermore, after several days it almost seemed as if the animals recognized each other's claims on a given food stake, for even an otherwise generally dominant animal, with a lead of several yards, backed off if the "owner" of the stake was behind him. (Sometimes the owner screamed at anyone who approached his stake.)

It should be mentioned, however, that the animals by no means had simple or invariant position habits. Their tendency to go to a particular place changed instantly if the food conditons or social conditions were varied sufficiently. This is seen most clearly in the next test, in which the payoff on each side of the enclosure varied randomly from trial to trial.

Now the 6 food stakes are distributed around the field in a semicircle, with the stakes at least 10 feet apart and all clearly visible from the door of the release cage. On a given trial, either 0, 1, 2, 3, 4, 5, or 6 of the stakes lie on the left of the field and the rest of the stakes (or none) lie on the right of the field. From laboratory studies one would expect that individuals would have a clear preference for going to whichever side holds the greater amount of food. But, obviously, this would not be the most adaptive solution in the present case, for to get food each animal must anticipate or predict well in advance where the others are going. How well can the group as a whole regulate the distribution of animals relative to the distribution of food? Can the group in effect match the number of animals in a given area to the number of "food units" in that area?

Under all but the two extreme conditions (where one side of the field held no food) the group nearly always split as soon as they emerged from the release cage. Each individual tended to go in whichever direction there were more baited food stakes (the range of scores here was from 73% to 86% for the six animals), but no individual was as consistent as the group majority (which scored 93%). Thus individual animals went to the greater food supply if, and only if, not too many others were also going there. These decisions were made within a few yards of the starting point. Frequently the whole group started first toward the larger food supply, only to come to a halt after a few yards, mill about, vacillate one way and the other, and then split up, one party reversing to go in the other direction, and varying in numbers according to the number of available food stakes.

Figure 7 shows the average results for 10 trials per condition (20 for the 3–3 condition). Except for Bandit (who still did not compete in the races, but who begged food from the victors), there is almost a perfect matching behavior on the part of the group. Indeed, such results obtained on almost every replication of the 7 conditions.

Another way to look at the results is to ask to what degree the spatial centroid (mean) of the group and the spatial dispersion (variance) of the group correlated with corresponding measures for the foods. Exactly 30 seconds after the start of the trial (by which time it was rare that more than one animal had actually gotten to a food stake), the respective coefficients are .74 and .50, and both of these values are highly significant, statistically speaking. (These are partial tau coefficients, determined by ranking the scores of the several conditions within each replication, and thus partialing out replication effects.)

Table I. Number of Trials Each Animal Obtained Food at Each of the Different Food Stakes When 3 Food Stakes Were Baited on Each Side of the Cage

Subject	L1	L2	L3	R1	R2	R3	Total
Shadow	2	3	2	10	7	8	32
Bandit	1	0	0	0	0	0	1
Belle	6	15	8	4	4	2	39
Polly	0	2	4	8	12	11	37
Bido	1	8	18	10	4	2	43
Libi	22	4	0	0	5	9	40
	32	32	32	32	32	32	

Food stake[a]

[a] The stakes were arranged in a semicircle, as shown in Figure 6, and are numbered here from front-left (L–1) to front right (R–3) around the semicircle.

Chi square (excluding Bandit) = 122.16, $df = 20, p < .001$.
Chi square for each subject except Bandit, $p < .05$.

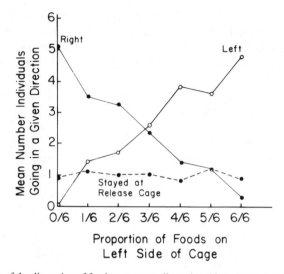

Fig. 7. Effects of the dispersion of food upon group dispersion. Note that except for failures to run there is a close matching between the number of animals going in a given direction and the number of foods in that direction.

Is this sort of group behavior best described as a "competition", in which each animal is out for his own good, or is it best described as a "cooperation" performance, in which the net result is food for everyone and almost no fighting? I leave this question to the philosophers. However, it is quite clear that in performing as they do, the animals are not acting independently of each other, but operating as a coordinated system.

To render this conclusion more convincing, an analogous type of test was conducted with our delayed response procedure. One pile of food is hidden on one side of the enclosure and shown to one leader and another pile of food is hidden on the other side of the enclosure and shown to a different leader. On control trials, the two piles are equivalent, and on experimental trials they differ in quantity (2 vs. 4 pieces) or in preference value (preferred fruit vs. nonpreferred vegetables).

In each of several experiments, the group majority accompanied the leader who was going to the better goal on an average of 80% of the trials, regardless of who the leader was or where the food was hidden. A majority of "errors" involved following a preferred leader (who was more apt to share food), i.e., the preference value of the food and the preference value of the leader were additive variables determining group choice. Usually the group split into two parties and went to both of the hidden goals simultaneously, and in the experiment with different quantities of food the number of animals following each leader roughly matched the amount of food. Clearly, such a result could not be achieved without some form of information exchange among animals. The major cues for this type of discrimination were, I believe, the tendency of the leaders to show stronger signs of anticipatory behavior (e.g., faster running speed, more vigorous tugging and signaling at followers, whimpering if no one followed) for a preferred versus a nonpreferred goal.

A very interesting question raised at the Erindale Conference by a member of the audience is whether a *single* chimpanzee who had been shown two piles of food differing in quantity could direct the group to split up and assign the appropriate number of foragers to each pile. If so, it would seem that the animals would be capable of military planning. Unfortunately, I never tried such an experiment. I would bet that the outcome would be negative, but, on the other hand, several years ago I (and many other primatologists) would have bet the same thing for the experiments just described in the previous paragraphs, so who knows?

Relations among Subgroups within a Group

The whole dynamic ecological system on this earth consists of many subsystems loosely coupled, and the subsystems themselves tend to consist of still smaller systems, again more closely coupled internally yet less closely coupled between one another, and so on. Thus in most species of primates we usually distinguish at least several "levels" of social organization: interindividual relations; subgroupings or family units composed of several individuals; larger groupings composed of several subgroups; and local populations or communities of groups. Principles analogous to dominance, possession, and spacing equilibria may operate at all levels, and a complete account of socioecological coordination would describe what is going on at all levels simultaneously, rather than trying to claim one level (e.g., the group as a whole) as *the* fundamental one. Stated otherwise, the levels of organization of which we are speaking signify only the level of the attention of the observer whose attention has been attracted by certain regularities of patterns that seem to prevail at that level.

Even casual observation is sufficient to detect the role of subgroupings and temporary coalitions in primate groups. For example, in my group of chimpanzees, few real altercations involved only a single pair of animals. Ordinarily, everyone came running. If the fight became a serious one, animals who had lived together the longest almost always sided with each other against relative strangers. In milder contests over an object, however, whoever had the object first seemed to be treated by the group as the "rightful owner"—for if this animal had the object taken from him by force, not only he but sometimes the whole group hooted and screamed at the thief, and someone tried to placate the loser by clinging to him, grooming him, or engaging him in gentle play. Sometimes, after being screamed at thus, the thief himself started to whimper and make overtures to play or to groom the loser (while still trying to retain the object, of course).

Another simple experiment illustrates the role of subgroup affiliations in foraging situations. Using our standard procedures, a group of eight chimpanzees (our old animals plus two strangers) is confronted with 2 sets of tin cans, which lie 300 feet apart and in opposite directions from the starting point, and which contain food. (On control or baseline trials they are tested with no special test object—i.e., they are simply turned loose from the release cage and are free to roam.) Given the data of previous experiments on group splitting and the fact that the present experiment was conducted more than a year later and the animals were consequently more mature and more practiced, it was a foregone conclusion that the aggregate would split once they learned that the tin cans contained food. The questions were: What proportion of the scatter between animals is attributable to stable subgroup differences? Will we see essentially the same pattern of splitting-then-regrouping at both the subgroup and the group level of analysis? That is, will both the subgroups and the group as a whole tend to return to their respective control or baseline (equilibrium) level of spacing once they have finished off the food?

For purposes of analysis, the eight animals were divided into three a priori subgroups—two trios and one pair—solely according to the differential amounts of time they had lived together before the test.

Figure 8 shows the moment-by-moment dispersion of the overall group of eight animals over the course of a 10-minute trial. The data are the average results for 20 trials per condition. Here group dispersion is measured by the group range, i.e., the simple distance between whichever two animals were farthest apart. Under control conditions the chimps usually came out of the release cage quickly and scattered a bit—undoubtedly because the release cage was relatively small compared to the group's usual spatial dispersion, and under such conditions of crowding, with no escape possible, the largest or most dominant animal often started picking on a relative stranger, and this in turn sometimes led to an all-out brawl between two subgroups. Once they had spaced out a bit, however, all was placid very shortly. Sometimes the animals who had just rushed away from each other screaming now all returned to the release cage and commenced to play—as if the crowding were positively attractive as long as an escape hatch was left open. The dispersion of the group after several minutes averaged to about the same values we saw in routine, everyday observations of the animals.

When food was involved, the pace was much faster. As in previous experiments, every chimpanzee watched every other, usually half of them went in one direction and half went in the other direction (in accordance with the distribution of the food), and within 30 seconds the group was scattered all over. After the food was consumed, all animals started to drift back together again until they reached the spatial limits or equilibrium conditions seen under control conditions. These limits were, incidentally, considerably larger than those seen in the data of Figure 4 at an earlier age, and the length of time the animals took before coming back together was also longer.

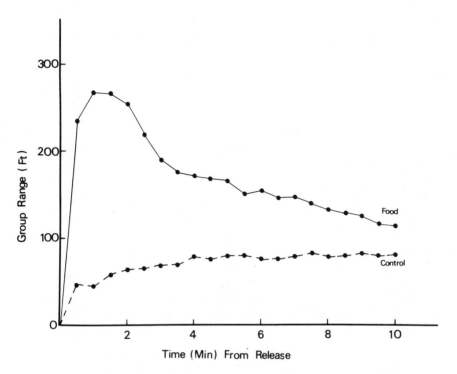

Fig. 8.   Dispersal-then-reaggregation in the group of eight chimpanzees. The food stakes were 300 feet apart.

Figure 9 partitions the total group scatter (under each condition at each instant in time) into two independent and exhaustive components: the scatter within subgroups, and the scatter between subgroups. (See Menzel, 1974 for the details of this analysis. It is comparable to analysis of variance but it can also be derived from the familiar Pythagorean formula for distance.) It can be seen that between-subgroup scatter is much larger than within-subgroup scatter, and that the former component explains most of the overall group's behavior. (However, each of these component processes follows essentially the same time trend as was seen in Figure 8 for the group process.) Animals who had been raised together did get farther apart when food was involved than they would have otherwise, and on some trials they went in opposite directions from each other if that was the only way to get food, but, *relatively speaking*, they still tended to stay closer to each other than to members of the other subgroups and to rejoin each other more rapidly after a separation. Naturally, not all pairs of animals within a given subgroup showed equally strong affiliative tendencies and not all subgroups were (internally) equally cohesive entities. Just as the group as a whole is a less strongly coupled subsystem than the subgroups which compose it, so also these

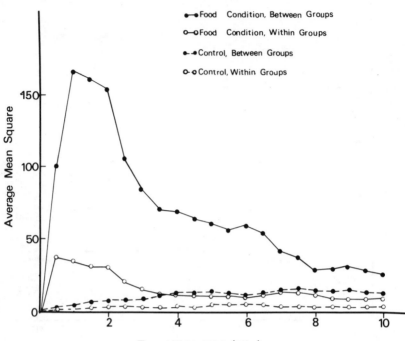

Fig. 9. Partitioning overall group dispersion in each test condition into two independent components: the scatter of animals within each of the three subgroups, and the scatter between the centroids
of the three subgroups. These components are strictly comparable to within-groups and between-
groups effects in analysis of variance.

subgroups tend to be less strongly coupled subsystems than the pairwise relationships which compose them.

A comparison of the distances between each pair of individuals under each
of several conditions revealed another interesting fact. Despite the large distance
scores in the food tests and the small distance scores in the other tests, the
relative size of these scores for the various pairs of animals were highly correlated (Pearson r, about .90) across test conditions. In other words, the structure
of the overall group and the general relationships between the parts of this whole
(i.e., individual animals) tend to remain the same despite large variations in the
absolute size (i.e., spatial area covered) of the configuration. The metric distances between an animal and his companions are probably much less important
than ordinal considerations—such as: Who is my nearest neighbor? Is he or
anyone else between me and my goal? Can I get there before they do? Where will
this put me then in relation to the group's general line of travel?

Conclusions

As far as we know, no monkeys or apes sit around the campfire in the evening like Kipling's wolves, let alone sit around a U.N. conference table for 24 years like people, to define what they mean by aggression or draw up formal social contracts or hold court against those who transgress the law of the pack. On the other hand, there can be little question that their social systems are orderly and predictable (i.e., lawful) and that under ordinary conditions they work. Would a group of chimpanzees that had been trained in sign language like the Gardners' Washoe, but otherwise raised in isolation from their kind, have any better basis for group cooperation and resolution of social conflicts than would normal "untrained" group-living chimpanzees? Except in very limited and contrived experimental environments, I doubt it. Would a society created from scratch by such language-trained animals differ substantially from that of animals without language? Again, I doubt it. In my opinion, formal language and species-specific displays are at best surface aspects of group communication and coordination; the core of our problem lies elsewhere.

Before there can be group communication, there must first of all be a sharing of goals, in the sense that each member of a group pursues his own goals only by taking into account the goals of the others, not only as facts about the world but as potential aspects of his own goal hierarchy. In other words, the social unit formed of many individuals in interaction must become a goal-seeking system in its own right (MacKay, 1969, p. 116). In primates, and unquestionably in man, this presupposes long-term familiarity with others of the same species, if not long-term familiarity with a particular social group and particular companions within that group (Miller, this volume; van Lawick-Goodall, 1973; Rogers, 1973).

Secondly, once social goal seeking has commenced, each individual must attach positive value to anything that brings the group up to date, to match the current state of the field of activity. In short, one of the goals of each individual must be to share information with the others, bringing their value systems and "cognitive maps" into agreement.

Finally, as the number of individuals in the group increases and the resources for which they strive (e.g., pieces of food) come in increasingly smaller packages which cannot be shared by all and which are distributed rather thinly over the home range, complete equality between individuals and close spatial cohesion between animals becomes impossible. To organize the goals of all individuals into a compatible group goal complex, each individual must do something a bit different if the whole is to form a stable system. Status hierarchies, roles, central coordination, and social rules of some sort become necessary.

All of these basic aspects of group communication are clearly present in many species that possess very different forms of ethological displays and no display systems that a linguist would call a real language. Speaking most generally, there is an infinitely large number of systems of individual information processing and social information exchange that might accomplish the biologically and socially "correct" results. (This is not, of course, to imply that any species can use any of these systems or that species do not differ in how many different systems they might use interchangably.) From the standpoint of Chomskian structural linguistics one system might seem more "elegant" and "sophisticated" than another, but from the standpoint of biological function and adaptiveness it is the results that count. For human beings, verbal language obviously provides a highly efficient mechanism for expressing to others (at least to those who share the same language and the same basic experiences) almost anything one cares to express. However, it is equally true that almost anything that man can say verbally he can also convey by other means as well, and that in our not infrequent instances of failure of verbal communication there is often nothing so persuasive as a good old-fashioned primate embrace or kick in the rump.

The discussion can now be brought to bear specifically on the problem of communication of aggression. In a free-ranging society in which the animals know each other extremely well and share most of their goals and seem intelligent enough and socially attentive enough to anticipate well in advance the sorts of situations which are likely to give rise to conflict, it is relatively rare that *specialized* communicative signals are necessary. The specialized communicative signals of most interest to ethologists and linguistically oriented psychologists seem to provide whatever *additional* information is required to reduce the uncertainty of the group (or of a particular individual) in cases where the situation would otherwise still be unclear. Waterhouse and Waterhouse (1973) estimated from their study of a zoo colony of rhesus monkeys that in adults almost 70% of all aggressive and dominance interactions involve no physical contact or obvious displays at all—they consist of a subordinate animal simply moving off or giving way to a dominant before anything further happens. It is only for the young of this species (as for human children) that interactions seem so unsubtle that about the only way to assess dominance is to observe direct physical conflicts (which usually center around preferred objects).

From the observations presented in this chapter and from my own studies of wild macaques (Menzel, 1966, 1969) and from Chance's (1970) analysis of group "attention structure," I suspect that Waterhouse and Waterhouse have, if anything, underestimated their monkeys. Their figures reflect our human limitations as observers as much as they reflect the behavior of the subjects. Monkeys and apes seem to be constantly taking account of their own position, the lay of the land, and the actions of many other individuals (especially close friends and those more dominant than they)—and adjusting their actions accordingly—long before any emotion-provoking situation develops. More often than not it is impossible for an observer to judge at any one instant whether or not a given animal is avoiding or approaching or giving way to one particular object or conspecific. Adult males in particular seem sometimes to actively inhibit emotional displays. In many cases the interpretation of a specific behavior as a sign of aggression or submission must rest on observation of long sequences of events, sometimes over a period of days (Hebb & Thompson, 1954) or across several appropriately varied experimental conditions (Menzel, 1966).

In short, to fully understand the communicative capacities of animals it is necessary in the last analysis for the human observer to become almost as familiar with them as individuals as they are familiar with each other, and in effect to view his study as a process of two-way communication between himself and the animals. In my opinion, two-way communication is improved when we stop viewing ourselves as superior beings and total outsiders. Rather than attempt to train animals to use our systems, or view their systems as a primitive form of our own, perhaps it would be best to proceed like an anthropologist studying a new culture and attempt first of all to learn what systems the animals are already using with each other.

References

Altmann, S. A. The structure of primate social communication. In S. A. Altmann (Ed.), *Social communication among primates*. Chicago: University of Chicago Press, 1967, pp. 325–362.

Ashby, W. R. Information flows within coordinated systems. In J. Rose (Ed.), *Progress of cybernetics*. New York: Gordon & Breach, 1970, pp. 57–64.

Bastian, J., & Bermant, G. Animal communication: an overview and conceptual analysis. In G. Bermant (Ed.), *Perspectives on animal behavior*. Glenview, Ill.: Scott, Foresman & Co., 1973, pp. 280–306.

Brown, J. L., & Orians, G. H. Spacing patterns in mobile animals. *Annual Review of Ecology and Systematics* 1970, *1*, 239–262.

Carpenter, C. R. *Naturalistic behavior of nonhuman primates*. University Park: Pennsylvania State University Press, 1964.

Chance, M. R. A., & Jolly, C. *Social groups of monkeys, apes and men*. New York: E. P. Dutton, 1970.

Fouts, R. Use of guidance in teaching sign language to a chimpanzee. *Journal of Comparative and Physiological Psychology*, 1972, *80*, 515–522.

Gardner, B. T., & Gardner, R. A. Two-way communication with an infant chimpanzee. In A. Schrier & F. Stollnitz (Eds.), *Behavior of nonhuman primates* (Vol. 4). New York: Academic Press, 1971, pp. 117–185.

Hall, K. R. L. Aggression in monkey and ape societies. In P. C. Jay (Ed.), *Primates: studies in adaptation and variability*. New York: Holt, Rinehart and Winston, 1968, pp. 149–161.

Hebb, D. O. Temperament in chimpanzees: I. Method of analysis. *Journal of Comparative and Physiological Psychology*, 1949, *42*, 192–206.

Hebb, D. O. & Thompson, W. R. The social significance of animal studies. In G. Lindzey (Ed.), *Handbook of social psychology* (Vol. 1). Cambridge: Addison-Wesley, 1954, pp. 532–561.

Hockett, C. F. Logical considerations in the study of animal communication. In W. E. Lanyon & W. N. Tavolga (Eds.), *Animal sounds and communication*. Washington: American Institute of Biological Sciences, 1960, pp. 392–430.

Kawai, M. On the rank system in a natural group of Japanese monkeys: I. Basic rank and dependent rank. *Primates*, 1958, *1*, 111–148.

Krushinskii, L. V. Animal behavior: its normal and abnormal development, New York: Consultants Bureau, 1960.

Kummer, H. Dominance versus possession: an experiment on hamadryas baboons. In E. W. Menzel (Ed.), *Symposia of the Fourth International Congress of Primatology* (Vol. 1). *Precultural primate behavior*. Basel: Karger, 1973, pp. 226–231.

Lorenz, K. *On aggression* New York: Harcourt, 1966.

MacKay, D. M. *Information, mechanism and meaning*. Cambridge: Massachusetts Institute of Technology Press, 1969.

Marler, P. Communication in monkeys and apes. In I. Devore (Ed.), *Primate behavior*. New York: Holt, Rinehart & Winston, 1965, pp. 544–584.

Marler, P. Aggregation and dispersal: Two functions in primate communication. In P. C. Jay (Ed.), *Primates: studies in adaptation and variability. New York: Holt, Rinehart & Winston, 1968, pp. 429–438.*

Mason, W. A. Determinants of social behavior in young chimpanzees. In A. Schrier, H. Harlow & F. Stollnitz (Eds.), *Behavior of nonhuman primates* (Vol. 2). New York: Academic Press, 1965, pp. 335–364.

McBride, G. A general theory of social organization and behavior. *University of Queensland Veterinary Science Papers*, 1964, *1*, 75–110.

Menzel, E. W. Responsiveness to objects in free-ranging Japanese monkeys. *Behaviour*, 1966, *26*, 130–150.

Menzel, E. W. Naturalistic and experimental approaches to primate behavior. In E. Willems & H. Raush (Eds.), *Naturalistic viewpoints in psychology*. New York: Holt, Rinehart & Winston, 1969, pp. 78–121.

Menzel, E. W. Communication about the environment in a group of young chimpanzees. *Folia primatologica*, 1971, *15*, 220–232.

Menzel, E. W. Leadership and communication in young chimpanzees. In E. W. Menzel (Ed.), *Symposia of the Fourth International Congress of Primatology* (Vol. 1). *Precultural primate behavior. Basel: Karger, 1973, pp. 192–225.*

Menzel, E. W. A group of young chimpanzees in a one-acre field. In A. Schrier & F. Stollnitz (Eds.), *Behavior of nonhuman primates* (Vol. 5). New York: Academic Press, 1974, pp. 83–153.

Mowrer, O. H. Learning theory and the symbolic processes. New York: Wiley, 1960.

Olson, D. R. Language and thought: Aspects of a cognitive theory of semantics. *Psychological Review*, 1970, *77*, 257–273.

Pavlov, I. P. *Conditioned reflexes* Oxford: Oxford University Press, 1927.

Premack, D. On the assessment of language competence in the chimpanzee. In A. Schrier & F. Stollnitz (Eds.), *Behavior of nonhuman primates* (Vol. 4). New York: Academic Press, 1971, pp. 185–228.

Rogers, C. M. Implications of a primate early rearing experiment for the concept of culture. In E. W. Menzel (Ed.), *Symposia of the Fourth International Congress of Primatology* (Vol. 1). *Precultural primate behavior*. Basel: Karger, 1973, pp. 185–191.

Rosenblueth, A., Wiener, N., & Bigelow, J. Behavior, purpose and teleology. *Philosophy of Science* 1943, *10*, 18–24.

Rumbaugh, D., Gill, T. V., and von Glaserfeld, E. C. Reading and sentence completion by a chimpanzee. *Science*, 1973, *182*, 731–733.

Sade, D. S. Some aspects of parent-offspring and sibling relations in a group of rhesus monkeys, with a discussion of grooming. *American Journal of Physical Anthropology*, 1965, *23*, 1–18.

Thorpe, W. H. The comparison of vocal communication in animals and man. In R. A. Hinde (Ed.), *Nonverbal communication*. Cambridge: Cambridge University Press, 1972, pp. 27–48.

Tinbergen, N. *The study of instinct*. London: Clarendon Press, 1951.

Tinbergen, N. War and peace in animals and man. *Science*, 1968, *160*, 1411–1418.

Tinklepaugh, O. L. An experimental study of representative factors in monkeys. *Journal of Comparative Psychology*, 1928, *8*, 197–236.

van Lawick-Goodall, J. Cultural elements in a chimpanzee community. In E. W. Menzel (Ed.), *Symposia of the Fourth International Congress of Primatology* (Vol 1). *Precultural primate behavior*. Basel: Karger, 1973, pp. 144–184.

von Frisch, K. The dancing bees (Isle, trans.). New York: Harcourt, Brace, 1955.

Waterhouse, M. J., & Waterhouse, H. B. Primate ethology and human social behavior. In R. Michael & J. H. Crook (Eds.), *Comparative ecology and behavior of primates*. London: Academic Press, 1973, pp. 669–688.

Wynne-Edwards, V. C. *Animal dispersion in relation to social behavior*. New York: Hafner, 1962.

CHAPTER 6

Nonverbal Expressions of Aggression and Submission in Social Groups of Primates[1]

Robert E. Miller

Department of Psychiatry
School of Medicine
University of Pittsburgh
Pittsburgh, Pennsylvania

Aggression and violence have both fascinated and repelled mankind since earliest recorded history. All of our histories, and our great legacy of drama and literature, are chronicles of war, civil strife, criminal acts of murder and rape, and accounts of man's inhumanity to man. The figures of history are, for the most part, men of violence—Alexander the Great, Genghis Khan, the Caesars, Napoleon, Wellington, and Hitler, to mention only a few. Those who have dared to speak out against aggression and to advocate that man use persuasion, reason, logic, and ethics to settle our human differences have, more often than not, been themselves imprisoned and tortured, burned at the stake, crucified, or certified to be insane for their heretical contention that aggression is not the only way to achieve happiness for the greatest number of people.

Perhaps it is because of the realization that our known weaponry could destroy the entire world many times over, or because of the constant exposure to news of violent crime, riot, and war; in any event, aggressive behavior has become an urgent subject of study by scientists throughout the world. Social scientists, neurologists, and biologists are attempting to uncover the causes and to suggest treatments for aggression.

[1] The experimental investigations reported in this paper were supported by a research grant (MH-00487) from the National Institute of Mental Health, United States Public Health Service, and by the Commonwealth of Pennsylvania.

In our attempts to understand the roots of aggression, it is quite natural that we have begun to examine the behavior of simpler organisms first and then to try and extrapolate from these species to the aggressive acts of man. Comparative studies are a tried and proven method of arriving at some fundamentally significant scientific theories, and animal models have been of tremendous importance to the development of many fields, e.g., immunology, genetics, physiology, etc. Clearly, many worthwhile experiments will continue to utilize animal subjects to trace specific neuronal pathways, hormonal influences, and biogenic amine levels in the expression of aggressive behavior.

I am not convinced that a comparative analysis will be able to resolve the "nature–nurture" controversy which, with respect to aggression, has been provoked by Lorenz in his book *On Aggression* (1966) and the Ardrey books, *African Genesis* (1961), *The Territorial Imperative* (1966), and *The Social Contract* (1970). Each of these books has attempted to demonstrate or to convince on the basis of somewhat selective materials obtained primarily from ethological studies of animal social behavior that man is innately aggressive, that his killer instincts cannot be controlled, and that only through massive sublimation activities such as sports can we avert or subdue our interpersonal aggressive drives. The nature point of view has been vigorously opposed by many such as Montagu and his collaborators in *Man and Aggression* (1968) and Russell and Russell in *Violence: Monkeys and Man* (1968).

The generalization from animal behavior to that of human societies is, at best, only tentative. More immediately relevant information would seem to deny the innate view of aggression in that cultural anthropologists have studied a number of primitive human societies (e.g., Pygmies, Hopi Indians, Eskimos) where overt aggression is extremely rare and where noncompetitive cooperation is the social norm.

It seems that a revival of the old innate-environmental discussion, while it raises polemics and proliferates publications, cannot contribute effectively to the study of aggression and its causes. As in the case of racial differences in intelligence, it can only raise again what has repeatedly proven to be an essentially untestable question.

The study of our closest phylogenetic relatives, the nonhuman primates, should provide some clues as to the quality and quantity of aggression that these species have evolved and their mechanisms for dealing with aggressive behavior. It is interesting to discover in reading the literature of the past 30 years that our concept of the brutal nature of the infrahuman primates has been drastically revised as more and more field studies of these fascinating animals have been completed. I suppose that it is a commentary on my own age that I remember vividly the annual visits of Martin and Osa Johnson to the small town in western New York where I grew up. They always appeared at a local theater to show their films of Darkest Africa, and their visit was of such an occasion that a school holiday was declared so that the children could attend their film lecture. They appeared on the stage in their safari garb with riding breeches and knee-high boots and always carried a spear or elephant-hide shield or some other dramatic display and narrated their spectacular wildlife films. It is hard to realize that only 35 years ago large portions of the continent of Africa were virtually unexplored and that it did take considerable ingenuity and courage to undertake an expedition to these remote areas. Their shots of the great apes, particularly the gorilla, showed an awesomely fierce and frightening beast—King Kong in the flesh. Today we know from extensive studies of the gorilla by Schaller (1963) that they are really timid and quite gentle creatures in spite of their immense size and incredible strength. They enjoy the most amiable social relationships with their fellows, freely mingling in small groups. These primates, at least, seem to display few innate aggressive tendencies in their natural habitat. Similarly, the chimpanzee as described by Goodall (1965) and Reynolds (1965) were found to be generally friendly and good-tempered animals. There are occasional neighborhood spats but serious fighting is relatively rare.

The early scientific studies of infrahuman primates seemed to confirm the prejudice that these animals were fierce and unrelentingly aggressive. The study of captive baboons in the London Zoo by Zuckerman (1932) depicted these animals as savage fighters that attacked and killed almost indiscriminately, even maiming infants in their mothers' arms. Despite the adequate supply of food and the safety from predation that the zoo afforded, these primates were intractably hostile. The pioneer of primate ethology, C. R. Carpenter, who performed many of the early studies of both New and Old World monkeys in their natural habitat during the 1930s, succeeded in moving a group of rhesus monkeys from their natural habitat in India to an island, Cayo Santiago, off the coast of Puerto Rico in 1938. There the animals were released and permitted to form natural groups. The initial observations of these animals revealed that there were quite high levels of aggression that occurred both within and between troops. Perhaps one of the reasons these monkeys were particularly violent immediately after their release is that they had just endured a very difficult and traumatic period of capture, transfer to holding pens aboard ship, and a rough voyage around the world. Further, the animals were not all members of the same group in India and were, therefore, strangers to each other in many cases.

While the first few years of study of this transplanted group of monkeys suggested that there was a considerable amount of aggressive behavior, particularly on the part of one very aggressive male, Diablo, continuing observation over the course of the past 30 years has revealed that these animals and their descendants have settled into a relatively stable social organization consisting of several bands of monkeys, each with its own home range on the island (Koford, 1963, 1965). While quarreling and fighting does occur, particularly in the vicinity of the provisioning sites, there is no indication that intractable, savage fighting is a regular feature of social encounters either within or between groups.

Since the middle 1950s there have been many extensive field studies of a variety of primate species in Asia, in Africa, and in Central and South America. These investigations have, for the first time, detailed the extraordinary social adaptations of the infrahuman primates and have revealed the significant differences not only between the various species, but also within the same species living under differing ecological conditions. The advance in our knowledge about animal behavior and particularly about primate behavior during the past 25 years is really remarkable. The more we have learned about these intriguing animals, interacting with each other in their natural habitat, the less they appear to be brutally aggressive or—in the case of the smaller and more tameable species—simple, amusing clowns. With the exception of the provisioned troops of animals such as the rhesus on Cayo Santiago, the chimpanzees, studied by Jane Goodall in the Gombe Stream Reserve, and the Japanese macaques studied and fed by the Japanese Primate Center, the field studies have shown that the infrahuman primates, just like all the rest of us, spend the greater part of their days in the serious business of working for a living, caring for their young, and defending themselves from predators. Each member of the troop must forage every day of his life from the moment he is weaned to the day of his death to provide himself with sufficient nutrients to maintain health and energy.

All of the infrahuman primates studied to date are social animals, that is, they live in close and continuous contact with conspecifics. However, the size and structure of the social grouping varies greatly from species to species and even within the same species in different ecological conditions. While gibbons form "humanlike" family groupings consisting of a male and his mate with their offspring (Carpenter, 1940), rhesus (Koford, 1965; Lindburg, 1971; Kaufman, 1967; Southwick, 1969), baboons (Hall & Devore, 1965; Devore & Hall, 1965), howler monkeys (Carpenter, 1965), Japanese macaques (Imanishi, 1957), and many other species congregrate in troops which may number in the hundreds. In many of these groups the animals, especially the females, may spend their entire lives within the same troop and remain permanently within a restricted geographical home range. The anthropoid apes, in particular chimpanzees (Goodall, 1965) and gorillas (Schaller, 1963), seem to form more loosely knit groupings and individuals are able to move from group to group with little difficulty.

A feature of most primate groupings is a social dominance hierarchy. While the behavioral expression and the degree of control exerted by the most dominant animal shows considerable variability from species to species, close observation reveals that some individuals are accorded unusual respect by the other members of the group and that they often control movements of the troop during the foraging expedition, limit the aggressive activities within the group, and coordinate defense of the troop against predators or intrusions by other groups of the same species. The most dominant animal is generally an adult male, or, in some cases, a group of two or three adult males who cooperate and share the leadership position. It is clear from many studies and in many species of animals from the rat to primates (Rose, Holaday, & Bernstein, 1971; Moyer, 1971) that the male hormone, testosterone, is a factor influencing aggressive behavior. In a classic series of studies on castrate male and female chimpanzees, Birch and Clark (1946, 1950; Clark and Birch, 1945, 1946) demonstrated that the administration of testosterone increased assertive behaviors in both male and female subjects. Estrogens, on the other hand, reduced aggressiveness in the male castrate but increased aggressiveness in the female, probably due to the irritation accompanying the engorgement of the sex skin. It has been found that prenatal administration of androgens to female fetal monkeys has a profound and persistent effect on the social behavior, producing an aggressive and masculinized female (Goy, 1968). Joslyn (1973) has recently shown that young female monkeys treated with testosterone from 6.5 to 14.5 months of age were able to attain dominance over their male companions and, further, that these changes in assertiveness persisted for at least a year after androgen treatments were discontinued. In another study, Mirsky (1955) found neither androgens nor estrogens had any significant effects on social dominance status in older rhesus monkeys castrated 2 months prior to treatment.

While maleness is clearly a factor in the establishment and maintenance of social dominance in primate groupings, it is also the case that adult females may achieve a social position within the group which commands deference not only from their subordinate female companions but also from the lower ranking males in the group. As it turns out, the relative social status of the female, at least in the macaques, is a crucial variable in the determination of the position her sons will ultimately achieve within the group. Sons of high-ranking mothers achieve high rank within their own peer group and ultimately, as they grow up, within the larger group of animals (Koyama, 1967; Kawamura, 1958; Koford, 1963, Sade, 1967). Furthermore, Sade found that the female offspring of rhesus monkeys as they became adults almost invariably ranked just below their mothers, even dominating the older females which had been present during their adolescence. It should not be assumed from these data that relative dominance is exclusively a genetic factor; in fact, the studies suggest that it is the communicative and protective behaviors of the dominant mother that enable her offspring to acquire very early in life an assertiveness over their less favored peers.

Social dominance behavior is manifested primarily through expressions of dominance and submission within the group. In the rhesus monkey there are a number of facial expressions, postures, movements, and vocalizations that are associated with social position and that, when evoked during social exchanges, tend to settle differences in priority to food, spatial location within the group, access to receptive females, etc. The overlord in a group of baboons or rhesus monkeys or Japanese macaques has a repertoire of graded threat expressions that can be used to intimidate subordinate animals when they invade his social space, create a disturbance within the group, or challenge his position of priority. A simple stare at the offender will often suffice to elicit a fear grimace and hasty withdrawal, but in more extreme circumstances, the more dominant animal may give an open-mouth threat, a shoulder-bobbing display, a quick charge, and, if he succeeds in catching the offender, a cuff or bite. Similarly, there is a series of expressions which reveal social submission: the fear grimace, sexual presentation (even by males), precipitous escape, and, when physically attacked, a high-pitched screeching vocalization. These communicative displays related to social dominance status have been described in detail by a number of ethologists (van Hooff, 1967; Moynihan, 1967; Ploog, 1967; Andrew, 1963).

In an early paper on social dominance in primates, Maslow (1940) presented a very bleak picture of the nature of social interactions among the Old World monkeys:

> Catarrhine dominance is rough, brutal, and aggressive; it is of the nature of a powerful, persistent, selfish urge that expresses itself in ferocious bullying, fighting, and sexual aggression. The subordinate animal is usually afraid of the dominant animal and is frequently completely terror-stricken and cowed. These animals never show anything that could possibly be called friendship for their fellows. (P. 316.)

In fact, however, when one looks carefully at Maslow's data, one sees that these damning conclusions were drawn from a very atypical sample of subjects. The paired comparisons were made between animals not only of different sexes but of widely differing ages, and even more specifically, of five different species that were pitted against one another. Subsequent field and laboratory data do not bear out these very pessimistic characterizations—in fact, most species of primates seem to live in relatively compatible groups where there may be some minor quarreling among neighbors and, occasionally, conflict between adjoining groups whose home ranges may overlap, but there is rarely serious fighting leading to injury and death. It is quite remarkable that the social dominance structure in a group of primates in the field may persist for many years without serious disruption and some males may retain their dominant position within the group well past their prime of physical power even when young, stronger males are present within the group. It is quite true that aggressive behavior may be augmented by various ecological or experimenter-induced variables but, under ordinary conditions, the infrahuman primates and especially the anthropoid apes seem to live in relative social harmony.

There are some variables which drastically augment aggression in troops of monkeys. Southwick (1969), in a review of his several field studies of rhesus in India, has emphasized the ecological factors in inter- and intragroup aggression. Social groups inhabiting forest areas were found to be considerably more peaceable than those located near agricultural fields and human villages. The rhesus troops that lived in and around a Hindu temple and depended upon tourists' and worshippers' offerings for their food were very belligerent, and fighting with serious wounding was observed. By far the most persistant and savage aggression, at least 50 times the level observed in forest troops, was reported in a captive group of 17 animals that Southwick established in Calcutta. It is also of interest to note that the social patterning of aggressive behavior differed markedly as a function of the ecology of the territory. In rural groups, adult males, adult females, and juveniles were equally likely to initiate an aggressive behavior. Adult males were most likely to threaten or attack adult females (32%) or juveniles (32%) with fewer aggressive acts against adult males (21%) or infants (16%). Rural females aggressed against other females (41%) or juveniles (41%), more rarely against adult males (12%), and infrequently against infants (6%). Juveniles behaved aggressively only with their peers (94%), only occasionally threatening adult females (6%) and never adult males or infants.

In the more crowded and socially disorganized setting of the temple, however, patterns of aggressive behavior changed markedly, with adult males displaying the most aggression, 64%; adult females, 29%; and juveniles only 8%. Temple males directed most of their agonistic behavior toward other males (35%) and juveniles (32.5%), females and infants receiving much less of their aggressive behavior (17.5% and 15%, respectively). Temple females directed their attacks at adult males (44%) and other females (33%), infants and juveniles receiving 11% in each case. Juveniles in the temple groups divided their aggressive attacks between other juveniles, 40%; adult females, 40%; and infants, 20%.

In the captive group males and females were about equal in the aggressive behavior (46.7% and 44% respectively), while juveniles were responsible for only 9% of aggressive behavior. The patterning of aggression in the captive group was similar to that of the temple groups except for adult females who aggressed principally against juveniles (61%). The intensive study of the captive group in Calcutta permitted the study of additional ecological variables. On the premise that competition for food would increase agonistic behavior, Southwick reduced available food by 25% with the result that agonistic behavior *decreased* significantly. A 50% reduction in food produced a still lower level of agonistic behavior. Not only was aggressive behavior diminished but there were also reductions in other social behaviors including sexual behavior, grooming, and play. In another set of experiments, Southwick investigated the effects of space on aggression. When cage space was reduced by 1/2, there was a significant increase in levels of aggression. Finally, Southwick introduced strangers into the Calcutta group with a most interesting result. The introduction of two new juveniles increased agonistic interactions by 400%. When two new adult females were added, aggressive behavior increased 1000%, and the introduction of two strange adult males increased agonistic interactions by 800%. It was particularly interesting to note that strangers were attacked primarily by residents of the group corresponding to their own class, i.e., juveniles attacked juvenile strangers, female adults attacked female strangers, and the attacks on strange males were initiated by resident males.

Other studies have confirmed that changes in group composition have marked effects on social behavior and, particularly, on levels of aggression; Carpenter (1942) and Bernstein (1964) have shown that removal of adult males from established social groups creates social disharmony and a reduction in the group's spatial movement. Perhaps the most dramatic confirmation of the introduction of strangers to an established social group was described by Hall (1964). An adult male and female baboon were added to an existing social group of 17 baboons in a zoo enclosure. Although the existing colony had lived in social harmony for many months, the introduction of adult strangers created totally chaotic conditions. Ultimately, after savage fighting, most of the animals were killed or died of their wounds.

One of the most interesting examples of the impact of environmental factors on the social relationships of primates is provided by the studies on the common langur of India. Jay (1963) observed the behavior of these monkeys in northern India. Her descriptions indicate that the animals live in bisexual groups of from 5 to 50 individuals but she noted that male-only groups ranging from 2 to 10 individuals were also found. The bisexual groups resisted the attempts of males living on the periphery to rejoin the social group. There was little aggressive behavior within the bisexual groups, and the picture is one of strong intragroup cohesion and a reasonably low level of aggressive behavior.

Sugiyama (1967) studied the langur in Southern India with a drastically different result. Here single adult males maintained a harem of adult females with infant and juvenile offspring. There were also bands of adult males and adolescent males in the area which had no access to females. These bands of males would, on occasion, rush toward and aggressively attack a harem leader, either killing him or chasing him from his female consorts. Typically, the dominant male from the unisex group then chased off his male comrades, who had assisted him in the coup d'etat, and took charge of the female harem for his exclusive possession. The most bizarre aspect of this accession of power occurred when the new leader, with no interference from the adult females in the harem, then selectively attacked and killed the male offspring of the former overlord—female infants and juveniles were spared. Through some biological mechanism, the adult females then came into estrus and were impregnated by the new leader even when the change in succession did not coincide with the usual breeding season.

In yet another study of the langur, Ripley (1967) conducted a field study in Ceylon. Four troops living in a cleared forest area were studied in 1962–1963. As with Jay's animals, these were mixed bisexual groups with juveniles and infants. While intragroup aggression was not marked, intertroop hostility was very high. In some instances raiding parties from one group would cross into territorial ranges of one or more groups, eliciting fighting and chasing from each of the invaded troops in turn. Ripley noted that the size of range compressed the population of langurs, thus increasing the likelihood of intertroop encounters.

In one species of monkey, then, the available data suggest that in northern India they are quite peaceable, in southern India extremely aggressive with an entirely different form of social organization, and, in Ceylon, highly antagonistic in intergroup encounters.

We have concentrated so far on aggressive interactions in primate groups since this is the organizing topic of this colloquium. It is important to point out, however, that there are strong and persistent affiliative tendencies that strengthen positive relationships within the group. Early in life, as Harlow, Rowland, & Griffin (1964) have demonstrated, the infant–mother and infant–peer relationships are extremely powerful social forces—crucial to the adequate social development of the monkey. As is well known (Mitchell, 1968; Harlow *et al.*, 1964), the infant rhesus monkey deprived of mother and peers suffers irreparable social pathology. As the infant begins the detachment process from its mother, peer relationships begin to play an important role. Within the first year of life the infants show differential play patterns as a function of sex (Seay, 1966), males engaging in vigorous rough-and-tumble play while females display more decorous forms of play. It is likely that the mock fighting, chasing, and mutual grooming which occupy the energies of juveniles determine the long-term relationships among the future leaders of the group. Adults, including the dominant males, are extremely tolerant of the playful activities of the young, permitting them to roll and jump boisterously on and around them. In adults, sexual behavior also serves to strengthen attachments and perhaps the strongest affiliative force in social groups of primates is that of mutual grooming. Grooming strengthens and confirms dominance relationships—subordinates grooming their social superiors more than vice versa (Sparks, 1969). During rest periods between meals, the primates spend a great deal of time in grooming behavior—a ''friendly'' and benign form of social interaction.

The field studies of infrahuman primates have contributed in a major way to our understanding of social, developmental, and ecological factors and their impact on the social group. It is clear that early laboratory and zoo studies produced a somewhat distorted view of social organization, particularly in that they suggested that these animals were extraordinarily aggressive. Yet, with the perspectives afforded by field studies, laboratory experiments on primates have an important place in research on aggression and other social behaviors. It is possible only in the laboratory setting to conduct some of the kinds of studies that focus on specific developmental, physiological, and hormonal factors which are significant to normal social development. The contributions of Harlow and his associates (Harlow *et al.*, 1964) to the understanding of the importance of early social relationships for the subsequent social adequacy of the adult monkey could not have been performed in the field. An isolated infant monkey simply would not survive in a natural setting, and thus only through the nurturance and protection of a modern laboratory would we have the insights into developmental phenomena that these studies have afforded. Field and laboratory studies should be complementary, each providing to the other the special advantages they can offer. Thus I would like now to move from our brief overview of studies in the natural habitat to some work we have conducted in our laboratory located in a high-rise building in an urban center—not even remotely resembling the natural setting for rhesus monkeys.

We became interested in social dominance behavior in laboratory-housed rhesus monkeys as a result of some investigations we were conducting on the effects of social interaction on discrimination learning (Miller & Murphy, (1956*b*).

Ten young male monkeys were subjected to dominance tests in the Wisconsin General Test Apparatus. Each of the monkeys was paired with every other monkey in WGTA, and over a series of trials the two members of the pair competed for food incentives such as bits of apple and raisin. Relative dominance was assessed in terms of the amount of food each animal obtained on these trials. The series of tests was repeated 12 times over a period of 20 months. The result revealed that social dominance status was a highly reliable phenomenon over this period of almost 2 years, and, in fact, the last 6 tests in the series showed an invariant relationship in social dominance (Miller & Murphy, 1956*a*).

We have also studied the social dominance relationships in monkeys subjected to a competitive perching task (Miller and Banks, 1962). The animals were first trained to sit on a 4-inch square wooden perch elevated from a grid floor. A conditioned stimulus consisting of a 1200-cycle tone was presented 6 seconds prior to and overlapping with a 2-second shock delivered through the grid. The monkey could avoid the painful shock by climbing on the perch within 6 seconds of CS onset. The stimuli were not response-terminated—i.e., the tone continued for a full 8 seconds and shock was present on the grid during the final 2 seconds of tone even though the animal was safely on the perch. When all of the monkeys within a group had attained an acquisition criterion for the perching response, they were placed in the apparatus in pairs. Since the perch was only large enough to accomodate a single monkey, the unsuccessful competitor was forced to remain on the grid and receive the unpleasant shock. Every animal was paired with every other animal in his test group, 15 trials were presented to each pairing, and this series of tests was repeated 12 times. Two groups of postadolescent male rhesus monkeys were subjected to the competitive perching dominance tests. In the first group of 6 animals there was a total of 180 pairings tested in the 12 dominance series. Even in this very competitive situation where the loser was required to accept a painful shock on each trial, only 11 fights occurred, and all but 3 of those were seen in the first 4 roundrobin series. In the remaining 169 pairings only expressive threats and submissive gestures were utilized by the pairs to make dominance determinations (Figure 1). In the second group of 8 monkeys, there were 33 fights in the 336 pairings. These fights were, once

GROUP I SOCIAL DOMINANCE HIERARCHIES

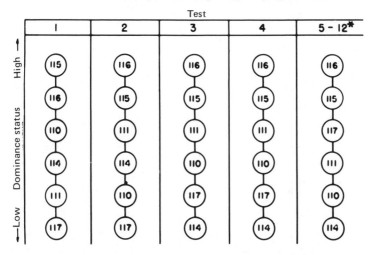

Fig. 1.   Social dominance status of a group of six monkeys over 12 dominance determinations. Social dominance was assessed by a competitive avoidance situation (Miller and Banks, 1962). The numbers within the circles are animal identification numbers. *Dominance was invariant for the final 8 dominance series.

again, seen in the early dominance series and dropped out rapidly as testing proceeded. There were some interesting individual differences in this second group of animals (Figure 2). Monkey #122 was a highly competitive and aggressive animal which contested vigorously for the perch and was involved in 60% of all fights observed. Number 126 was involved in 42% of the fights—primarily as a victim. He adopted an exaggerated submissive behavior—squealing and presenting to the dominant partner on each CS presentation. He would scuttle backward toward the animal on the perch, thrusting his buttocks into the dominant partner's face, a behavior which frequently elicited an attack. Monkey #124 developed a most interesting and unique behavior during the tests. While displaying high levels of submissive behavior, he would gradually approach the animal on the perch. Cautiously, he would move first one hand and then a foot onto the perch and slowly but surely, over the course of several trials, would crowd the more dominant animal to the grid. Once on the perch, he proved to be very tenacious and would resist all efforts of his partner to dislodge him. Surprisingly, this tactic was quite successful and the displaced animals threatened but rarely attacked #124 once he was on the perch.

In our next experiments (Miller, Murphy, & Mirsky, 1955), we decided to attempt to shift these stable dominance relationships by making the dominant animal fear and avoid a subordinate in a procedure we called interanimal conditioning (Murphy, Miller, & Mirsky, 1955). The same 10 animals that had

GROUP II COMPOSITE DOMINANCE RANKS

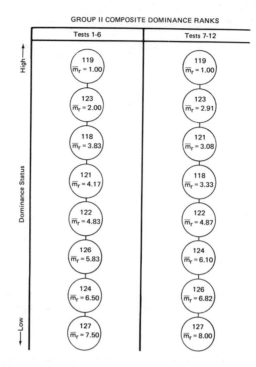

Fig. 2. Social dominance status of a group of eight rhesus monkeys. Dominance was measured in a competitive avoidance situation with 12 round-robin determinations. The top number in a circle is the animal identification number and the lower number is the ordinal rank of the individual over 6 consecutive determinations.

been tested in 12 food-getting dominance determinations were used in this study. The ninth-ranking male was chosen to be the target animal and we attempted to raise his dominance status. The procedure was very simple. The target animal (#53) was placed in one compartment of a two-compartment box, and the animal to be conditioned was placed in the other compartment. The compartments were separated by a one-way vision device. The target animal could never see the conditioning subject. However, the device allowed the subject to see the target animal during the conditioning trial. The floor of the conditioning subject's compartment was composed of a grid that could be electrified to produce a painful shock. Mounted on the one-way vision panel was a bar that permitted the conditioning subject to terminate the shock and, simultaneously, sight of the target animal. If a bar press response were made within 5 seconds of exposure of the target animal, the conditioning subject avoided shock and terminated sight of the target subject. Control trials were also administered with the target animal removed from his compartment and no shock delivered to the conditioning subject. Conditioning subjects were thus trained to an acquisition criterion to perform an avoidance response upon seeing the target subject but not to respond in the absence of the target subject. Conditioning was conducted in a sequential fashion. Conditioning sessions were conducted for 6 days, then food-getting dominance tests for the entire group were conducted the next week, followed in turn by further conditioning, etc.

The first week animal #57 was conditioned to avoid #53 and, in turn, other animals in the group were trained to avoid the target animal. As Figure 3 indicates, this avoidance training, where dominant monkeys learned to associate pain with sight of a particular individual, was reflected in changes in the social dominance hierarchy within the group. Ultimately, the target animal succeeded in achieving the fourth rank—a significant rise from his former position of ninth. The behavior of the target animal was interesting in that, as animals that had been superior to him in the past displayed fear grimaces, gaze aversion, and presentation gestures, the target monkey assumed a swaggering, prototypic dominance behavior. These social changes persisted throughout the conditioning period and for some weeks thereafter, but as the avoidance response extinguished in conditioned subjects, the target animal was again forcibly relegated to his former position of submissiveness.

A second study (Murphy and Miller, 1956), performed in a similar manner with naive animals, confirmed that interanimal conditioning was effective in reversing dominance relationships. Again, the original status was reestablished as the avoidance response was permitted to extinguish (Figure 4).

It was this early set of studies on social dominance that compelled us to embark on a new track, the study of nonverbal behaviors in monkey and man. It quickly became apparent that interactive encounters in a social dominance setting were mediated primarily through subtle glances, facial expressions, postures, and movements rather than intense and persistent fighting. In an attempt to clarify the nature and process involved in the expression of these cues and their reception and interpretation by other animals, we designed a series of studies to isolate nonverbal behaviors for detailed examination. Through a number of revisions, we finally developed a method, "cooperative conditioning," which seems to provide a useful tool in the investigation of nonverbal behavior (Miller, 1967).

In the "cooperative conditioning" paradigm each of the experimental subjects is first trained to perform a simple instrumental conditioned response, e.g., pressing a lever upon receipt of a visual stimulus in order to avoid the delivery of a noxious shock. Such conditioning is quite rapid in the rhesus monkey and the individual subjects rather quickly attain a criterion of acquisition. Since the animals are usually restrained in primate chairs during training and throughout the subsequent social tests, it is practicable to obtain measures of cardiac rate during testing periods.

When each of the animals has achieved the criterion of acquisition, the cooperative conditioning tests are begun. One subject is designated as the stimulus animal or "sender." It is placed in a conditioning chamber where the

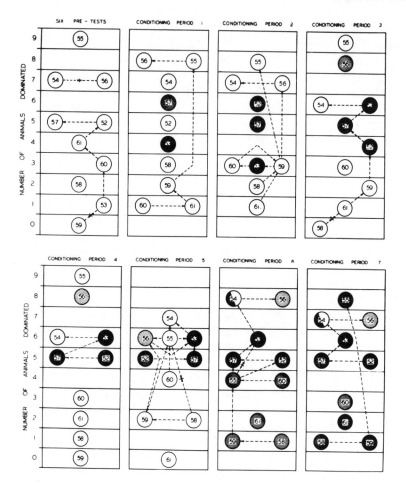

Fig. 3. Sociograms of the dominance relationships within a group of ten monkeys prior to and following successive conditioning periods. Dotted arrows indicate discrepancies in the dominance hierarchy, i.e., animals lower in the hierarchy which dominated animals higher in the group. Ties are shown by joined arrows. The solid black circle is the conditioned stimulus monkey, #53. Striped circles represent monkeys conditioned to avoid sight of #53 during the conditioning sessions that preceded these dominance determinations. Animal #56 was also conditioned to avoid monkey #54 in an attempt to reverse that dominance relationship. (From *Journal of Comparative and Physiological Psychology*, 1955, *48*, 394.)

conditioned stimulus can be presented during testing sessions and the appropriate reinforcements delivered but where the bars required to perform the instrumental response have been removed. A second trained subject, the "responder," is placed in a second test room which contains the appropriate bars to make an instrumental response and the reinforcement devices but which lacks the equipment required to present a conditioned stimulus. Thus, the stimulus animal is provided with the stimulus which indicates *when* an instrumental response is required but is unable to perform that response in the absence of the manipulandum. The responder has the bar which permits an appropriate response but lacks the stimulus which indicates when it is required. Both animals are equipped with reinforcement devices so that they share equally in the consequences of a conditioning trial. A closed circuit television camera is focused on the head and face of the stimulus subject and the picture is transmitted to the responder subject throughout the test session. Thus successful performance of a conditioned response requires that the "sender" display a facial expression upon receipt of a conditioned stimulus which is detected and properly interpreted by his paired "responder" which can then perform the instrumental response.

A series of previous studies (Miller, 1967; 1971) has shown that the cooperative conditioning method is a sensitive tool for the study of specific expressive cues and for the investigation of relationships between physiological responses and social communication in the monkey. Normal monkeys are as effective in response to the facial expressive cues of another monkey in avoidance situations as they are to the original visual stimulus used during the training phase. It has also been shown that the heart rate response of the responder animal was similar in latency and intensity to that obtained during original instrumental conditioning sessions. Studies with color films of stimulus animals which could be shown for repeated sessions with a group of responders enabled us to specify the particular expressive cues that elicited consistent instrumental responses in viewers (Miller, 1967).

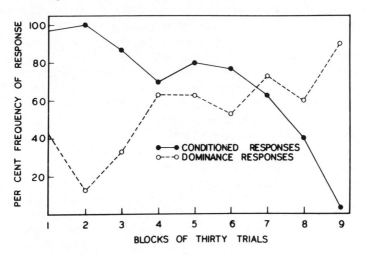

Fig. 4. Conditioned avoidance responses throughout extinction and number of pieces of food obtained in a socially competitive situation by a typical monkey. (From *Journal of Abnormal and Social Psychology*, 1956, *53*, 247.)

In a previous paper (Miller, Caul, & Mirsky, 1967) it was shown that early isolation destroyed the ability of monkeys to send or receive adequate social messages. It has been repeatedly demonstrated that social isolates do not form normal social attachments in terms of dominance, grooming, sexual, or maternal behavior. In fact, their most prominent symptom is that of hyperaggression extending to attacks upon infants, females, and even clearly superior adult males (Deets & Harlow, 1971). The most bizarre expression of this hyperaggressiveness is extreme self-mutilation in which isolates bite deeply into their own abdomen or limbs. We have suggested that the complete lack of nonverbal fluency in isolates is a most important factor in their inadequate and distorted social behavior and, further, that social experiences during the first year of life are required for the monkey to acquire the essentials of nonverbal behavior.

The aggressive quality of social interaction in primate groups is reversibly altered by the administration of psychoactive drugs. As I indicated last year, the administration of a psychotomimetic agent to one monkey of a group of three vastly increased the amount of aggressive behavior that occurred in the group (Miller, Levine, & Mirsky, 1973). On the other hand, a stimulant administered to one of a group of three animals enhanced the positive aspects of social behavior while markedly reducing aggression. These psychoactive drugs, which altered the course and nature of group social interactions, also changed the transmission and reception of nonverbal cues in the cooperative conditioning task, lending support to the notion that effective nonverbal behavior is the sine qua non of successful group interactions.

An experiment is currently under way to determine the acute and chronic effects of delta-9-THC on nonverbal communication and group social behavior of monkeys. Prior to the administration of the drug, we have been obtaining baseline measures of both cooperative conditioning and unrestricted social interaction. Six rhesus, all of them adolescent males, are currently being tested. They were experimentally naive but familiar with each other prior to testing. The animals were first placed in primate restraining chairs and trained to perform a conditioned avoidance response. They were then paired in all possible combinations in the cooperative conditioning paradigm (Miller, 1967), and with six animals there are 30 such pairings.

In a previous paper (Miller, 1974) it was shown that monkeys which were exceptionally good "senders" in the cooperative conditioning experiments were very insensitive "responders" to the facial expressive cues from other monkeys. Likewise, poor senders were exceptionally good responders. It was pointed out that these findings were in accord with those reported by Lanzetta and Kleck (1970) for male college students. In addition, it was observed that good senders were invariably submissive in a free-social situation, while good responders occupied intermediate ranks in the social dominance hierarchy. Dominant animant animals were average senders and responders—not showing much differentiation in these two aspects of social communication.

On the basis of performance as senders and responders in the present group of six monkeys, a sociogram depicting adequate channels of social communication was constructed (Figure 5). As you will note, some pairings seemed to share mutuality in the cooperative conditions task—both animals sending and responding well to each other's facial expressions. In other cases, one animal may send well to a particular partner but is unable to receive from him. Also there are a couple of pairings where no successful communication occurred in either direction. The animals have been arranged in the sociogram according to their performance as senders and responders. From our previous data we would predict that good senders are submissive, good responders are in middle ranks, and animals that are approximately equal in sending and responding are domin-

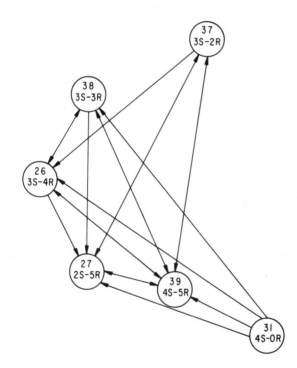

Fig. 5. Sociogram depicting the performance on cooperative conditioning in a group of six monkeys. Arrows indicate the direction of communication between pairs of animals. Although all possible pairings were tested, only those pairs showing significant levels of communication are shown by directional arrows. The top number in each circle is the animal identification number and the lower set of figures is the number of pairings in which the animal transmitted significantly to others followed by the number of pairings in which the animal received significantly from others. The sociogram is arranged from top to bottom in accord with predictions of their dominance status from the nonverbal data, i.e., it was predicted that #37 would be most dominant, followed by #38, etc. The lateral displacement has no significance but was introduced to eliminate confusion from crossing lines.

ant. Thus Figure 5 represents our prediction of social dominance status from nonverbal performances alone.

The second phase of this experiment was conducted in a double-blind fashion by my colleague, Allyn Deets, who was trained by Harlow at Wisconsin and is an expert at observing and scoring ongoing social interactions in groups of monkeys. The six monkeys were studied in social groups of three, and all possible trios were studied—a total of 20 groups in all. The monkeys were observed 5 days per week, and on every day two new trios were observed. Each of the 20 trios was observed twice, every trio being observed once before any trio was observed a second time. Every day the members of a trio were allowed to interact with one another by removing panels that divided large observation cages into three separate sections. Data collection began immediately, with the three monkeys being scored one at a time in succession, each for 12 minutes. At the end of a daily session the members of the trios were separated again into individual compartments.

A total of 49 separate categories of behavior were scored during these trio interactions, but for this discussion we are concerned only with the data relating to aggressive and submissive behavior. For purposes of demonstration, I have added the frequency counts for four forms of aggressive behavior—threatening, physical attack, pursuing, and clasp-pull-bite responses—and five forms of submissive behavior—fear grimacing, grinning and lipsmacking, rigid submission responses, fleeing, and screeching. The frequency counts for these categories were added as simple, unweighted sums. Direction of response was also recorded, i.e., not only the initiator of behavior but also the recipient to whom it was directed was noted. This permitted calculation of the difference between the number of aggressive acts delivered by a particular individual and the number of aggressive behaviors directed against that individual. Figure 6 shows the results of this analysis for both aggressive and submissive behaviors. The predictions derived from the nonverbal communication data conformed well with the actual social dominance hierarchy obtained in group testing. Only one animal, #31, failed to behave socially in predicted fashion—rather than being the most submissive animal he actually was in the fourth position in both aggressive and submissive behavior.

The two animals at the bottom of the hierarchy, #39 and #27, were quite different in their use of specific submissive expressions. Monkey #39 almost invariably displayed fear grimacing in the presence of other animals. Animal #27, however, had a greater tendency to respond to superiors with grinning and lipsmacking, which appear to be appeasement and greeting gestures. This monkey had roughly eight times as many lip smacks as any other animal in the group.

Threat was the most commonly employed aggressive behavior—constituting 74.4% of all aggressive acts. The relatively mild clasp-pull-bite category made up 18.4%, pursuits 2%, and actual physical attacks only

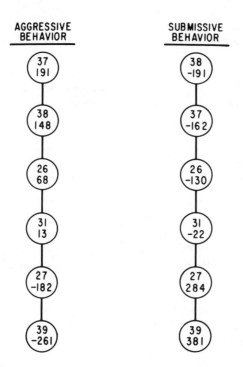

AGGRESSIVE
BEHAVIOR

SUBMISSIVE
BEHAVIOR

Fig. 6.   Social dominance status in a group of six monkeys as determined by the expression of
aggression and submission when they were tested in all possible trios in a free social situation. The
top number in each circle is the animal's identification number. The lower figure in each circle is the
number of acts initiated *by* the subject minus the number of acts directed *against* that subject. Thus,
for example, monkey #38 initiated 148 more aggressive acts against the other five animals than were
directed against him. Similarly, monkey #38 received 191 more submissive acts from his partners
than he initiated towards them.

5% of aggressive behaviors. Thus, even in these confined groups, there was a
low level of actual physical assault, and aggression was expressed primarily
through communicative facial expressions and postures. Similarly, the two forms
of submissive facial expressions, fear grimacing (49%) and grinning and lipsmacking (26%), were the most prevalent submissive acts. The subordinate fled
(10%), screeched (8%), or rigidly submitted (4%) on other occasions when
dominant animals approached.

   I should reiterate that the data cited above were only the categories related to
aggressive and submissive behaviors. The positive and affiliative acts—play,
social grooming, etc.—which constituted by far the largest amount of social
behavior, are not reported in this chapter. Thus, in terms of total social behaviors
that were observed and categorized, actual physical aggression was much less
frequent than the preceding percentages would suggest.

As Figure 6 suggests, there are great variations among animals in the use of aggressive and submissive expressions. At one extreme of the hierarchy, #39 was never observed to display aggressive behavior in the free social situation. His expressions were always submissive and he was the recipient of the greatest amount of aggressive behavior from his partners. Monkey #38, on the other hand, was never seen to give a submissive response to another animal. Animals in the center of the hierarchy generally were aggressive to those below them and submissive to those above.

The results indicate that one can make rather specific predictions about a subject's performance in a social group from information about his facility at transmitting clear and overt affective expressions and his ability to perceive such nonverbal messages from others. The data from this and earlier experiments suggest that animals that are low in social status are exceptionally effective senders of facial expressive cues, those in the middle of the hierarchy are sensitive to nonverbal expressions of others, and the most dominant animals are intermediate in their ability to both send and receive expressive cues from others. It is not known at this time how individual subjects have acquired a measure of "specialization" in the sending or receiving of nonverbal cues; a developmental study of a group of individuals over a period from infancy to adulthood would be required to determine the social history of these communicative expressions. It does appear, however, that nonverbal skills may reduce intragroup aggression markedly. Submissive monkeys display frequent and clearly discriminable facial expressions that are readily perceived and interpreted by those higher in the social dominance hierarchy. The subjects in the middle of the hierarchy respond sensitively to expressive cues of others in the social group and may then anticipate and perhaps forestall aggressive attacks. It was noteworthy in this respect that, in our previous study (Miller, 1974), the monkey intermediate in dominance in a squad of three animals formed a cohort relationship with the dominant animal against the submissive. When the dominant threatened the submissive the middle animal joined in the threat; when the dominant animal presented for grooming the middle animal immediately began grooming, chasing the submissive animal away if it attempted to groom.

Now, in conclusion, I'd like to speculate briefly regarding the implications of both field and laboratory studies of infrahuman primates for the control of aggression in man. There is no question that studies of the neural substrates of aggressive and/or violent behavior, such as those reported in the recent summary and evaluation by Goldstein (1974), should be continued and extended. It has been amply demonstrated that humans with subclinical seizure disorders, abnormal EEG patterns, or invasive tumors in certain areas of the brain may suddenly explode in irrational, seemingly undirected, and shocking violence. They may assault and kill total strangers in a rampage such as that which occurred at the University of Texas a few years ago. These individuals, if they can be identified in time, can be treated with appropriate drugs or surgical intervention. Other factors affecting the expression of aggression in man, such as the effects of alcohol or excessive use of stimulants, may prove to be important but difficult to control in modern society. Certainly, if alcohol alone could be eliminated or limited in use, thousands of violent assaults, injuries, and deaths could be averted. However, abnormal brain function, whether a consequence of individual pathology or action of toxic drugs, is probably responsible for only a fraction of total human aggression.

If our studies of the infrahuman primates have any bearing on the problem of human aggression, the most significant etiological variable must be the early socialization processes of infants and juveniles as they work out, without risk of serious injury, their social interaction with peers. The young child must learn or be instructed by his elders to control aggression and to express assertiveness in socially acceptable ways. Inherent in this view is that the child must recognize and respond appropriately to those subtle, expressive cues that reveal hostility and rising anger in associates so that his own behavior can be modified to avert an outbreak of violence.

In a recent paper Deets and Harlow (1971) have proposed a unified view of the interactions between biological and social factors in the maturation and development of aggression in primates. There is a considerable body of evidence from the Wisconsin studies of social isolation that there is a definite maturational sequencing in the emergence of social tendencies in the infant monkey. During the first 3 months of life the predominant social interactions are affiliative. The infant–mother dyad is close and affectionate and the infant unhesitatingly approaches other animals within the social group. At about 3 months of age, the infant monkey begins to show a maturation of fearful, withdrawal reactions from strangers and environmental novelty. Aggressive behavior does not appear in the behavioral repertoire until late in the first year of life. In the normal monkey-rearing situation, the growing infant is provided with maternal and other social support throughout this period when these processes are maturing in sequence and as a result he may learn to make appropriate emotional responses to various social and environmental situations. For example, the infant, during the maturation of fearful behaviors, learns to avoid certain kinds of potentially dangerous stimuli and to ignore other innocuous cues. Similarly, when aggression begins to emerge, both affiliative and fear responses are available to the young monkey, and these facilitate the acquisition of appropriate behaviors within the peer group during aggressive play. Thus the infant learns his unique position within the social group—which animals he may aggress against without painful retribution and which he should defer to with appropriate fear expressions.

The Wisconsin studies have shown that disruption of social learning opportunities during any or all of the developmental sequences through social isolation produces aberrant behavior in the animal after the isolation experience is terminated. Animals isolated during the first 3 months of age show exaggerated fear responses upon removal from isolation but affiliative tendencies are still sufficiently strong so that these animals eventually develop normal social behaviors. Animals isolated for 6 months were both nonaffiliative and hyperfearful in subsequent tests. Animals isolated from 6 to 12 months, when aggression first emerges and social controls over its expression are learned, proved upon release to be normally affiliative and fearful but extremely aggressive in their social relationships.

There is evidence (Deets & Harlow, 1971) that a similar maturational sequencing of affective responses occurs in the human child, though, of course, on a different time scale. Unfortunately, only the first two sequences, affiliation and fear, have been examined in detail and the maturation of aggression and the processes of development of social controls have not been intensively studied in preschool children. Deets and Harlow suggest that important, lifelong aggressive patterns develop in the infant sometime during the first 3 or 4 years of life and suggest that developmental studies of aggression during this period are urgently needed.

Our studies of the nonverbal communication of isolate monkeys (Miller *et al.*, 1967) revealed that animals deprived of social interactions during infancy were totally deficient in sending and especially so in the receiving of expressive cues from other monkeys. This absence of nonverbal fluency was coupled with marked social disturbance, notably including extreme hyperaggressiveness directed at inappropriate targets. These animals, which had been isolated for the first year of life, are extremely anomalous in their own facial expressions, e.g., two of the male isolates have never been observed to display a fear grimace or an open-mouth threat in the 7 years in which they have been in our laboratory. We have found them to be quite dangerous to work with in that laboratory personnel cannot predict when they may attack since they show no premonitory facial expressions.

Studies of the infrahuman primates have revealed that adequate socialization of the young, strong group cohesion with effective leadership, and the elaboration of clearly discriminated expressions of dominance and submission have produced stable social groupings that are maintained for long periods of time with minimal intragroup violence. One might anticipate that the study of nonverbal fluency in man may similarly reveal that aggression is importantly related with the failure of subjects to perceive and interpret subtle expressions of irritation and annoyance in others so that behavior can be modulated in time to prevent an escalation to anger. It would be particularly interesting to study the developmental course of the sending and receiving of nonverbal expressions so that one could relate early social experience with subsequent nonverbal performances. Since aggressive behavior almost invariably is accompanied by highly visible nonverbal as well as verbal responses, the study of the gradations of expressions that culminate in overt hostility would seem to be important for the understanding of human aggression.

Acknowledgments

I would like to express my sincere appreciation to the several colleagues who have participated in various phases of this research program. Dr. I. A. Mirsky supported and contributed to the investigations throughout the program. I would especially like to thank Dr. Allyn Deets, who has lent his expertise in the study of group social behaviors in monkeys during the past three years of this project, and Dr. H. E. King, who graciously consented to present this paper to the symposium when I was unable to attend.

References

Andrew, R. J. The origin and evolution of the calls and facial expressions of the primates. *Behaviour*, 1963, *20*, 1–109.

Ardrey, R. *African genesis*. New York: Atheneum, 1961.

Ardrey, R. *The territorial imperative: A personal inquiry into the animal origins of property and nations*. New York: Atheneum, 1966.

Ardrey, R. *The social contract*. New York: Atheneum, 1970.

Bandura, A. *Aggression: A social learning analysis*. Englewood Cliffs, N.J.: Prentice-Hall, 1973.

Bernstein, I. S. Role of the dominant male rhesus monkey in response to external challenges to the group. *Journal of Comparative and Physiological Psychology*, 1964, *57*, 404–406.

Birch, H. G., & Clark, G. Hormonal modification of social behavior: II. The effects of sex-hormone administration on the social dominance status of the female-castrate chimpanzee. *Psychosomatic Medicine*, 1946, *8*, 320–331.

Birch, H. G., & Clark, G. Hormonal modification of social behavior: IV. The mechanism of estrogen-induced dominance in chimpanzees. *Journal of Comparative* and *Physiological Psychology*, 1950, *43*, 181–193.

Bronson, F. H., & Desjardins, C. Steroid hormones and aggressive behavior in mammals. In B. E. Eleftheriou & J. P. Scott (Eds.), *The physiology of aggression and defeat*. New York: Plenum Press, 1971, pp. 43–63.

Carpenter, C. R. A field study in Siam of the behavior and social relations of the gibbon (*Hylobates lar*). *Comparative Psychology Monographs*, 1940, *16*, 1–212.

Carpenter, C. R. Societies of monkeys and apes. *Biological Symposia*, 1942, *8*, 177–204.

Carpenter, C. R. The howlers of Barro Colorado Island. In I. DeVore (Ed.), *Primate behavior: Field studies of monkeys and apes*. New York: Holt, Reinhart, and Winston, 1965, pp. 250–291.

Clark, G., & Birch, H. G. Hormonal modification of social behavior: I. The effect of sex-hormone administration on the social status of a male-castrate chimpanzee. *Psychosomatic Medicine*, 1945, *7*, 321–329.

Clark, G., & Birch, H. G. Hormonal modification of social behavior: III. The effects of stilbesterol therapy on social dominance in the female-castrate chimpanzee. *Bulletin Canadian Psychological Association*, 1946, *6* (1).

Deets, A. C., & Harlow, H. F. Early experience and the maturation of aggression. In V. P. Rock (Chm.), *Value and Knowledge Requirements for Peace*. Symposium presented at the annual meeting of the American Association for the Advancement of Science, Philadelphia, December, 1971 (Washington: AAAS, 1972, Audiotape No. 94 –71 IV).

DeVore, I., & Hall, K. R. L. Baboon ecology. In I. DeVore (Ed.), *Primate behavior: Field studies of monkeys and apes*. New York: Holt, Rinehart, and Winston, 1965, pp. 20–52.

Geen, R. G. *Aggression*. Morristown, N.J.: General Learning Press, 1972, pp. 1–23.

Goldstein, M. Brain research and violent behavior: A summary of the status of biomedical research on brain and aggressive violent behavior. *Archives of Neurology*, 1974, *30*, 1–35.

Goodall, J. Chimpanzees in the Gombe Stream Reserve. In I. DeVore (Ed.), *Primate behavior: Field studies of monkeys and apes*. New York: Holt, Reinhart, and Winston, 1965, pp. 425–473.

Goy, R. W. Organizing effects of androgen on the behaviour of rhesus monkeys. In R. P. Michael (Ed.), *Endocrinology and human behaviour*. London: Oxford University Press, 1968, pp. 12–31.

Hall, K. R. L. Aggression in monkey and ape societies. In J. D. Carthy & F. J. Ebling (Eds.), *The natural history of aggression*. New York: Academic Press, 1964, pp. 51–64.

Hall, K. R. L., & DeVore, I. Baboon social behavior. In I. DeVore (Ed.), *Primate behavior: Field studies of monkeys and apes*. New York: Holt, Reinhart, and Winston, 1965, pp. 53–110.

Harlow, H. F., & Bromer, J. A. A test-apparatus for monkeys. *Psychological Record*, 1938, *2*, 434–436.

Harlow, H. F., & Harlow, M. K. The affectional systems. In A. M. Schrier, H. F. Harlow, & F. Stollnitz (Eds.), *Behavior of nonhuman primates: Modern research trends* (Vol. 2). New York: Academic Press, 1965, pp. 287–334.

Harlow, H. F., Rowland, G. L., & Griffin, G. A. The effect of total social deprivation on the development of monkey behavior. *Psychiatric Research Reports*, 1964, *19*, 116–135.

Imanishi, K. Social behavior in Japanese monkeys, *Macaca fuscata*. *Psychologia*, 1957, *1*, 47–54.

Jay, P. The Indian langur monkey (*Presbytis entellus*). In C. H. Southwick (Ed.), *Primate Social Behavior*. Princeton, N.J.: Van Nostrand, 1963, pp. 114–123.

Joslyn, W. D. Androgen-induced social dominance in infant female rhesus monkeys. *Journal of Child Psychology and Psychiatry*, 1973, *14*, 137–145.

Kaufmann, J. H. Social relations of adult males in a free-ranging band of rhesus monkeys. In S. Altmann (Ed.), *Social Communication among Primates*. Chicago: University of Chicago Press, 1967, pp. 73–98.

Kawamura, S. Matriarchal social ranks in the Minoo-B troop: A study of the rank system of Japanese monkeys. *Primates*, 1958, *1*, 149–156.

Koford, C. B. Ranks of mothers and sons in bands of rhesus monkeys. *Science*, 1963, *141*, 356–357.

Koford, C. B. Population dynamics of rhesus monkeys on Cayo Santiago. In I. DeVore (Ed.), *Primate Behavior: Field studies of monkeys and apes*. New York: Holt, Reinhart, and Winston, 1965, pp. 160–174.

Koyama, N. On dominance rank and kinship of the wild Japanese monkey troop on Arashiyama. *Primates*, 1967, *8*, 189–216.

Lanzetta, J. T., & Kleck, R. E. Encoding and decoding of nonverbal affect in humans. *Journal of Personality and Social Psychology*, 1970, *16*, 12–19.

Lindburg, D. G. The rhesus monkey in North India: An ecological and behavioral study. In L. Rosenblum (Ed.), *Primate behavior: Developments in field and laboratory research* (Vol. 2). New York: Academic Press, 1971, pp. 1–106.

Lorenz, K. *On Aggression*. London: Methuen, 1966.

Maslow, A. H. Dominance-quality and social behavior in infra-human primates. *Journal of Social Psychology*, 1940, *11*, 313–324.

Miller, R. E. Experimental approaches to the physiological and behavioral concomitants of affective communication in Rhesus monkeys. In: S. Altmann (Ed.), *Social Communication Among Primates*. Chicago: Univ. of Chicago Press, 1967, pp. 125–134.

Miller, R. E. Experimental studies of communication in the monkey. In L. Rosenblum (Ed.), *Primate behavior: Developments in field and laboratory research*. New York: Academic Press, 1971, pp. 139–175.

Miller, R. E. Social and pharmacological influences on nonverbal communication in monkeys and man. In L. Krames, P. Pliner, & T. Alloway (Eds.), *Nonverbal communication: Comparative aspects*. New York: Plenum Press, 1974, pp. 77–101.

Miller, R. E., & Banks, J. H. The determination of social dominance in monkeys by a competitive avoidance method. *Journal of Comparative and Physiological Psychology*, 1962, *55*, 137–141.

Miller, R. E., Caul, W. F., & Mirsky, I. A. The communication of affects between feral and socially isolated monkeys. *Journal of Personality and Social Psychology*, 1967, *7*, 231–239.

Miller, R. E., Levine, J. M., & Mirsky, I. A. Effects of psychoactive drugs on nonverbal communication and group social behavior of monkeys. *Journal of Personality and Social Psychology*, 1973, *28*, 396–405.

Miller, R. E., & Murphy, J. V. Social interactions of rhesus monkeys: I. Food-getting dominance as a dependent variable. *Journal of Social Psychology*, 1956, *44*, 249–255 (a).

Miller, R. E., & Murphy, J. V. Social interactions of rhesus monkeys: II. Effects of social interaction on the learning of discrimination tasks. *Journal of Comparative and Physiological Psychology*, 1956, *49*, 207–211 (b).

Miller, R. E., Murphy, J. V., & Mirsky, I. A. The modification of social dominance in a group of monkeys by interanimal conditioning. *Journal of Comparative and Physiological Psychology*, 1955, *48*, 392–396.

Mirsky, A. F. The influence of sex hormones on social behavior in monkeys. *Journal of Comparative and Physiological Psychology*, 1955, *48*, 327–335.

Mitchell, G. D. Persistent behavior pathology in rhesus monkeys following early social isolation. *Folia Primatologica*, 1968, *8*, 132–147.

Montagu, M. F. A. *Man and aggression*. New York: Oxford University Press, 1968.

Moyer, K. E. A preliminary physiological model of aggressive behavior. In B. E. Eleftheriou & J. P. Scott (Eds.), *The physiology of aggression and defeat*. New York: Plenum Press, 1971, pp. 223–263.

Moynihan, M. Comparative aspects of communication in New World monkeys. In D. Morris (Ed.), *Primate ethology*. London: Weidenfeld and Nicolson, 1967, pp. 306–342.

Murphy, J. V., & Miller, R. E. The manipulation of dominance of monkeys with conditioned fear. *Journal of Abnormal and Social Psychology*, 1956, *53*, 244–248.

Murphy, J. V., Miller, R. E., & Mirsky, I. A. Interanimal conditioning in the monkey. *Journal of Comparative and Physiological Psychology*, 1955, *48*, 211–214.

Ploog, D. W. The behavior of squirrel monkeys (*Saimiri sciureus*) by sociometry, bioacoustics, and brain stimulation. In S. Altmann (Ed.), *Social communication among primates*. Chicago: University of Chicago Press, 1967, pp. 149–184.

Reynolds, V., & Reynolds, F. Chimpanzees in the Budongo Forest. In I. DeVore (Ed.), *Primate behavior: Field studies of monkeys and apes*. New York: Holt, Reinhart, and Winston, 1965, pp. 368–424.

Ripley, S. Intertroop encounters among Ceylon gray langurs (*Presbytis entellus*). In S. Altmann (Ed.), *Social communication among primates*. Chicago: University of Chicago Press, 1967, pp. 237–253.

Rose, R. M., Holaday, J. W., & Bernstein, I. A. Plasma testosterone, dominance rank, and aggressive behavior in male rhesus monkeys. *Nature*, 1971, *231*, 366–368.

Russell, C., & Russell, W. M. S. *Violence: Monkeys and man*. London: Macmillan, 1968.

Sade, D. S. Determinants of dominance in a group of free-ranging rhesus monkeys. In S. Altmann (Ed.), *Social communication among primates*. Chicago: University of Chicago Press, 1967, pp. 99–114.

Schaller, G. B. *The mountain gorilla: Ecology and behavior*. Chicago: University of Chicago Press, 1963.

Seay, B. Maternal behavior in primiparous and multiparous rhesus monkeys. *Folia Primatologica*, 1966, *4*, 146–168.

Southwick, C. H. Aggressive behaviour of rhesus monkeys in natural and captive groups. In S. Garattini & E. B. Sigg (Eds.), *Aggressive behavior. International Symposium on the Biology of Aggressive Behavior, Milan, 1968*. Amsterdam: Excerpta Medica Foundation, 1969, pp. 32–43.

Sparks, J. Allogrooming in primates: A review. In D. Morris (Ed.), *Primate ethology*. Garden City, N.Y.: Doubleday and Co., 1969, pp. 190–225.

Sugiyama, Y. Social organization of hanuman langurs. In S. Altmann (Ed.), *Social communication among primates*. Chicago: University of Chicago Press, 1967, pp. 221–236.

van Hooff, J. A. R. A. M. The facial displays of the catarrhine monkeys and apes. In D. Morris (Ed.), *Primate ethology*. London: Weidenfeld and Nicolson, 1967, pp. 9–88.

Werthan, F. *A sign for Cain: An exploration of human violence*. London: Robert Hale, 1966.

Zuckerman, S. *The social life of monkeys and apes*. London: Kegan, Paul, Trench, Trubner, and Co., 1932.

CHAPTER 7

Nonverbal Communication: The Effect of Affect on Individual and Group Behavior

Benson E. Ginsburg

Professor of Biobehavioral Sciences
University of Connecticut
Storrs, Connecticut

The Problem: What Does an Animal Communicate and How Can We Know?

"I think, therefore I am," may also be paraphrased "I feel, therefore I am." The essence is the conscious process of self-awareness. In the final genetic continuum, one is not sure where thought begins or where affect comparable to that which we as humans are capable of experiencing begins, or, for that matter, where consciousness begins. Yet, without being scientifically precise about it, we are on firm ground in attributing thought, affect, and consciousness to each other and consciousness and affect to our dogs—but do they think? And is a snail capable of affect? Or is an ameba "conscious?" If so, how can we know it?

The properties that I attribute to your mind are reflections of what I know about myself. Your moods are more real to me through my own introspection than by means of what you can report. Your anger may be manifest and you may verbalize it with great eloquence, but I can only understand what you feel when you feel angry through having felt that way myself. I believe my dog experiences something similar, but I do not attribute an analogy of that feeling to the snail. Can my dog or cat experience grief or sadness? Can I vicariously experience or understand the compulsion of a psychotic or the anxiety of a neurotic if I have never subjectively passed that way myself? How communicate the sensation of childbirth to a man so that he may truly know what it is? Does the nursing rat or

161

bitch experience mother love in anything like the sense in which the human does? And how do we communicate our feelings to one another? Conversely, how can we mask them? By what means can we induce a desired emotional response in ourselves, in another person—or in an ape, a dog, or a cat?

For us as verbal beings, there is a premium on communication by spoken language. However, at the level of affect, the verbalizations are redundant. If I have never felt whatever it is that you feel, your words will not communicate your feelings to me in the same sense that they would had I experienced them. Even if I have shared in the emotions you are expressing verbally, I must still judge whether you feel them and mean them or whether you are dissembling, and I will use other and often nonverbal cues in order to make this decision. One may say that he or she loves another, but the truth of this statement will be judged by a multitude of other cues: a glance, a smile, a touch, and certain consistencies of behavior over time. Here, as with verbal cues, a real understanding and sharing of the affect is only possible if one has also experienced it. We not only anthropomorphize the animals that we observe, but we anthropomorphize each other. Nor can we escape such anthropomorphisms in our attempts to be ''scientific'' in our analysis of the behavior of higher mammals without ignoring the essence of what that behavior is all about. Wright (1953) essentially restated the problem of the psychophysical parallelism as applied to these dimensions of behavior when he pointed out that the so-called objective, descriptive analysis of behavior as seen from outside the individual, and the subjective, introspective approach overlap by an order of magnitude approaching 100%. We can test our assumption that other human beings feel the same emotions we do, using a combination of these approaches, but we cannot truly assess the subjective dimensions of the emotional life of a gorilla, for example, without assuming, as Darwin did in *The Expression of the Emotions in Man and Animals*, that our phylogenetic homologies impart credence and an order of validity to our anthropomorphic analogies.

On the neurological level, we know where to stimulate in the mammalian brain in order to induce a variety of emotional reactions. For all the differences in detail, there are homologous structures in a series of mammalian brains, let alone primate brains. To know that an electrode placed in a comparable area of my brain and the brain of a cat can stimulate us both to show rage does not by itself prove that the cat is feeling what I am feeling when we are both thus stimulated. The homology of structure, the analogy of motor patterns, and the tracing of similar changes in similar pathways is not identical with the affect, and though I can never know whether the cat is acting as an automaton or is feeling something akin to what I would feel under similar conditions, the latter is the more attractive and parsimonious assumption. In spite of the plausibility of this assumption, the behavior does not necessarily have the meaning that I might like to impute to it on the very reasonable basis that similar motor behaviors resulting from stimulation in homologous structures in me and in the cat have similar representations in those neural structures having to do with my affect, and that congruence for these two sides of the triangle imply congruence for the third—the (conscious) use to which the behavior is put.

There is the further question of the elaboration of these higher cortical mechanisms at the level of mobilizing the behavior for communicative purposes in a social situation, and of controlling its expression because of prior experience and/or anticipated consequences. If a fish or a mouse or a monkey with augmented testosterone levels is thereby driven to heightened displays of aggression, is man any more or less autonomous with respect to the extent that he is driven or controlled by these homologous evolutionary legacies, or may his behavior be different even where the mechanisms appear to be similar? Perhaps, though this may be the case, his autonomic signs may more accurately signal his affect? In spite of all our self-conscious experience with these problems at the human level, we are still not sure of ourselves in our own interpretations and communications of affect. With other animals, we can only infer that affect is a necessary construct from anthropomorphizing and from observations that are more consistent with this inference than with any other.

The Model: Social Behavior of Wolves

In this chapter, we shall be primarily concerned with the communication behavior of a wild social species, the North American gray wolf (*Canis lupus*). Because it is a social species that lives in a cooperative pack, there is a premium on its communication behavior, since the activities of the pack are initiated, coordinated, and redirected by such behavior. Social roles are established and maintained in this way, as are social bonds, including sexual, filial, and parental relations. Pack membership is both signaled and recognized. The capacities to communicate intent and to form individual and group bonds are also related to the potential for domestication. Just as wolves form affiliative relations with each other, so do dogs form these with people. They communicate hostility, fear, suspicion, playful intent, and a range of other "moods" to us. That these are indeed moods, each implying an impetus toward or a readiness for a certain type of behavior, is corroborated in a statistical sense by the behavioral sequelae following the signal. Not every dog showing seemingly equivalent threat behavior will follow this with an attack even when the eliciting set of stimuli appears to be the same and to afford a commensurate opportunity for following the presumed intent with the expected deed. The point is that it happens often enough for the two to be associated and to permit the inference to be made that the one is likely to be followed by the other.

Nor are we, the humans in the interaction, capable of determining the *Canid*'s intent without experience — vicarious or direct. This is a circumstance that is often lost sight of because of our familiarity with domestic forms, and, by extrapolation, with the similar-appearing behavior of their wild relatives. But suppose we were to be confronted with an angry giraffe; would we recognize his signals?

Prerequisites for Communication

The association of the signal with the mood or affect and, in turn, with the appropriate act, is established by experience in these contexts, whether the eye of the beholder belongs to a human investigator or to a conspecific. We have, for example, reared a female cub in complete visual isolation from the age of 3 weeks to 10 months. When she was first introduced to other wolves, she did not recognize their threats, greetings, or dominance postures and reacted inappropriately. Her own vocalizations and body postures contained a suitable repertoire of wolf behavior, but she did not use these in appropriate combinations or contexts and was thus not "understood" by other wolves. By being forced to interact with them under restraint from the time she emerged from isolation, she managed to put her communication system in place in 4 or 5 days. She had the genetic potential, but this was, by itself, not sufficient to insure that she would be able either to communicate or to understand.

For us, as for the isolate wolf, it is by observing wolf behavior in context that we learn there are dominance postures, threat postures and vocalizations, and submissive postures and vocalizations, as well as body language for play solicitation, sexual solicitation, and many other aspects of communication.

We have kept wolves together as cubs without adults and they have developed an intact communication system typical of wolves that have had adult tutors, entirely out of their own genetic potential and experiences with each other (Rabb, Woolpy, & Ginsburg, 1967; Woolpy & Ginsburg, 1967; Woolpy, 1968; Ginsburg, 1968). By contrast, raising a wolf in social isolation virtually from birth produces an animal that has all of the appropriate components of meaningful social communicative behavior but is unable to put these components into a proper pattern and is also unable to use them in the proper social context. It does not, for example, understand a threat from another wolf until it has gained sufficient experience with this behavior and its aftermath to learn to recognize it. At first its only response is a startled avoidance to the attack itself. However, if such an isolated animal is introduced to its conspecifics immediately when it emerges from isolation and under appropriate restraint, it not only learns the meaning of the communicative behavior of normally reared animals, but it also organizes its own behavior so that after about 4 days of such exposure it is both responding and communicating effectively. The isolate now knows when it is being threatened and will either threaten back or make submissive and appropriate appeasement gestures. It knows when it is being solicited for play, and it can develop normal courtship and sexual behavior. Until the social context was provided and "understood," the isolate exhibited fragments and patterns of communicative behavior that conveyed no meaning. If such an animal is permitted to persist in its out-of-context patterns, it becomes more difficult for these to become organized and integrated into an effective communication system. If the behavior develops in the proper social context, either in the ordinary course of events or in controlled encounters immediately after emerging from isolation, one can establish a lexicon of body postures. This was done by Charles Darwin in his book on *The Expression of the Emotions in Man and Animals*. It was also done for the wolf by Schenkel (1947) and by a number of other investigators. This lexicon is good enough for the human observer to use in analyzing individual and group behavior in a pack of wolves. One can see the dynamics of the pack in the behavior and predict from their communications what is going to happen. It is also a reliable lexicon for human comportment in the presence of an unfamiliar wolf. If the tail is high, the incisors bared, and the ears forward, it is a full-blown threat. If the ears are laid back and the tail is lower and the teeth are more broadly bared, it is an ambivalent threat and the animal may still back off if approached, or even allow itself to be handled. Since part of what we do is to attempt to form social bonds with adult wild wolves, it is important for us to be attuned to their language, and we find it to be reliable.

Physiological Correlates of Communication: Inadequate Criteria

By contrast, as most of us know from common experiences, a domestic dog has many of the same body postures. However, unlike the wolf, who means what he says and says what he means, the dog may or may not mean it, and less frequently, he may or may not say it. To understand what a threatening dog behind a barrier is going to do should one enter his enclosure, it is necessary to know the dog. It is necessary only to observe what the wolf is "saying."

An obvious explanation for the difference is in the selective premium placed on communication behavior in a wild social species. Selection pressure has thus both produced and preserved the stereotypy and reliability of the communication behavior in the wolf. In the domestic dog, selection pressure has been relaxed, and while the behaviors occur as a legacy from the evolutionary past, they do not necessarily retain the meaning they once had in the wild. If the motor patterns can thus be divorced from their ancestral meanings, to what extent can they be used as indicators of affect? A wolf showing a full-blown threat will, if challenged, carry out what that threat implies. Some dogs will, and some will not. Many dogs threaten fearsomely from their side of a barrier, but should a stranger enter, he or she is immediately accepted as a friend and the dog becomes playful and affectionate. Assuming that the wolf feels what I imagine I would feel in a situation where I was making vigorous threats and was prepared to carry them through to a physical attack, what about the dog, who at the moment of threatening appears to be every bit as much aroused? If we know that the dog does not "mean" this threat, we can measure activity, muscle tone, degree of physiological arousal, a host of autonomic responses, the level of various steroid hormones in the blood and brain, the blood glucose level, and the turnover of key neural transmitters. We might then attribute a causal relationship to any differences that we find in any of these indicators if these differences correlate with the two distinct behaviors: threat with friendly aftermath if challenged as against threat with hostile aftermath when challenged. Suppose, as is the case with a number of these measures, we find no differences in autonomic and other responses between a threat that will be carried out and a seemingly equivalent threat that will not be. What does this tell us about the underlying conscious affective state of each of these animals during the time the threat is being made? Were I to judge this in the same way that I would judge the behavior of a person, it would be my guess that the affect is the same during the threat phase and that a difference in affect only arises with the difference in the subsequent behavior.

The Body Language of Wolves: A Social Lexicon

Crisler (1958) has described the wolf as "head oriented" by contrast with the dog, who is "rump oriented" with respect to other wolves or dogs. This is particularly so in courtship, where the male wolf will run muzzle to muzzle with the female and will do a courtship dance in front of her, bouncing with his chest to the ground and his rump high. If she accepts the courting male, the female will stand with her tail averted and permit the male to mount and copulate. In attempting to breed a female dog to a male wolf when the female is in full season, there is often a miscommunication that is great enough to prevent the mating from taking place. The male wolf will attempt to court the female in the manner described. The female dog, however, will often behave inappropriately and paw at the male or attempt to mount him, instead of responding first in playful fashion and then by standing with the tail averted. The male dog, put with a female wolf that is in season, will attempt to mount without courting and will frequently not be accepted.

In the organized pack, the role of communication behavior is responsible for much of the pack's cohesiveness, for the individuation of social roles, and to provide an organized framework for the various specialized activities that the individuals must carry out with respect to one another in the pack organization (Rabb et al., 1967; Ginsburg, 1966, 1968, 1972; Woolpy, 1968). There is typically a dominant male and a dominant female. The female will dominate the other females by direct aggression, particularly during the mating season. The dominant male is responded to both as an individual and as a result of his physical demeanor. He is responded to as an individual since other wolves in the pack will give way to him regardless of his particular carriage at the moment. In social situations that involve his control over the pack, he signals his intent in the usual way—by approaching with tail held high and ears up and looking in the direction of another wolf whose activities he is seeking to affect. It is very seldom necessary for an actual physical encounter to occur, and when this does happen in cases involving the dominant male, the encounters are brief and bloodless. Encounters involving the dominant female with other females, particularly during the mating season, may result in actual bodily harm.

The organization of the pack extends to most aspects of behavior. In the captive groups that we have studied, hunting was, of course, not observed. However, all other aspects of normal behavior did occur and are substantially the same as those observed in the field (Ginsburg, 1966; Mech, 1962). Communication is largely in the form of body language, and we find that the accompanying vocalizations are less attended to than the bodily postures. For example, growling can be just as intense and identically pitched when a threat is ambivalent as when a threat is full-blown. The major signaling differences in the two instances will be the position of the ears, lips, and tail. The behavior of other wolves toward the one who is threatening will, in this instance, be controlled not by the intensity of the growl, but by the body language. This language is adequate to signal and control the young in many situations, to beg for food (on the part of the young, who are then regurgitated to by the parents), for greetings among familiar animals and for threats both within the pack and to strangers, and for the control of reproductive and mating behavior. The vocalizations also play a role in signaling the cubs, in greeting behavior, hunting, and territoriality (Pimlott, Shannon, & Kolenosky, 1969).

Communication, Pack Organization, and Population Control

In the three well-organized packs that we have studied, there was seldom a season in which every female capable of mating was actually bred. Control is exerted by the dominant female, who tracks down other females when they come into heat and attacks them physically when they engage in sexual activity with males. During several seasons, the first female to come into heat was savagely attacked by the dominant female and once her hind legs were torn to such an extent that she could not stand and receive a male. Later, this omega female, who was a virtual outcast for several weeks, regained her status in the pack by joining the dominant female when her litter was born and acting as a maiden aunt or dry nurse. Control by the dominant male is more interesting, involving as it does communication rather than overt fighting. Most of the females in the pack preferentially solicit the dominant male when they come into breeding season.

When they accept another male after a period of courtship, they will attempt to leave him and go to the dominant male when he is close by. Generally they turn on the male they have accepted with a threat or a mild attack and run to the dominant male. This will occur in any stage of mating, including copulation. The dominant male seldom accepts these overtures, which are made in a manner similar to solicitation of play, that is, by pawing at the male, running with him, licking at his muzzle, or greeting. The presence of the dominant male thus disrupts the mating behavior of the pack in this purely passive way involving the manner in which the females respond to him. He also disrupts the breeding more directly by slowly approaching a pair in courtship or coitus in what appears to be a natural manner, although the tail is high, the ears are forward, and his gaze is directed at the courting or copulating pair. In the precoital situation, a subordinate male will dismount regardless of the stage of sexual activity. After a successful copulation, however, the subordinate male will no longer give way in the same manner, although the female will still turn on him and go preferentially to the dominant male. Instead, the consort male now remains in physical proximity to the female and may interpose his body between her and the dominant male, exhibiting piloerection, holding his tail high, but appearing to direct his threat behavior at the female. He generally faces away from the dominant male.

The Executive Male: Sex without Issue

While most of the sexual activity centers around the dominant male in the manner described, actual counts of successful matings as indicated by ties show that the dominant male is not the primary sire in a pack. When a succession in dominance occurs and a new dominant male is firmly established in his role, his mating performance as judged by actual completed copulations resulting in a tie declines by comparison with his previous performance as a high-ranking subdominant animal. Dominance in the male appears to be associated with "leadership," "authority," "territoriality," and sexual fun and games, but not with leaving the most progeny. The male succeeding to dominance has usually been high in the hierarchy and among the most active and effective sires prior to his achieving dominance.

The Pack as Kingmaker

The organization of the pack, from feeding the young to controlling mating, is achieved by communication among the group. The pack is cooperative and generally peaceful. Threats to the dominant male are usually not made by a single subdominant individual, but by a group of males, of which one is the principal challenger. Usually, when the dominant male meets the challenge by threatening, some of the other males back off and the principal challenger, who is left without a militant following, generally gives way. The process of challenging dominance is thus "democratic" and not a matter of a contest between two individuals in the manner depicted in Jack London's *Call of the Wild*, although female dominance is typically established through individual encounters.

Taming a Wolf

We have also worked with the socialization of adult wolves to human handling (Ginsburg, 1966, 1972). Generally there are four phases to this endeavor. In the first phase, the captured and confined animal is frantic. It tries to get as far away from the investigator as possible. It defecates, urinates, salivates, trembles, and attempts to escape. When it has become familiar with the routine and its surroundings, it attempts to keep a distance between itself and the investigator, but there is very little communication. It is as though the animal were pretending that the investigator is not there. In the next phase, the animal acknowledges the presence of the investigator and communicates as it would to another wolf. During this phase we generally attempt to interact with the animal by hand feeding, petting, and otherwise seeking bodily contact. This results in threats, which, if not-full blown, are ignored by an experienced handler. The animal may grab or tear at the handler's clothing and may occasionally warn one of us by actually grabbing his person. In such instances, one simply does not move and the warning results, at worst, in a bruise. From this stage, greeting may be elicited and social behavior gradually instituted. In dealing with an aggressive phase, an experienced handler decides how far he can go entirely according to the way in which the wolf is communicating its intentions. He must also be able to distinguish an intended greeting, which involves mouthing the face of the handler, from even an ambivalent threat, since the results would be quite different. Our method for approaching the animal at this time is generally from a sitting or crouching position, and the method for turning off an attack is simply to remain low and not to move. Attempts to intimidate a threatening wolf will either cause the attack to be more severe or will badly frighten the animal so that the process of attempting to socialize him is set back considerably. Attempts at simulating the submissive gestures of a subdominant animal are not effective. In watching wolves encountering each other in a situation involving hostility, we wonder whether in addition to monitoring tail position, ear position, fang baring, and general demeanor, the autonomic signs are not also being monitored, and in particular, whether the yellow eye of the wolf may not be an aid to such monitoring. Tranquilized animals are responded to as though there is some difficulty in communication. Depending on the stage of the dose response curve, a tranquilized wolf (on Librium, Chlorpromazine, or Meprobamate) may attack the handler without the usual warning (Ginsburg, 1972). In our normal interactions with unsocialized or semisocialized wolves that are in an aggressive phase, we are confident that our general bearing and, in particular, the smoothness and naturalness of our movements are being monitored. All of us have been in encounters that were stressful and fear-inducing for us, and the animals have not usually reacted to us according to the degree of fear we are experiencing, but rather according to the extent to which we could control our movements. Thus they are monitoring our body language even as they (and we) monitor theirs.

I have argued earlier in this chapter that this communication behavior is largely genetically determined. It occurs without tutors from the wild in cubs that have been brought up together. It is not innate in terms of its production or of being responded to, since an isolated wolf does not seem to realize when it is being threatened or solicited for other purposes and, even when he learns this, it may take him some time to respond appropriately. It is also our experience, however, that if such an isolated animal is introduced to its conspecifics immediately after it emerges from isolation and is permitted to interact under restraint, it learns to decode as well as to signal appropriately in approximately 4 days.

The Role of Early Experience in Determining Later Behavior

Since the discovery of the phenomenon of imprinting (*Praegung*) by Heinroth and its detailed investigation by Lorenz (1937), Tinbergen (1951), Hess (1959), and many others, the role of early experience in the determination of later behavior has received a great deal of attention. Early deprivation in children has been shown to influence their later behavior and the work of Harlow, Harlow, and Hansen, (1963) has demonstrated that profound and seemingly irreversible deficits in behavior can be induced by early deprivation in rhesus macaques. Fuller (1963) has reported long-term effects of early isolation on behavior, and Scott (1962) has done a series of developmental studies in dogs resulting in the definition of a "critical period" for socialization spanning approximately the fifth to the twelfth week. Rosenzweig (1971) has shown that rats brought up in an impoverished environment form fewer neural connections than do those reared in enriched environments. Bloom (1964), in following the development of children, indicates that a great deal of their intellectual capacity and personality is set well before school age. Denenberg (1969), Levine and Mullins (1966), and others have presented evidence that early handling in mice and rats produces profound effects on later behavior via adrenal cortical hormones, whose levels are affected by the handling. These hormonal changes, by analogy with the work on the role of early androgen administration in the determination of male sexual behavior (Young, Goy, & Phoenix, 1964; Harris,

1964), are thought to change the brain, during a labile period in development, so that the later behavior is altered. All of these data and approaches taken together could be interpreted to mean that important potentials for behavior are molded during quite early development and remain relatively immutable later on. If this were true, we should have to concentrate on behavioral prophylaxis from the moment of conception until age 4 or 5 in our own species, and from approximately 5 to 12 weeks in the dog. Education, the peer group influence in college, life experiences later on, and even psychotherapy would be confounded by age 5—let alone later—with an individual whose intellectual and personality profile had already passed through its most malleable period and was now relatively set.

The socialization to human handling of adult wild animals and the successful structuring of the social behavior of a wolf isolated from its conspecifics until the age of 10 months by means of immediate and controlled experiences with normal wolves constitute evidence that all is not necessarily lost if the early experience has been suboptimal or even bizarre. Perhaps, as J. P. Scott has suggested in a personal communication, there is a circumscribed period of high behavioral lability that amounts to a displaced critical period when an isolate is first brought into social contact with other animals or a wild animal is confronted with a new environment, including human handlers.

Behavioral Taxonomy: Communication

Recently Shaw (1975) did a field study of the red wolf in Texas. There appear to be two subspecies in that area, but they intergrade sufficiently for morphological characteristics to constitute a problem for the taxonomist who may attempt to distinguish them on this basis. Red cell antigen and serum protein analyses have so far failed to provide any adequately distinguishing markers. Because one subspecies is generally smaller and of a more slender body build, the hypothesis that it resulted from hybridization with the coyote has been entertained.

In the realm of communication behavior, the coyote and the wolf differ in many respects. Wolves, including red wolves, snarl with the lips pulled back, baring the incisors and canine teeth. Coyotes typically gape, with the mouth wide open, while emitting a hissing sound. Our F_1 coyote-beagle hybrids snarl rather than gape.

Shaw found that the smaller species of red wolf has a gape threat, while the larger shows the snarl. This adds considerable credibility to the hypothesis that coyote hybridization has been involved. While we do not know whether a coyote × red wolf F_1 would show the gape rather than the snarl, our experience with coyote × beagle hybrids suggests that they would not, and that repeated hybridizations and possible selection would most likely have been necessary to establish the gape as a component of communication in a population of hybrid origin. It is interesting to speculate whether the motor component (gape vs. snarl) is genetically associated with the preferential decoding of the behavior. At present we do not yet know whether an isolate snarler would as easily learn to respond to either the gape or the snarl, and vice versa. Whether this difference in threat behavior serves as an isolating mechanism for the two populations in the field and/or as a bridging behavior for continuing hybridization behavior with the coyote is also a matter of speculation. Work is in progress on the former question, and we hope that the latter will also receive attention in the near future.

Social Behavior and Breeding Structure

As was also mentioned earlier, the domestic dog, while showing the appropriate signaling behavior, may or may not mean what he appears to be saying, whereas a normal wolf both says what he means and means what he says. This would indicate that selection pressure is necessary to keep all components of the behavioral system operative, and thus that they are under genetic control. This also argues that it has high adaptive value in nature, serving as it does to permit an effective pack structure to develop and to be maintained. Such a structure copes with the ordinary problems of living, including hunting, care of the young, care of sick or injured animals belonging to the pack, courtship, mating, and behavioral contraception. It conserves energy and prevents injury, since most matters of social disputes and control can be settled without an overt fight. It also serves as a barrier to random mating, which, if it occurred, would be a most conservative genetic mechanism by contrast with the system that actually obtains in wolf packs. In this system, the population is broken up into small subpopulations for breeding purposes, where different combinations of genes have an opportunity to be "tried out" in different parts of the population and where recessive genes can come to expression because of the considerable inbreeding that is involved within a pack. This makes for a system that promotes more rapid evolution and which in turn places a high selective value on the efficacy and intactness of the communication system (Ginsburg, 1968; Wright, 1939).

References

Bloom, B. S. *Stability and Change in Human Characteristics*. New York: John Wiley and Sons, Inc., 1964.
Crisler, L. *Arctic World*. New York: Harper, 1958.
Denenberg, V. H. The effects of early experience. In S. E. Hafez (Ed.), *The Behavior of Domestic Animals*. London: Bailliers, Tindall, and Cassell, 1969, pp. 95–130.

Fuller, J. L. Effects of experimental deprivation upon behavior in animals. *Proceedings of the World Congress on Psychiatry* (Montreal), 1963, *3*, 223–227.

Ginsburg, B. E. Social behavior and social hierarchy in the formation of personality profiles in animals. In J. Zubin (Ed.), *Comparative Psychopathology, Animal and Human. Proceedings of the American Psychopathological Association*, 1966, *22*, 95–114.

Ginsburg, B. E. Breeding structure and social behavior of mammals: a servomechanism for the avoidance of panmixia. In D. C. Glass (Ed.), *Biology and Behavior Series, Genetics*. New York: Rockefeller University Press and Russell Sage Foundation, 1968.

Ginsburg, B. E. Anxiety: a behavioral legacy. In R. Porter (Ed.), *Psychology, Emotion, and Psychosomatic Illness*. Ciba Foundation Symposium (Vol. 8, new series). Amsterdam: Elsener, 1972.

Harlow, H. F., Harlow, M. K., & Hansen, E. W. The maternal affectional system of rhesus monkeys. In H. Rheingold, (Ed.), *Maternal behavior in mammals*. New York: John Wiley and Sons, Inc., 1963.

Harris, G. W. Sex hormones, brain development and brain function. *Endocrinology*, 1964, *75*, 627–648.

Hess, E. H. Imprinting. *Science*, 1959, *130*, 133–141.

Levine, S., and Mullins, R. F., Jr. Hormonal influences on brain organization in infant rats. *Science*, 1966, *152*, 1585–1592.

Lorenz, K. The Companion in the Bird's World. *Auk*, 1937, *54*, 245–273.

Mech, L. D. The ecology of the timber wolf (*Canis lupus L.*) in Isle Royale National Park. Unpublished doctoral thesis, Purdue University, 1962.

Pimlott, D. H., Shannon, J. A., & Kolenosky, G. B. *The Ecology of the Timber Wolf in Algonquin Provincial Park*. Research Report (Wildlife) No. 87. Department of Lands and Forests, Ontario, Canada, 1969.

Rabb, G. B., Woolpy, J., & Ginsburg, B. E. Social relationships in a group of captive wolves. *American Zoologist*, 1967, *7*, 305–311.

Rosenzweig, M. R. Effects of environment on development of brain and of behavior. In E. Tobach (Ed.), *Biopsychology of Development*. New York: Academic Press, 1971.

Schenkel, R. Ausdrucks—Studien an Wolfen. *Behaviour*, 1947, *1*, 81–129.

Scott, J. P. Critical periods in behavioral development. *Science*, 1962, *138*, 949–958.

Shaw, J. Ecological and taxonomic investigations of an endangered species, the red wolf (*Canis rufus*). Unpublished doctoral dissertation, Yale University School of Forestry, 1975.

Tinbergen, N. *The Study of Instinct*. New York: Oxford University Press, 1951.

Woolpy, J. H. The social organization of wolves. *Natural History*, 1968, *77*, 46–55.

Woolpy, J. H., & Ginsburg, B. E. Wolf socialization: a study of temperament in a wild social species. *American Zoologist*, 1967, *7*, 357–363.

Wright, S. Gene and organism. *American Naturalist*, 1953, *87*, 5–18.

Wright, S. *Statistical Genetics in Relation to Evolution*. Paris: Hermann, 1939.

Young, W. C., Goy, R. W., & Phoenix, C. H. Hormones and sexual behavior. *Science*, 1964, *143*, 212–218.

CHAPTER 8

Animal's Defenses: Fighting in Predator–Prey Relations

Stanley C. Ratner

Michigan State University
East Lansing, Michigan

This chapter deals with a special case of fighting among animals. It deals with fighting and associated behaviors when a prey animal is attacked by a predator. An analysis of these behaviors serves at least two purposes. On one hand, it leads to the examination of defensive behaviors that probably have different evolutionary and functional meanings from defensive behaviors involving conspecifics. On the other hand, it permits comparison between these two types of fighting behaviors—the behaviors of fighting predators and fighting conspecifics. Investigators of each process may learn from the other. For example, investigators have their attention drawn to questions such as: the similarity in fighting with a predator and fighting with a member of the same species, the uses of threat displays in the two situations, and the sequences of defensive reactions in the two situations.

The Framework of the Analysis

The first thing that will be done to understand the behaviors involved in predator defenses will be to establish a procedure for the analysis. A special procedure is necessary when investigators are dealing with behaviors that involve large numbers of species and take a large number of forms. A procedure that is effective for such an analysis is called the comparative method, (Ratner, 1967).

While the idea of the comparative method is elaborated and defended in other publications (Denny & Ratner, 1970, p.7; Ratner, 1972), we will use it at the present time as a tool in order to learn something about defenses of animals. However, as a guide to thinking about comparative method, it can be considered to be like any other method, a tool that is used to work on a problem. So, the comparative method can be used in the same way as the quantitative method—not as an end in itself, but as a set of procedures to guide thinking and research. The comparative method is used when the investigator faces behaviors that have diversity. Defensive behaviors clearly appear to be diverse, especially if they are considered in terms of the forms they take and the number of species that show them. Defenses range from postures to bites and from insects to bears.

Table I shows the sequence of steps taken by the investigator who is using the comparative method. The first step, Stage I, involves amassing casual information about the behavior and, if possible, examining published reports that deal with the behavior. This step helps to get perspective on the diversity of the behavior, its functions, and mechanisms possibly associated with the behavior. Stage I is reminiscent of the "hip boot" stage of biology in which naturalists roamed fields and ponds getting ideas about biological objects and entered sketches and descriptions into reports. Stage II, an unfamiliar one for many psychologists, involves establishing the way to talk about the behaviors that are under investigation. In a word, it is necessary to know what you are talking about before you can make progress in understanding. Further, it is necessary to have the event in some perspective from Stage I in order to be effective at Stage II. Thus, the application of Stage II implies the development of a classification—a language—for the description of defensive behaviors and the postulation of mechanisms for the action of these behaviors. General criteria influence the classification of behaviors. Among them are: emphasis on functional classification as opposed to structural classification; classification along dimensions, such as time, energy, or economic value; validity of classification, which requires that

Table I.   The Stages Approach to Comparative Analysis

Order		
I	Background information	Search for informal and formal information sources
II	Taxonomy	Develop functional classification system
III	Research preparations	Specify valid and reliable examples of each class
IV	Variables	Identify variables that affect classes
V	Origins and comparisons	Trace origins of classes and compare classes
VI	General theory	Identify general mechanisms that relate all classes

the class reflect the facts of the background information as opposed to cultural traditions or unrepresentative samples.

Stage III, called development of research preparation, means that the investigator identifies the research setting including the animal, its history, and the measuring procedures that provide a good example of the behaviors that have been identified from Stage II. In other words, the investigator of predator defenses needs a research preparation that does for him what the fruit fly preparation did for genetics and the Skinner box preparation did for learning.

The fourth stage of comparative analysis is the most familiar to experimental psychologists. At Stage IV the investigator identifies the variables that affect the behavior or process he is studying. A number of descriptive variables immediately suggest themselves for investigation. Among them are the age of the animal, the sex of the animal, the species of the animal, and the past history of the animal. The actions of many of the descriptive variables are ordinarily of a practical significance rather than a theoretical significance. However, each behavioral process ordinarily has special variables whose actions are suggested from Stage I and whose effect has theoretical significance in terms of understanding mechanisms. Thus, Stage IV serves both as a way to demonstrate the effects of variables that may affect the behavior and as a way to uncover the dynamics of the behavior. Stage IV requires knowledge about research preparations, appropriate classes of behavior, and a solid perspective from Stage I.

Comparative Method and Predator Defenses

Now, what can this framework tell us about the predator defenses of animals? The application of Stage I yields the idea that predator-prey relations are very general and crucial in the lives of animals, including invertebrates. From the point of view of the predator, the analysis deals with their food and the behaviors associated with food getting. From the point of view of the prey (the point of view that will be emphasized in this discussion), the analysis emphasizes behaviors associated with keeping the predator from his food.

What can the prey do to reduce his vulnerability? Reviews of reports from naturalists and other students of behavior reveal a number of things about the answer to this question. (1) The review of background sources suggests that the point of view of the prey is less frequently and less vigorously examined than the point of view of the predator. In other words, more is said about the predator than about the prey. (2) The language to describe the action of the prey is both incomplete and personalized for particular investigators. Investigators have generated large vocabularies that are not widely used, so a search of the research literature requires a lot of browsing. (3) The browsing route seems to yield the most information when reports of the natural history of the general biology of a genus of animals or class of animals is the topic of the text. So, for example, the classic work by Noble, *The Biology of Amphibia* (1954) includes a section on defenses against predators, as does Pope's treatise, *The Great Snakes* (1961). In addition, some investigators have dealt at length with defensive behaviors. These include Armstrong (1942), Volgyesi (1963), Cott (1940), Ratner (1967), and Gilman and Marcuse (1949).

Analyses of these and other descriptions of predator defenses strongly support several generalizations about the behavior of the prey. (1) Postures, movements, colors, and secretions are among the signals used by the prey animal. These signals seem to say to the predator: "I am not prey and I am certainly not food." (2) The prey has other strategies in addition to signaling. Escape is among them and with few exceptions all reports of predator-prey relations state or imply escape as another response used by the prey. As a signal, escape movements ordinarily lead the predator to chase or to attack. If the chase and attack are successful, the prey fights, and if the predator's success continues, the prey dies or becomes immobile. (3) Members of a species typically react to predators with a number of responses that appear to occur in a relatively reliable sequence. In addition, the responses and their sequence for a prey animal appear to be influenced by a companion sequence of responses of the predator that serve as stimuli for the prey animal. These actions can be considered analogous to the sequence of mutual responses described by Tinbergen (1953) in the courting and copulation of fish. Thus, the model of Tinbergen will be used as a first approximation for the description of predator defenses.

The variety of responses and the variety of animals that use them call for some system of classification that at the same time suggests the mechanism for the behavior. It is assumed that prey animals make somewhat predictable and stereotyped responses to predators and some of these responses appear to act as signals, much the way threat displays of monkeys act as signals to other monkeys. One way to organize these observations about prey and predator is to use a descriptive language suggested by the work of ethologists, such as Spalding and later investigators (Denny & Ratner, 1970, p.204).

As seen in Figure 1, the reactions of the prey animal can be described in terms of three behavioral components where each component is composed of a number of stimulus and response elements.

Several things are important about Figure 1. The horizontal axis refers to defensive distance—the distance between the prey and the predator. While a metric value is obviously implicit in the scale of defensive distance, none except zero is included. This is done because the metric value depends on a number of parameters, including the species that is the prey and the species that is the predator. Hediger (1964, p.34) has compiled data on one response in the sequence of the preconsummatory component. He writes about *flight distance* as the distance between prey and predator at which the prey flees from the predator. He notes, for example, if the predator is man, that howler monkeys in the wild

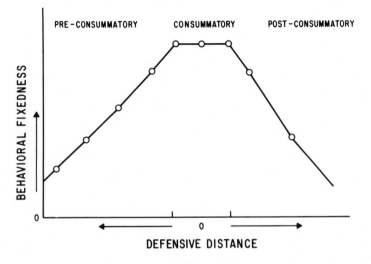

Fig. 1.   Behavioral components of predator defense as a function of the defensive distance between
the prey and predator.

flee if the man comes closer than 25 yards; the ostrich flees if the predator comes
closer than 150 yards, and the fiddler crab flees if the predator comes closer than
10 yards. Notice also from Figure 1 that as the defensive distance becomes less
than the flight distance, other responses are elicited. As the distance decreases to
zero, all of the responses that occur are responses in the preliminary (preconsummatory) component of predator defense. Then when the distance becomes
zero, other responses occur, and so on through a postconsummatory sequence.
The third idea implicit in Figure 1 is that the stereotypy, or fixedness of
responses, increases as the defensive distance approaches zero and is maintained
there. Further, the degree of stereotypy after reaching its highest level then
decreases in the final (postconsummatory) component of the sequence.

   The Preconsummatory Component.   Freezing is the first conspicuous response of the prey animal in the preconsummatory component of predator
defense. The response of freezing is almost ubiquitous across species and across
stimuli. Many animals freeze at any sudden stimulus change. The posture
associated with this response element has not been studied extensively, but
casual reports and observations suggest that when an animal freezes it ceases
ongoing movement and then slowly explores the environment using equipment
appropriate to the species. Rabbits may freeze in mid-step, may freeze while
squatting, or may freeze mid-nibble. Since this response is conspicuous and
appears to be the first response in the sequence, we are considering it. However,
the remaining elements that will be discussed will be those that have signal value
for other individuals. In most cases, the individual that is signaled is the

predator, but in some cases the response signals the predator and at the same time signals members of the animal's own species.

As is evident from Table II, there has evolved a variety of defensive responses that function in the preliminary component of predator defenses. Some of these responses can be described in terms of the prey telling the predator that it is something other than food; other of the responses, particularly those that have little or no signal value, can be described in terms of the prey showing the predator that it has disappeared. As mentioned previously, all of these can be described as preliminary strategies that occur when the defensive distance is greater than zero.

The first strategy noted in Table II is called *injury feigning* or disablement reaction. This is a response that has evolved to a high level among a number of birds such as meadowlarks, killdeer, and ducks. (It may be the reaction shown by younger brothers and sisters who fall and writhe with apparent pain when the older sibling rushes at them.) A bird that is reacting by feigning injury may run or fly weakly in an erratic pattern with one leg or one wing extended and unused. Figure 2 illustrates the extended wing posture. Injury feigning is a powerful and almost obvious stimulus for the predator. The predator dashes after the prey, following it in its erratic and helpless-looking flight. From the point of view of

Table II.   Analysis of Responses with Signal Functions for Behavioral Components of Predator Defense

Response	Animal	Other details	Reviewer
Preconsummatory component			
Injury feigning	Ground-nesting birds	Near nest	Armstrong (1942)
Mimicry	Insects	Batesian, Mullerian	Cott (1940)
Mobbing	Passerine birds	Flying predators	Hinde (1970)
Attack directing	Beetles	Unpalatable structure	Cott (1940)
Threat posturing	Moths	Expose structure	Cott (1940)
Projecting and secreting	Beetles	Delays predator	Maier and Maier (1970)
Consummatory component			
Contact secreting shedding	Earthworm, bird, salamander	Fear molting, autotomy	Denny and Ratner (1970), Noble (1954)
Fighting	Common among species	Struggling	No reviews
Death feigning, animal hypnosis	Common among species	Immobile	Maier and Maier (1970)
Postconsummatory component			
Postimmobility escape	Common among species	Sudden escape	Ratner (1967)

Fig. 2.   Example of injury feigning, a preconsummatory response, shown by the night hawk. (Adapted from Armstrong, 1942.)

the prey, the predator is being led away from the nest. Thus injury feigning is typically observed when birds are nesting.

The second response, *mimicry*, is described in exacting detail by Cott (1940) and appears in several ways among prey animals. "In Batesian mimicry a relatively scarce, palatable, and unprotected species resembles an abundant, relatively unpalatable or well protected species" (p. 398). That is, the defense involves living on the bad reputation of the model. "In Mullerian mimicry, a number of species, all possessing *some* disagreeable feature, come to resemble each other," or as Cott says (p. 398), in Mullerian mimicry "the mimic shares the repellent features of its models, and the enemy is taught by a real warning." Mimicry as a preliminary defensive action is especially conspicuous among insects. Notice that mimicries only sometimes involve postures and movements when the prey takes a posture to look like something else. Thus, only in some cases does this defense involve a signal to the predator.

Mobbing is another predator defense that requires some comment. In this case, when the predator is approaching the prey, the prey animal gives a distinctive call while dashing toward the predator. The call brings other members of the species into the mobbing act and these individuals also call and dash toward the predator. Soon the predator is surrounded and hounded by calling and dashing figures. The survival value of this strategy for the species is almost intuitively evident and the annoyance of the predator is also evident, as when a hawk or a crow is mobbed by songbirds.

The responses of *threat posturing* and *attack directing*, if they occur, appear relatively late in the sequence of preconsummatory movements. That is, they appear as the defensive distance moves close to zero. Threat posturing, much like the response in fighting among members of a single species, involves the prey taking a posture that exposes some strongly marked area of the body. Figure 3 shows the threat posture of the mantis in which the wings are elevated and dark circles surrounded by yellow rings are quickly exposed. This defense is also commonly seen among species of butterflies that assume a posture and reveal two large eye shapes.

Attack directing, also described by Cott (p. 386), involves presenting to the predator some distasteful, irrelevant, or dangerous structure that directs his attack toward this structure. For example, the large beetle *Antia* raises its body and exposes large posterior spots when a predator is close. If the attack continues, *Antia* ejects a strong acidic secretion that can sting the hands or face of a human. Analogous reactions are seen in a number of sea creatures when attack is imminent. They may wave brightly colored papillae that are injurious in some species, distasteful in some, and readily regenerated in others. Similarly, the wart hog, when a predator closes the defensive distance, quickly backs into a hole that it may find or evacuate by rapid digging and then shows its wart-covered face and tusks. The tusks are reputed to be powerful weapons.

Fig. 3.   Defensive threat response of the mantis when a predator closes the defensive distance. (Adapted from Cott, 1940.)

Threat posturing and attack directing are relatively stereotyped for a species as implied by their closeness to the consummatory components of predator defense.

Projecting substances and secreting substances are the final response elements of the preconsummatory component noted in Table II. These response elements appear in some species when the defensive distance is greater than zero and appear in others when the defensive distance becomes zero. The data regarding these defenses are casual in terms of detailed and accurate descriptions of their occurrences. However, impressions from research in our laboratory (Ratner & Boice, 1971) and from casual reports are that projecting substances and objects typically occurs when the defensive distance is greater than zero, while secreting substances typically occurs when the distance is at zero. Thus, for example, some birds project stomach contents or cloacal contents when the predator is still some distance from them (Vogel, 1950). Skunks project secretions up to 3 m and species of cockroaches and beetles, including the bombardier beetle, project chemicals several body lengths. Chimpanzees, gorillas, and species of monkeys respond to predators that are some distance from them by throwing objects, including feces (Maier & Maier, 1970).

Defensive secreting, assumed to occur when the defensive distance is zero, is widespread among species and takes many forms. Some substances that are secreted are toxic to the predator, as is seen among millipeds that secrete toxic benzoquinones and among beetles (*Apheloria corrugata*) that secrete hydrogen cyanide gas. Other substances that are secreted are primarily unpleasant and cause the predator to back away temporarily. Examples of this defensive reaction include "reflexive bleeding," seen in the Mexican bean beetle, and mucous secreting, seen in earthworms and some amphibians. Defensive secreting also functions to make the prey slippery and possibly more difficult to hold. Thus, when the predator closes the distance to zero, a strategy is useful if it functions to lead the predator to make movements that are incompatible with holding the prey or if it makes the prey difficult to hold.

In summary then, the first behavioral component in the interaction between predator and prey involves a number of responses that occur in sequence for a number of species as the defensive distance changes between the individuals. Each of the prey's responses have signal value to some extent. In addition, the form and function of the responses become more clear and predictable as the defensive distance decreases. The first responses involve *detection of the predator* and *escape*, both of which have generalized signal value. If these fail, the responses shift to deception and warning, including attack directing, threat posturing, and projecting substances. Obviously, all of these fail at some time for some individuals of the species, so the defensive distance between the prey and the predator becomes zero and remains there for many individuals. When this happens the behavioral sequence moves to the consummatory component.

The Consummatory Component. Elements of the consummatory component of predator defense are also noted in Table II. These responses are separated
from those of the preconsummatory component primarily because of their behavioral fixedness within members of the species. These responses are like
mounting and thrusting for sexual behavior, or licking and swallowing for
drinking behavior. These are the culmination of the behavioral sequence.

As noted in Table II, and depending on the species, three conspicuous
responses may occur if the defensive distance between the prey and the predator
is held at zero. Many species move to a second line of defensive secretions,
which we will call *contact secreting.* Some amphibians release special substances that differ from mucous, e.g., earthworms release coelemic fluid that has
a *pH* of 8.5–9.0 and differs from the preconsummatory secretion. Many birds
release their feathers. The response of releasing feathers we have called *fear
molting* and believe that it is analogous to *fear shedding* that is seen in some
mammals. Fear shedding may be seen if an untamed bird or a small mammal is
suddenly grabbed and picked up. Feathers or hair may be seen coming from the
animal. In its most dramatic form, some animals shed portions of their
bodies—the response of *autotomy,* as reported for salamanders and lizards
(Noble, 1954). In these cases, biological adaptations have occurred so that the
tail or portion of the tail can be readily separated from the body. For example,
observers have reported cases in which a hawk struck and grabbed a pigeon and
departed with talons full of feathers, and a cat grabbed a lizard and departed with
only the tail. Spine shedding by porcupines appears to be an analogous reaction.
The signal value of this type of defensive reaction is difficult to evaluate at this
time since investigations of the response and the subsequent responses of the
predator are not available. But, in general, fear molting and shedding seem to say
that ''the prey is not what it seems to be.''

If contact secreting and shedding are unsuccessful and the defensive distance remains at zero, then the prey animal typically begins fighting. Pill bugs
fight, chaffinches fight, rats fight, and so forth. The question of the similarity in
the sequence and form of these fighting movements as compared with intraspecific fighting is an open one. At this time it will simply be noted that fighting is
one of the conspicuous elements in the consummatory component of reacting to
predators and introspecific aggression.

Defensive Immobility. As fighting continues between the prey and the
predator, the prey animal may make one more conspicuous response; Darwin
called this response death feigning. Other investigators and naturalists have
called it other things, including: tonic immobility, animal hypnosis, catalepsy,
trance reaction, and defensive immobility. Interest in defensive immobility has
generated a literature of more than 250 papers beginning in 1646 with a report by
the Jesuit priest, Father Kircher, who observed the response under special conditions with chickens and described it in terms of the birds' fear and fascination.

In general, defensive immobility can be described as the prey becoming very still, very flaccid, and unresponsive to stimulation. In a particular case, it is called playing possum and has been reported in many field situations (Keefe & Wooldridge, 1967). Defensive immobility has been used to the advantage of the human in a number of ways. For example, large crabs are dealt with by the Japanese by first imposing defensive immobility on the animal. In addition, a common observation among people who band birds is that the bird may fight strongly and then become absolutely still in the bander's hand. While the band is very easy to apply at this time, the workers are reminded that the animal may appear to have died, but the bird need only be thrown into the air and it will probably recover and fly away.

Figure 4 shows the posture of a domestic chicken during immobility after it has been attacked and held by a human predator. This posture is common for a number of avian species and is analogous to that of mammals.

The first characteristic of defensive immobility to be considered is its generality across the species. Published reports indicate that scores of animals of different species show the response if they are attacked and held by a predator (Gilman & Marcuse, 1949; Ratner, 1967). In these reports, the investigator is ordinarily the predator, and the prey species range from invertebrates (such as stick bugs, pill bugs, crabs, and spiders) to amphibians, birds (including the domestic pigeon and chicken) to coyotes, sheep, and monkeys. However, laboratory and field tests indicate that some species show little evidence of

Fig. 4. Defensive immobility (animal hypnosis) of the chicken when a predator has held prey for 10–15 seconds. (Adapted from Gallup, Nash, Donegan, & McClure, 1971.)

immobility. Examples of these animals are the crustacean, *Porcellio scaber*, the wolf, and the wren. It is expected that other species also respond to predators but fail to show defensive immobility.

Survival Value of Immobility. Several questions about this response come immediately to mind. The foremost question is how can immobility function as a defense against predators? A firm answer to this question is unavailable, but a general answer can be given that is congruent with the facts that are known about the reaction. In addition, the answer can be viewed in terms of some general assumptions about behavior. One such assumption is that any response that is widespread among species, shows a fixed form within the species, and involves a particular posture probably has adaptive significance and serves as a signal. The primary evidence to support this assumption comes from examining field reports of predator and prey interactions, which indicate that a prey animal may escape from a predator following defensive immobility.

Table III shows the results of these analyses for three species of prey and two types of predators. Notice that the numbers of animals that escape following defensive immobility are surprisingly large and probably not typical. But even if these frequencies were reduced threefold, they suggest that the response is effective. Population ecologists and evolutionists suggest that a characteristic with as little as .1% additional survival value can lead to selection for the characteristic. Defensive immobility appears to enhance survival. At least it enhances escape from predators.

The mechanism for the effectiveness of defensive immobility is probably like the mechanism for other signals. They change the behaviors of the participants. Defensive immobility typically leads the predator to reduce his attention toward the prey and to relax his guard. This takes several forms. Sargeant and Eberhardt (1975, in press) report that the red fox frequently put the duck down when it became immobile and sometimes rolled the duck with its paw or mouthed it gently. I have found that when carrying a bird from the trap to the laboratory, I held it tightly while it fought and struggled; then I relaxed my grip somewhat when the animal became immobile. In the case of the pill bug, *Armadillidium vulgare*, I searched the ground and if I saw a pill bug I attempted

Table III.   Number of Prey Escaping Following Defensive Immobility

Prey	Predator	Number caught	Number escaping	Observer
Pill bug	human	70	5	Ratner*
Chaffinch	human	35	3	Ratner*
Duck	red fox	50	29	Sargeant & Eberhardt[†]

*From field notes
[†]1975, in press

to pick it up. If it became immobile and rolled into a tight ball it occasionally rolled from my fingers and became lost in an area otherwise covered with small round stones, bits of earth, and bits of bark.

Defensive immobility of ducks and the other birds was observed to lead to relaxation on the part of the predator. In the case of the pill bug, defensive immobility made the prey difficult to hold and difficult to see. In addition, the pill bug was less available as a food object since it became a round object with a hard shell.

Other Characteristics of Defensive Immobility. Sixty years of research have exposed many other characteristics of defensive immobility which suggest that it is a response with profound biological and behavioral consequences. Klemm (1971) and others have shown that the EEG of animals during immobility resembles the EEG during early stages of sleep. Severing higher neural centers interferes with the occurrence of immobility according to McGraw & Klemm (1969).

Defensive immobility appears very weakly in the immature members of a species (Ratner & Thompson, 1960; Borscheldt & Ratner, 1973). Analgesia typically accompanies defensive immobility, as has been noted by Ratner (1967) and Gilman and Marcuse (1949). Heart rate during immobility rises to extreme values according to studies by Ratner (1967, p. 567) and Eyer (1974). In addition, muscle tone is characterized by waxy flexibility during immobility, a characteristic that has given rise to several of the labels for the reaction.

Behavioral characteristics associated with defensive immobility have been studied extensively by Gallup and his co-workers. Recent papers include reports by Gallup (1972); Gallup, Creekmore, and Hill (1970); Gallup, Nash, and Ellison (1971); and Gallup, Nash, Potter, and Donegan (1970). Their findings and the findings of others indicate that the duration of defensive immobility of birds, for example, may be greater than 1 hour, but a number of variables affect these durations. Among these variables are the proximity of the predatory stimulus, such as a hawk or glass eyes located near the prey; presenting an aversive stimulus, such as electric shock just prior to attack; changing the opportunity to escape prior to attack by the predator; and the presence of members of one's own species during the time of immobility.

Clearly, defensive immobility is a complex response that is affected in its intensity by a number of psychological variables. In the context of this chapter it is considered to be the final response in the consummatory sequence involving reacting to predators.

As noted in Table II, one conspicuous response appears in the postconsummatory component of this sequence. This is the response of postimmobility escape. For birds this response takes the form of a sudden righting movement followed by flight. Birds in the laboratory frequently manage to escape from the experimenter by this strategy. Postimmobility escape can not be reliably predicted from any preparatory movements as far as can be determined from careful observation in the laboratory.

Summary of the Analysis of Predator Defenses

Prey animals make a variety of responses as the defensive distance between the predator and themselves is decreased. These responses are examined by the comparative method and found to consist of a relatively reliable sequence of responses, some of which have signal value for the predator and for members of the prey's species. The sequence is described in terms of preconsummatory, consummatory, and postconsummatory components. Research preparations, including species that show the responses, sources of background information about the responses, and some of the characteristics of the responses are also presented.

The main signal functions of responses in the preconsummatory components of predator defense can be described as follows:

Freezing: "Something has changed."
Injury feigning: "Look at me."
Mimicry: "I am not what I seem to be."
Mobbing: "Call for help."
Attack directing: "Take this."
Projecting and secreting: "Wait a moment."

The signal functions of the responses in the sequence of consummatory and postconsummatory components of predator defense can be described as follows:

Contact secreting (including fear molting, shedding, and autotomy): "Take this."
Fighting: "My last chance to get away."
Defensive immobility: "Now you can relax."
Postimmobility escape: "I have recovered."

Relations between Predator Defense and Aggression

The question that remains concerns the relations between behaviors and signals involved in predator defense and behaviors and signals involved in intraspecific aggression. At this time only a few of the major points of congruence between the behavioral classes will be considered. (1) It seems clear that both behavioral classes involve preconsummatory, consummatory, and postconsummatory components. (2) Numerous observations and reports are available about the preconsummatory and consummatory components. These reports show that threatening postures, movements, and other displays appear in the preconsummatory component of both predator defense and intraspecific aggression. However, as is true for many classes of behavior, little data are available about the characteristics of the postconsummatory component of predator defense and aggression. (3) Fighting appears to be a conspicuous response of the consummatory component that is observed in both predator defense and aggression. Other responses, such as contact secreting and contact shedding or molting, are known to occur in predator defense and may occur in both classes. (4) Submissive postures sometimes shown by the vanquished fighter may share some characteristics of defensive immobility, but again the data are incomplete.

References

Armstrong, E. A. *Bird display*. Cambridge, England: Cambridge University Press, 1942.

Borscheldt, P. L., & Ratner, S. C. Development of freezing and immobility, predator defenses, in the bobwhite quail (*Colinus virginianes*). *Behavioral Biology*, 1973, *8*, 83–92.

Cott, H. B. *Adaptive coloration in animals*. New York: Oxford University Press, 1940.

Denny, M. R., & Ratner, S. C. *Comparative Psychology*. Homewood, Ill.: Dorsey, 1970.

Eyer, J. C. Heart rate in bobwhite quail during freezing and tonic immobility. Unpublished doctoral dissertation, Michigan State University, 1974.

Gallup, G. G., Jr. Mirror-image stimulation and tonic immobility in chickens. *Psychonomic Science*, 1972, *28*, 257–259.

Gallup, G. G., Jr., Creekmore, H. S., & Hill, W. E., III. Shock-enhanced immobility reactions in chickens: Support for the fear hypothesis. *The Psychological Record*, 1970, *20*, 243–245.

Gallup, G. G., Jr., Nash, R. F., & Ellison, A. L., Jr. Tonic immobility as a reaction to predation: Artificial eyes as a fear stimulus for chickens. *Psychonomic Science*, 1971, *23*, 79–80.

Gallup, G. G., Jr., Nash, R. F., Donegan, N. H., & McClure, M. K. The immobility response: A predator-induced reaction in chickens. *The Psychological Record*, 1971, *21*, 513–519.

Gallup, G. G., Jr., Nash, R. F., Potter, R. J., & Donegan, N. H. Effect of varying conditions on immobility reactions in domestic chickens (*Gallus gallus*). *Journal of Comparative and Physiological Psychology*, 1970, *73*, 442–445.

Gilman, T. T., & Marcuse, F. L. Animal hypnosis. *Psychological Bulletin*, 1949, *46*, 141–165.

Hediger, H. *Wild animals in captivity*. New York: Dover, 1964.

Hinde, R. A. *Animal behaviour* (2nd ed.). New York: McGraw-Hill, 1970.

Keefe, J. F., & Wooldridge, D. *The world of the opossum*. New York: J. B. Lippincott, 1967.

Klemm, W. R. Neurophysiologic studies of the immobility reflex ("animal hypnosis"). In S. Ehrenpreis & O. C. Solmitsky, (Eds.), *Neurosciences Research* (Vol. 4). New York: Academic Press, 1971, pp. 165–212.

Maier, R. A., & Maier, B. M. *Comparative animal behavior*. Belmont, Cal.: Brooks-Cole, 1970.

McGraw, C. P., & Klemm, W. R. Mechanisms of the immobility reflex ("animal hypnosis") III. Neocortical inhibition in rats. *Communications in Behavioral Biology*, 1969, *3*, 53–59.

Noble, G. K. *The biology of amphibia*. New York: Dover, 1954.

Pope, C. H. *The great snakes*. New York: Knopf, 1961.

Ratner, S. C. Comparative aspects of hypnosis. In J. E. Gordon (Ed.), *Handbook of clinical and experimental hypnosis*. New York: Macmillan, 1967.

Ratner, S. C. Comparative psychology: Some distinctions from animal behavior. *Psychological Record*, 1972, *22*, 433–440.

Ratner, S. C., & Boice, R. Behavioral characteristics and functions of pheromones of earthworms. *Psychological Record*, 1971, *21*, 363–371.

Ratner, S. C., & Thompson, W. R. Immobility reactions (fear) of domestic fowl as a function of age and prior experiences. *Animal Behaviour*, 1960, *8*, 186–191.

Sargeant, A. B., & Eberhardt, L. E. Death feigning by ducks in response to predation by red foxes (*Vulpes fulva*). *American Midland Naturalist* (1975, in press).

Tinbergen, N. *Social behaviour in animals*. London: Methuen, 1953.

Vogel, H. H. Observations on social behavior in turkey vultures. *Auk*, 1950, *67*, 210–216.

Volgyesi, F. A. *Hypnosis of man and animals* (2nd ed.). Baltimore: Williams & Wilkins, 1963.

Index

191